TOWARDS THE ETHICS OF A GREEN FUTURE

What are our obligations towards future generations who stand to be harmed by the impact of today's environmental crises? This book explores ecological sustainability as a human rights issue and examines what our long-term responsibilities might be.

This interdisciplinary collection provides a basis for understanding the debates on the provision of sustainability for future generations from a diverse set of theoretical standpoints. Covering a broad range of perspectives such as risk and uncertainty, legal implementation, representation, motivation and economics, *Towards the Ethics of a Green Future* sets out the key questions involved in this complex ethical issue. The contributors bring theoretical discussions to life through the use of case studies and real-world examples. The book also includes clear and tangible recommendations for policymakers on how to put the suggestions proposed in the book into practice.

This book will be of great interest to all researchers and students concerned with issues of sustainability and human rights, as well as scholars of environmental politics, law and ethics more generally.

Marcus Düwell holds a chair in philosophical ethics at Utrecht University, and is the Director of the university's Ethics Institute. His research focuses on ethics of human rights, ethics of future generations and bioethics.

Gerhard Bos's research is directed towards the conceptual underpinnings of human rights and the implications for long-term responsibilities. He worked at the Ethics Institute at Utrecht University as a postdoctoral researcher, and coordinated the ESF Research Networking Programme 'Rights to a Green Future' (2011–2015).

Naomi van Steenbergen divides her research time between moral psychology, ethics and climate justice. She is currently co-editing a book on practical self-understanding. Besides her research and teaching in philosophy, she works as a literary and academic translator.

ROUTLEDGE STUDIES IN SUSTAINABILITY

For a full list of titles in this series, please visit www.routledge.com/Routledge-Studies-in-Sustainability/book-series/RSSTY

TOWARDS THE ETHICS OF A GREEN FUTURE

The Theory and Practice of Human Rights for Future People

Edited by Marcus Düwell, Gerhard Bos and Naomi van Steenbergen

Routledge
Taylor & Francis Group
LONDON AND NEW YORK

earthscan
from Routledge

First published 2018
by Routledge
2 Park Square, Milton Park, Abingdon, Oxon OX14 4RN

and by Routledge
711 Third Avenue, New York, NY 10017

Routledge is an imprint of the Taylor & Francis Group, an informa business

British Library Cataloguing-in-Publication Data
A catalogue record for this book is available from the British Library

Library of Congress Cataloging-in-Publication Data
Names: Dèuwell, Marcus, 1962- editor. | Bos, Gerhard, editor. | Steenbergen, Naomi van, editor.
Title: Towards the ethics of a green future : the theory and practice of human rights for future people / edited by Marcus Dèuwell, Gerhard Bos and Naomi van Steenbergen.
Description: Abingdon, Oxon ; New York, NY : Routledge, 2018. | Series: Routledge studies in sustainability | Includes bibliographical references and index.
Identifiers: LCCN 2017061087 (print) | LCCN 2018015028 (ebook) | ISBN 9781315115788 (eBook) | ISBN 9781138069312 (hbk) | ISBN 9781138069329 (pbk) | ISBN 9781315115788 (ebk)
Subjects: LCSH: Environmental ethics. | Sustainability--Moral and ethical aspects. | Human rights.
Classification: LCC GE42 (ebook) | LCC GE42 .T68 2018 (print) | DDC 179/ .1--dc23LC record available at https://lccn.loc.gov/2017061087

ISBN: 978-1-138-06931-2 (hbk)
ISBN: 978-1-138-06932-9 (pbk)
ISBN: 978-1-315-11578-8 (ebk)

Typeset in Bembo
by Taylor & Francis Books

CONTENTS

CONTRIBUTORS

Dieter Birnbacher is Professor Emeritus of philosophy at the University of Düsseldorf, Germany. He is a member of the Central Ethics Commission of the Bundesärztekammer (German Medical Association) and a member of Leopoldina, National Academy of Sciences. His publications include books on action theory, ethics, medical ethics and environmental ethics as well as on Wittgenstein and Schopenhauer.

Gerhard Bos's research looks at the conceptual underpinnings of human rights and their implications for long-term responsibilities. He coordinated the ESF Research Networking Programme 'Rights to a Green Future' (2011–2015). He is currently co-editing a number of books, including *Human Dignity in Philosophy and Applied Ethics – China and the West* (Cambridge University Press, forthcoming). Further relevant publications include 'A Chain of Status: Long-term Responsibility in the Context of Human Rights', in G. Bos and M. Düwell (eds), *Human Rights and Sustainability: Moral Responsibilities for the Future* (Routledge, 2016).

Ileana Dascălu holds a PhD in philosophy from the University of Bucharest, Romania, with a thesis on equality of opportunity in an intergenerational context. She is currently a lecturer at the Faculty of Philosophy of the University of Bucharest, working on political philosophy and philosophy of education.

Marcus Düwell is Director of the Ethics Institute of Utrecht University, the Netherlands. He is a member of the board of Utrecht University's Institutions of Open Societies, editor-in-chief of the journal *Ethical Theory and Moral Practice* (Springer) and vice-president of the Helmuth Plessner Society. Recently, he directed bigger research projects on human dignity as foundation of human rights, Western and Chinese concepts of human dignity, practical self-understanding, future generations and climate ethics. He is co-editor of the *Cambridge Handbook of Human Dignity* (Cambridge University Press, 2014); *Human Rights and Sustainability* (Routledge, 2016); and author of *Bioethics: Methods, Theories, Domains* (Routledge, 2012).

Adrian-Paul Iliescu is a Romanian philosopher, doing research in the analytic (Wittgensteinian) tradition in political philosophy and applied ethics. His most important book is *Wittgenstein: Why Philosophy Is Bound to Err* (Peter Lang, 2000). Among his more recent papers are 'How Is Equality Possible? An Analysis of the Idea of Intrinsic Equality', *Transylvanian Review*, 32(1) (2013); and 'The "Missing Link": Polarization and the Need for "Trial by Jury" Procedures', in D. Birnbacher and M. Torseth (eds), *The Politics of Sustainability: Philosophical Perspectives* (Routledge, 2015). He currently focuses on social justice and intrinsicalism.

Karsten Klint Jensen is a PhD and Associate Professor of philosophy at Umeå University, Sweden. His research lies primarily in ethical theory and applied ethics. A dominant theme has been the interface between ethics and other disciplines, e.g. economics, decision theory, animal welfare studies, environmental science, risk assessment and risk perception studies. He has participated in several major national and international interdisciplinary research projects. A common theme of his contributions to these projects is the uncovering of the values underlying disagreement and conflict between stakeholders.

Lukas H. Meyer has pursued research on justice and responsibility in space and time. He is Director of the Institute of Philosophy of the University of Graz, Austria, head of the interdisciplinary doctoral programme 'Climate Change', funded by the Austrian Science Fund, and the leader of research projects on aspects of intergenerational justice, historical injustice and climate ethics. Meyer is one of the founding editors of the journal *Moral Philosophy & Politics* (De Gruyter). His books include *Historische Gerechtigkeit* (De Gruyter, 2005); *Intergenerational Justice* (Oxford University Press, 2009, ed. with Axel Gosseries); *Legitimacy, Justice and Public International Law* (Cambridge University Press, 2009); and *Climate Justice and Historical Emissions* (Cambridge University Press, 2017, ed. with Pranay Sanklecha).

Thierry Ngosso is a Cameroonian philosopher and business ethicist. He holds a PhD in philosophy from the University of Louvain, Belgium. He is currently writing his habilitation dissertation entitled 'Climate Responsibility of Firms as Primary Agents of Justice' at the Institute for Business Ethics of the University of St Gallen. He is also Visiting Professor of political and moral philosophy at the Department of Philosophy of the Catholic University of Central Africa (Cameroon).

Elina Pirjatanniemi is Professor of constitutional and international law at Åbo Akademi University in Turku, Finland. She is also the Director of the Institute for Human Rights at the same university. She is an expert on human rights, as well as asylum and migration law, and on the relationship between human rights and criminal justice. She is also docent in criminal law at the University of Turku, Finland. Her publications cover several areas of law, with a particular emphasis on human rights, the environment and criminal law.

Adriana Placani is Assistant Professor in political philosophy at the Institute of Philosophy, University of Graz, Austria. Her current research focuses on normative questions in the philosophy of risk, with a special emphasis on the assignation of moral responsibility for risk impositions.

Fabian Schuppert is lecturer in political theory and philosophy, as well as Deputy Director of the Centre for the Study of Risk & Inequality at Queen's University, Belfast, UK. He received his PhD from Queen's in 2010, before taking up a postdoctoral position at the Centre for Ethics in Zurich. Fabian works on issues in climate justice, risk ethics, resource governance and political philosophy.

Joachim H. Spangenberg is Research Coordinator at the Sustainable Europe Research Institute SERI Germany, Cologne, and Senior Scientist at the Helmholtz Centre for Environment Research, Leipzig. With a PhD in economics, but an academic background in biology (MSc) and ecology, he is an inter- and transdisciplinary researcher by education and dedication. He works on sustainable development strategies, scenarios, models and indicators, including the limits of economic growth, environmental conflicts, sustainable consumption and ecosystem services and their valuation. Joachim serves on the Executive and Steering Committees of several academic associations, and on the Scientific Committee of the EEA.

Naomi van Steenbergen holds a PhD in philosophy from the University of Essex, UK. She divides her research time between moral psychology and climate justice. She is currently editing a book (with Marcus Düwell and Jos de Mul) on practical self-understanding. Besides her research and teaching in philosophy, she works as a literary and academic translator.

Klaus Steigleder is Professor of applied ethics at the Institute of Philosophy I and Director of the interdisciplinary master's programme 'Ethics – Economics, Law, and Politics' at the Ruhr-Universität, Germany. The current focus of his research is on economic ethics, climate ethics, energy ethics and risk ethics.

Harald Stelzer is Professor of political philosophy at the Institute of Philosophy, University of Graz, Austria. The current focus of his research is on decision-making under uncertainty from the perspective of normative theory as well as in applied ethics, with a special focus on climate engineering.

May Thorseth is Professor of philosophy at NTNU Norwegian University of Science and Technology, department of Philosophy and Religious Studies. She is director of NTNU's Programme for Applied Ethics, and a co-editor of *Etikk i* *praksis* [*Nordic Journal of Applied Ethics*] (Norwegian University of Science and Technology Library). Thorseth is co-author of *The Politics of Sustainability: Philosophical Perspectives* (Routledge, 2015). Current research includes ethics projects in the research projects *Frogs, Fuel, Finance or Food? Cultures, Values, Ethics, Arguments and Justifications in the Management of Agricultural Land* (FORFOOD), and *Managing the Transition to a 'Smart' Bioeconomy* (BIOSMART), both funded by the Norwegian Research Council.

Danielle Zwarthoed is a lecturer at the Catholic University of Louvain, Belgium. Her current research focuses on how education should dispose people to care for distant future people, on the relationships between material resources consumption and autonomy, and on the ethics of family reunification law.

1

INTRODUCTION

Gerhard Bos, Marcus Düwell and Naomi van Steenbergen

What do we owe to future people? Is there anything we should do now in order to do what is right for them? If so, what? How are we to realise the necessary changes in politics, law, the market and in our personal lives? Those questions are unavoidable in light of the environmental challenges that we face today: pollution, resource depletion, destruction of ecosystems, reductions in biodiversity and climate change – to name just a few. Those challenges may well become even more pressing in the future due to an unprecedented growth of the world population. Meeting these challenges would require the present generation to act now, to restrain itself and to realise fundamental changes in various aspects of its existence for the sake of preventing environmental hardship for future people. We face the question of what responsibilities we have for preventive action, as we are confronted with phenomena that threaten the possibilities of future people to exercise central human capacities and fulfil basic needs that we consider of central importance for human beings. Indeed, current environmental changes imperil the future of realising and protecting mutual recognition between human beings in a civilised world.

There is a broad consensus among scientists across the globe that the climate is changing due to anthropogenic causes, despite various uncertainties about the exact nature of the impact of this change across the globe and the possible developments it will give rise to. Given such an unprecedented scientific consensus on climate change, the phenomenon of human-induced climate change will be an important point of reference in this book, even though we will take other ecological challenges into consideration as well. However, the main focus of the book will be to contribute to a normative analysis of the challenge to understand ourselves as responsible in a long-term perspective.

1 Why ethics?

Meeting these ecological challenges will probably require new technologies for energy production, recycling of scarce resources, etc. It is also likely to require new forms of governance and policymaking. Even today, a lot of developments in research and international politics are driven by the attempt to find solutions to those ecological challenges. Still, it seems obvious that we cannot handle those challenges as a mere technological or management problem. We have to conceive of this challenge in the first instance as a moral one, which is to say that we are confronted with the question to what extent we have a moral responsibility to limit possible dramatic consequences to the extent that we are able to do so.

Some may wonder whether it is necessary to write an entire book about the ethics of climate change and long-term responsibility. Is there not a huge consensus that we ought to do something about climate change? Perhaps we don't always act accordingly, but do we not all agree that it would be better to act sustainably? Perhaps some people may think that it is already too late to avoid disastrous consequences of climate change, and they may wonder whether the international climate conferences really make sense or whether their individual contributions are really significant. But apart from dogmatic climate change deniers, no reasonable human being would defend the position that we should just forget about future people and treat the planet to our liking. All kinds of agreements, such as the Sustainable Development Goals, formulate this broadly shared global consensus, even on a global scale. So, what's the point of ethics?

Ethics is generally understood as the discipline that investigates and explores the nature and legitimacy of moral convictions and moral commitments. Conceiving of climate change as an ethical challenge means that this consensus about a moral duty to act sustainably calls for further theoretical consideration and academic scrutiny. A first indication that the moral consensus about climate change is fragile could stem from the observation that despite the rhetorical consensus about climate change, the discrepancy between our knowledge about climate change and our actual changes in behaviour is significant (see Chapter 9). Even though we have known about these challenges for decennia, they do not seem to have high priority. This could just be an indication that human beings are weak creatures – or as Kant once said: 'out of the crooked timber of humanity no straight thing was ever made'. But this lack of action could, on closer examination, also result from a lack of imagination about how we should shape social, political and economic life in ways that would be appropriate to the challenges in question. If our entire lifestyle – the way we eat, travel, use energy, organise cities, etc. – is part of the problem, then what options are there for sustainable solutions? And even if we were to know what a sustainable lifestyle would look like, would it be compatible with the moral obligations we have towards those currently alive? Is it possible to realise a sustainable lifestyle and maintain the openness of liberal societies with all the liberties that citizens have learned to appreciate and may even be right in viewing as indispensable? Will it not be necessary to establish stronger supranational, technocratic institutions that will weaken democratic legitimacy and nurture populist tendencies? And will a sustainable policy be compatible with the legitimate expectation of poor countries to economic development and prosperity?

These questions are not just technical or pragmatic questions. They are questions about the way we should understand our moral responsibilities in a long-term perspective, questions of how to conceive of the place of duties regarding a sustainable lifestyle in the context of our moral self-understanding in general. Ethical questions normally arise when traditional certainties are no longer obvious. Responsibilities with regard to the future is such a case in which moral certainties are undergoing a transformation. And they are particularly pressing since there are no prudential reasons to take care of future people. We can do something for future people, but we cannot expect anything in return. We may care about our children or grandchildren, but why should we care about people in a remote future? Perhaps the ethics of climate change is such a tough issue to face exactly because it asks us to rethink a moral order that we thought to be self-evident and to wonder how we can understand our moral commitments in a more consistent and coherent way. This book tries to take a step in this direction.

2 A rights-based approach

In the past, it was often claimed that responsibility for the environment could only be plausibly taken up if we abandoned some normative commitments that are deeply rooted in the self-understanding of modern liberal societies. Scholars assumed that it was the fault of modernity that we ended up in this ecologically unsustainable situation. If this is the diagnosis, then the therapy would probably be to abandon the normative starting points of modernity and replace them with some kind of holistic worldview that sees human beings in harmony with nature instead of standing in an instrumental relationship to nature. It can hardly be denied that the way nature was treated in the last two centuries has deeply problematic sides. Nor can it be denied that the current political and legal institutions are not well equipped to provide appropriate responses to those challenges. To that extent, the current situation is certainly a challenge for the established normative order. But a diagnosis of the dysfunctional elements of the current normative order has to ask carefully which elements of the modern world are responsible for the current situation. Is it an anthropocentric worldview that sees the human being as entitled to use nature for instrumental purposes? Is it the idea of a liberal society as such that has to be condemned? Is it the capitalistic form of the economy? Is it the idea of sovereignty of modern nation states and the corresponding competition between states that is responsible for this situation?

We cannot go into all the details of those discussions, but it is clear that all possible answers to this have consequences for the normative framework that an ethics of climate change can embrace. This book takes a rights-based framework as its starting point. That means that it starts from an ethics that conceptualises moral and political commitments in terms of rights of human beings and correlative duties of others. Such a rights-based ethics assumes that human beings have rights that all other human beings and particular political institutions have to respect. There are several reasons for such a choice. First of all, the current normative order – at least in liberal societies – is a rights-based order. Most contemporary constitutions are explicitly or implicitly based on a bill of rights and the international order works on the basis of the human rights regime. International treaties, including agreements about sustainability and climate policy, have been directly or indirectly developed on this normative basis. This does not mean that no ethical criticism of this regime is possible, but it does mean that a rights-based ethics has some continuity with the existing normative order. Second, if we consider the characteristic features of modernity – such as state sovereignty, capitalism and human rights – we have reason to think that it is not the idea of individual rights that is to blame for current ecological challenges. The idea of human and civil rights rather rests on normative responses to fundamental aberrations of the modern world, such as exploitation, wars and genocides. We have reason to see it as an achievement that political national orders as well as the international order should not overrule the will and the basic interests of human beings, and that they should therefore function on the basis of respect for individual rights, democracy and rule of law. Finally, from the perspective of ethical theory, we have reason to assume that the idea of 'rights' is better equipped for a defensible normative theory than ethical approaches that would base norms and their enforcement on the idea of respect for nature, the ecosystem or the like (see Chapter 2 for a more detailed discussion).

Nevertheless, the decision to work from a rights-based approach calls for some disclaimers. First of all, it is deeply contested as to what extent it is possible to extend a rights-based approach to future people. Does someone having a right not at least presuppose that this person exists? How can those who have not even been born yet have rights? These are important questions, which we have to discuss in some detail (see in particular Chapter 2). Second, such a commitment to human rights does not mean that the authors of this book assume that the current political and legal institutions are capable of providing appropriate solutions for contemporary challenges. Quite the opposite: the authors are engaged in an attempt to figure out what more appropriate political and legal institutions could look like. The founders of current institutions, including the human rights institutions, have designed these institutions as answers to quite different problems than the current ecological challenges. Third, to emphasise the rights of human beings does not exclude the possibility that we may have duties with regard to animals and perhaps even with regard to inanimate nature. This is not only true because protection of the ecological environment will in many cases be advantageous for the living conditions of animals. There will probably be good independent moral reasons to care about animals as well. We cannot go into detail with regard to this huge debate. In this context, it will have to suffice to stress that a rights-based ethics does not exclude the possibility that we have duties with regard to animals or nature itself; its only implication is that whatever these duties may be, they will have to be compatible with the duties that we have with regard to the rights of human beings. Fourth, one may be concerned that a rights-based ethics will involve certain problematic commitments, for instance that it means embracing a kind of individualistic conception of society that works on the assumption that human beings are atomistic individuals who do not care about each other and who establish rights as fortresses between them. Or, one could wonder to what extent rights are just a Western construct that implicitly signals a hidden colonialist attitude. It certainly cannot be denied that a lot of articulations of the idea of human rights display the features targeted by those criticisms. Nevertheless, there is reason to assume that such criticisms are not fatal for rights-based approaches in general. But this is also a topic that deserves a more elaborate discussion. For our context, it may suffice to emphasise that we see it as a task of the ethical discussion to deal with all the possible criticisms of a rights-based ethics, but that in this book, we only focus on the question what a rights-based ethics may mean for long-term responsibilities with regard to future people. That is probably enough for one book, since climate change is one of the main challenges of our time, and whether human rights remain a viable candidate for the normative order of the twenty-first century will depend to a great extent on the question whether the human rights idea can offer convincing answers to this challenge.

3 Towards a comprehensive view of the ethics of climate change

When we say that we focus on the ethics of climate change, we are not just focusing on a philosophical debate, but try to sketch the most important aspects for the endeavour of understanding what a comprehensive ethics of climate change would entail. This necessarily requires an interdisciplinary approach to the ethics of climate change. Such an interdisciplinary endeavour is necessary considering that our long-term responsibility with regard to future people is a challenge that will require us to rethink the social, political and legal order in general. If we have duties not just to current people but also to future generations, what does that mean for the legal order, for the economy, for democracy and for our individual lifestyles? Understanding the rights of future people does not merely require a sophisticated philosophical argument to show that it makes sense to speak about rights in a future-oriented way. It rather calls for us to spell out in some detail what this would mean for important parts of our social and political life. The chapters in this book do not aim to cover all aspects relevant for the topic; rather, they can be thought of as case studies of the most important aspects. In that regard, they are at the same time representative studies that show what a future interdisciplinary ethics of climate change could look like. One should, however, keep in mind that rethinking our current world in the light of a rights-based ethics of climate change will have implications for the very way we understand ourselves as human beings who stand in relationships of responsibility on a global and intergenerational scale. We probably do not even have a fully developed idea of what that would entail. In that sense, this book is just a step in such a direction.

The book starts with a more detailed discussion of the concept of rights (Chapter 2) and subsequently homes in on the problems of risks and uncertainty in the context of a rights-based ethics (Chapter 3). This topic is particularly pressing since it is often assumed that a rights-based approach is unable to deal with the idea of risk in general. The ability to protect rights seems to presuppose that we know what consequences our actions have. How can one protect rights under circumstances of risk and uncertainty? The chapter discusses the challenges a rights-based risk ethics has to face and gives indications of what possible answers could look like. It is evident that it is crucial for the entire endeavour of the book that a rights-based ethics has something to say in this context, because nearly all challenges in a long-term perspective are confronted with risks and uncertainties. Those uncertainties will not only be discussed on an abstract level; Chapter 4 will take a closer look at the scenarios that scientists develop in order to get a view of the future. It is of course indispensable to develop an understanding of the different ways the future may develop, but the chapter critically discusses some presuppositions that are made in the development of those scenarios. This chapter emphasises the need for developing those scenarios in a self-reflexive mode and for being open to revision.

Talking about rights is not just a matter of ethics; the aim, obviously, is their implementation within a concrete legal order. Chapter 5 investigates to what extent the existing human rights provisions have elements that allow for the inclusion of future people in the human rights regime. This chapter does not only aim at detecting such future-oriented elements within the different human rights regulations, but also identifies a future-oriented tendency within the human rights regime that became increasingly clear over the last decades and that will probably be a reason to rework this regime in the years to come. Chapter 6 discusses one possible element of such a future human rights regime: the idea of representing future people in political institutions. If human rights provisions are to take future people into account, this implies that it is not just up to the discretionary power of current political institutions to care about the future. Rather, future people should be represented within the structure of political institutions itself. This chapter gives an overview of important discussions about this idea and sketches the obstacles such an idea faces. It provides an abundance of material concerning concrete political and legal discussions about this topic. Chapter 7 investigates the particular circumstances and duties of developing countries in light of our current ecological challenges. On the one hand, developing countries face pressing problems right now, and they may be thought to be unable to afford caring for anything other than the present. On the other hand, the future generations of poor countries are likely to be among those hit hardest by climate change and environmental degradation. This chapter discusses the implications of the historical and current situation of developing countries for the future-oriented policies that they ought to adopt.

Chapter 8 provides an assessment of climate economics on the basis of a rights-based ethics. The chapter tries to show the difficulties of neoclassic economics in tackling the very topic of future-orientated economic thinking in the first place and tries to indicate some alternative ways of thinking about the problem. Chapter 9 gives an outline of the so-called 'motivational problem' within climate ethics. This problem indicates that there is a significant gap between the insight that we ought to act sustainably and our actual actions. This problem has to do not only with insights and knowledge, but also with the problem of motivation, which is obviously particularly significant in the context of future-oriented questions. Chapter 10 discusses the governance of a 'green future'. This chapter aims at analysing governance-related problems with regard to our topic on a structural level and illustrates those problems in light of a couple of concrete case studies. Chapter 11, finally, proposes a research agenda; a variety of aspects that are important for future research about a comprehensive ethics of climate change and rights in an intergenerational perspective.

The book is the result of a collaborative activity. Still, each author is responsible for his or her own chapter. The editors tried to edit the entire book in such a way as to achieve a certain level of coherence between the different parts. Such thematic coherence does, however, not exclude the possibility that authors have different theoretical and methodological starting points. Nevertheless, we are of the opinion that the book presents the problem under a coherent perspective. The book is directed towards a quite diverse audience – not just philosophers or lawyers, but rather scholars and students from all disciplines that deal with the normative dimensions of climate change and other ecological challenges. The reader should keep in mind that there are many more discussions about those normative dimensions than one would probably think. Ultimately, the very idea of 'sustainable development' is a normative idea: that we ought to act in such a way that by fulfilling our needs we ensure that future people are still able to fulfil their own needs.[1] As such, the whole idea of sustainability presupposes that we have duties with regard to future people, which means that everybody who deals with sustainability should be interested in this book. The authors did their best not to presuppose sophisticated philosophical terminology or argumentation, or – if necessary – to explain this argumentation. We hope that a broad group of scholars, students, policymakers, politicians and interested laypersons will benefit from reading this book.

Acknowledgements

This book has been realised in the context of the European Science Foundation (ESF)-funded networking programme 'Rights to a Green Future' (2011–2015). The scholars who participated in this network are from various disciplines and come from all over Europe; they aim to identify long-term environmental responsibilities in the context of human rights and to discuss related governance issues with regard to their legal, political, ethical and philosophical dimensions. We want to thank the ESF for their generous support of this network. We want to thank the Netherlands Organization for Scientific Research for additional financial support for the project 'Human Dignity as the Foundation of Human Rights?', which was important for a successful realisation of the current project. We want to thank all participants in the network and all participants in the network's workshops for their collaboration in such an open spirit. We want to thank Naomi Jacobs and

Leon van Rijsbergen for the excellent support while editing this book and we want to thank Leila Walker from Routledge for her patience with us. We hope that this book will contribute to next steps on the way to a future that takes human rights in an intergenerational perspective seriously.

Note

1 World Commission on Environment and Development, *Our Common Future*, Oxford: Oxford University Press, 2009, p. 43.

2

WHY *'RIGHTS'* OF FUTURE PEOPLE?

Marcus Düwell and Gerhard Bos

1 Introduction

Modern law conceptualises normative regulations in terms of 'rights'; modern legal systems are based on the idea that the law has to protect the rights of individuals. This implies that governmental restrictions on the exercise of our liberties have to be justified with reference to the impact of actions on individual rights. This rights-based idea of law is also the basis of the international normative order in so far as states have bound themselves internationally to such a respect of individual rights and international political institutions are explicitly built to enforce those rights. In international treaties, states have bound themselves to respect the rights assigned to human beings as such. Which is to say, individuals have these rights independently from the legal systems under which they fall.

Over the last years, philosophers had important discussions about the concept, justification, scope, legitimacy and various other aspects of human rights (see, e.g. Gewirth 1996; Donnelly 2003; Griffin 2008; Buchanan 2014). Some have seen human rights as merely a utopian framework (Moyn 2012) or have predicted the 'endtime of human rights' (Hopgood 2013). Often it was criticised that human rights have been interpreted as a moral framework, seen in continuity with older natural law and natural rights approaches (Beitz 2009). It was particularly emphasised that the modern human rights system has a new quality as a *political* and *practical* instrument. Human rights are formally accepted by states and international treaties are the result of political negotiations, which are enforceable and not just declarations of moral convictions without enforcement mechanisms. It was emphasised that we do not understand human rights if we do not focus on their practical purposes and functions (see Beitz 2009; Cruft et al. 2015).

At the same time, there is undeniably a moral dimension to the entire idea as well to the practice of human rights: human rights are historically developed as response to oppression, exploitation and atrocities against human beings. Wars of the twentieth century, colonial exploitation of the globe and the holocaust formed the background to the commitment of the international community to human rights, a commitment that must be understood as a moral statement. Despite all possible differences in moral and political opinions, human rights articulate the shared conviction as to how human beings should be treated and how they should not be treated: they should not be killed, tortured or humiliated; they should have a certain legal status and they should have access to at least some of the means necessary to live lives on their own.

This moral dimension of human rights, in particular, however, has provoked important controversies: does it really make sense to speak about 'rights' in moral terms? Are rights not necessarily bound to the legal sphere? Do they not necessarily presuppose some legal body that grants these rights? And if they have a moral dimension, what precisely is the connection between a moral and a legal understanding of rights? And does it really make sense to discuss morality primarily in terms of rights instead of duties or virtues? And if it makes sense to talk about moral rights: what do we have a right to? Whose duty is it to ensure that these rights are protected? It can hardly be individuals that carry the burden of all misery and shortcomings of the world. And if these rights impose duties on all of us, on what basis do we have such duties? Despite these discussions, however, it is clear that respect for rights of human beings belong to the normative core of modern societies; nearly all states on earth have formally committed themselves to the protection of those rights (though whether they respect them in practice is another story). In international law, other legal frameworks exist as well, it is generally assumed that there is a normative priority of the human rights regime in the sense that those other frameworks at least should not contradict human rights requirements; often they form a concretisation of human rights provisions to specific regulatory areas.

This latter point is relevant for the context of this book, which is concerned with anthropogenic climate change, threats to biodiversity, pollution, depletion of natural resources and a range of other topics that constitute a relevant concern for the future. How, though, are those topics related to the idea of rights, indeed of human rights? At first glance, it might seem that human rights merely regulate the way in which human beings are treated by the state or the way in which human beings treat each other. Human rights seem to have nothing to say about the way we should treat nature or deal with a changing climate. However, if we widen our perspective even slightly, it should be clear that human rights and institutional responses to environmental degradation and climate change are in fact intimately connected. First of all, the lives and living circumstances of people all over the world are already endangered at this very moment by problems such as pollution, droughts and extreme weather events. What happens in the natural environment is in many cases tightly connected to the lives of people. Moreover, it is not at all self-evident that the scope of application of the human rights framework should be restricted to our contemporaries and to current problems and conflicts. If we are today destroying natural resources and changing the climate in a way that will have a strong impact on the lives of future people, we should at least consider the possibility that this might be relevant in terms of rights we should grant them in response to their being human beings.

Nevertheless, as clear as it might be that environmental matters impact human lives, present and future, this does not by itself answer the further question whether we should rely on the human rights framework to regulate problems such as climate change. For some people, in fact, the environmental crisis affirms their scepticism about the very idea of human rights as a means to address urgent problems. Some will reason that since future people do not yet exist, it is entirely unclear that we are able to violate their rights at all. Even if we would have to care about future people, why should we think that our behaviour today would harm them? Others will wonder whether the whole idea of rights isn't an expression of the very same anthropocentric idea that has in the past been used to justify the exploitation of nature. Wouldn't it be better to replace this entire moral concept by a less anthropocentric framework? And are not human rights a very individualistic idea, while answers to the ecological crisis require concepts that aim at the protection of collective goods instead of individual liberties? Is not the fact that we exercise our individual liberties so unrestrained the main reason for the ecological crisis? Should we not see ourselves as a global community if we are to protect the planet's future when it is at risk, instead of embracing an individualistic framework that continues to focus on the protection of individual freedom, even when the planet and its future inhabitants are at risk?

We can easily see that these concerns are not merely related to the question how we should regulate matters of sustainability. Central questions of our political and moral self-understanding in general are at stake. In this chapter, we will discuss questions of an *ethics of rights*, in general terms, and then with regard to rights related to the environment and with regard to future people (section 2). Subsequently, we will discuss criticisms of a rights approach and alternatives for discussing ecological challenges (section 3). Finally, we will sketch some topics for future discussions (section 4).

2 An ethics of rights?

2.1 Why rights?

Human rights approaches are anthropocentric in at least two ways. First, human rights place the *human being at the centre of moral and legal consideration*. They justify duties by reference to human interests and rights. Second, ethical and legal practices that concern human rights are always *human practices*. That is, human rights are anthropocentric in both their object and their origin. This does not mean, though, that they automatically authorise human beings to use nature and animals for arbitrary goals. Only very few rights approaches hold that human beings can exploit nature to whatever purpose.

Rights as such are also not necessarily *egalitarian*. In earlier times, only free citizens would be rights holders, and most human beings would not have this status.[1] It was only in modern times that the idea arose that each human being should be entitled to rights equal to those of all others. Human rights contrast with other kinds of rights in the sense that they recognise all human beings as equal; they universally apply to all human beings as such. They protect something that is not dependent on any sovereign power who could grant these rights or take them away; rather, these rights are inalienably connected to our person.

Rights are in those discourses normally understood as '*claim-rights*' which means that a right is not just a *privilege* or a *liberty*. A claim-right presupposes that the other has strict obligations correlated to my right (Hohfeld 1964). From a historical perspective, the modern idea of (natural) rights developed primarily with the function of protecting the rights holder against the arbitrary use of power. That means rights give human beings a status vis-à-vis the state that forms a *limitation to the legitimate use of power*. The individual should not be dependent on gracious acts of powerful others that grant them their liberties. On the contrary: nobody – no individual person, church or state – should be entitled to possess another human being (see, e.g., John Locke 2016). Some *libertarians* (e.g. Nozick 1974) have concluded that this would imply that the state would have only a very minimal function – basically to ensure that nobody interferes directly with the exercise of the liberty of individuals.

But one can see claim-rights not only as a factor for limiting legitimate exercise of power but rather also as a necessary element in the justification of the necessity of the existence of a state in the first place. The protection of rights could be seen as the reason why we need a state at all. Some have argued that this protection of rights entails much more than just protection against interference with an individual's freedom. That is to say: human beings also have rights to get some form of support in exercising their liberties. They would distinguish between *negative rights* (rights against illegitimate infringement by others) and *positive rights* (rights to get some support in whatever it is we have a right to) (Gewirth 1996). To think about concrete examples, one can think that negative rights would protect human beings against interferences from others who, say, want to hinder me in my articulating an opinion; while positive rights enable individuals to make use of their freedom by giving them access to education, or to support them if they have special needs.

But what do we have a right to? There are at least two basic answers to this (Hart 1955). So-called '*interest theories of rights*' say that we have rights to those things in which human beings have the (most basic) interests. We all have an interest in staying alive, having some security, exercising our freedom, having some well-being or at least access to the necessary means to it. According to these theories, it is those basic interests that we have rights to, and correspondingly, the state has to take any measures necessary to protect these. Interest theories vary regarding the extent to which interests are protected – the idea of 'basic interests' can be understood broadly or more limited – and the extent to which the state is supposed to have an active role in their protection.[2]

'*Will theories of rights*' argue that rights holders have to be seen as sovereign over themselves, and that others have to respect this sovereignty. Rights protect the *ability* of right holders to govern their own lives. This does not of course mean that they are under an enforceable duty to make use of this ability: right holders can choose to refrain from exercising certain rights. Someone can decide not to make use of his right to free speech his entire life; this person would probably be a bit boring, but no rights would be violated as long as it was up to him to speak up or not. As long as nobody infringes on my opportunity to speak freely, there is no problem from the viewpoint of this rights-based approach, if I desire not to use it. This does imply that others have no right to directly hinder a rights holder in enjoying the freedom under his or her right. It implies more, however. To be able to exercise one's will, one needs access to information about the consequences of one's actions, a certain degree of education, and to some basic means that are necessary for the realisation the goals one wills. Here, too, there are discussions about the question how far such rights should go, and to what extent human beings have the right to be supported in the possibility to realise their freedom. In any case it is not clear that a 'will theory' would only be restricted to protecting individuals in as much as they are already exercising their will. That is to say, there are also positions that claim that states have (far-reaching) duties to enable people regarding the exercise of their will, to enable development of reflected views on what they might want, what might be important goals for them to realise.

This distinction between an interest theory and a will theory of rights is just a very basic distinction of different families of rights theories. The different rights theories vary in different regards. They will have different views with regard to the scope of rights: to how much of the realisation of our interests or of our will are we entitled? Is there a threshold level of realisation in terms of which we may distinguish what is and what is not a violation of rights? How can we determine such a threshold? (See Chapter 3 on this problem.) Rights theories will voice different opinions with regard to a possible hierarchy of different rights. It is not plausible to assume that all rights are of the same level of importance (we will come back to this), it may be acceptable to infringe on someone's private property if the life of another person is at stake. In any case, rights theories have different perspectives on this. Likewise, there are different views on the question who should be seen as the carrier of rights-correlated duties. It is clear that some rights can (as a matter of fact) only be protected by states or other collective actors. However, that does not hold for all rights in the same way. Rights theories differ in this regard as well. That said, the overall ground for the state's role in respecting and enforcing a specific right goes well beyond its being the (only) body capable of doing so: it seems the very notion of a right implies its being a legal entity that is enforced by the state.

This latter issue has to do with the question whether it makes sense to speak about 'moral rights' or whether rights just belong to the domain of law and politics. For this context, it will suffice to say that there are positions that would say that we have duties towards each other on the basis of moral rights. But we can also think about 'moral rights' in the sense of reasons for establishing political institutions and respective legal regulations. In the first sense of moral rights we could say I have a duty not to lie to you because you have a moral right to be treated with respect. Such a concept does not offer direct reasons for actions of the state – at least further considerations would be required. We would speak about 'moral rights' in the second sense if we e.g. say 'refugees have a right to asylum' and we mean by that that states have a duty to create laws that protect that right. In that sense we would see moral rights as the moral basis of legal rights, as reasons to create respective legal provisions.

There are also different positions regarding the interpretation of human rights. A standard position emphasises a difference between human rights and moral rights in general and civil rights. As already said, human rights have a moral dimension but nevertheless they are at the same time expressed in international treaties and regulations. In that sense they are part of positive law. But unlike regulations within domestic law they are provisions primarily directed towards states to organise their domestic law according to human rights requirements. In that sense, their primary enforcement would be the task of states while human rights courts and similar international bodies have a subsidiary task to supervise this enforcement and to take – under specific condition – measures if states fail to fulfil their duties.

A huge discussion deals with the question why human beings should have those rights. There are some positions that hold the view that this practice is historically developed the way it is and we should refrain from attempting to give a moral justification beyond this contingent development (Beitz 2009; Raz 2010). All we can do is to reconstruct those rights as a central element of modern self-understanding. Of course, we can reconstruct a logic behind these rights, e.g. we can try to show that human rights are protecting human agency, the ability to act which is important for human persons in general (Griffin 2008). Or it is argued that it is a central feature of modernity that human beings have to be treated with equal respect which implies that they can expect a justification for the way they are treated, and the human rights regime embodies this right to justification (Forst 2007). In a Kantian line we can argue that it is part of a reflected self-understanding of human beings that we understand ourselves as obliged to treat humanity always with respect. Because all human beings have status as beings with dignity, their rights should be respected. In this line one would offer a transcendental argumentation that tries to show that human rights are based in the reflected self-understanding of human agents in general. And because human beings deserve respect, the goods they need to develop their agency and realise their goods have to be protected (Gewirth 1978; Beyleveld and Bos 2009; Düwell 2017).

2.2 Rights and the environment

All the different human rights approaches are confronted with the question: in what ways are environmental goods relevant to them? It is clear that, traditionally, human rights were developed as protection for human beings against arbitrary behaviour of states and against abuse from other human beings. It is not a coincidence that human rights were declared directly after the atrocities of the holocaust and the Second World War (Morsink 2000). But if we assume that establishing human rights means granting human beings the status of human dignity (i.e. the status as a being that has a right to lead life according to his/her own goals), then this normative commitment bears constructive and critical potential in situations that are fundamentally different to that of the mid-twentieth century. In the twenty-first century we are perhaps less threatened by totalitarian regimes (even so that threat can never be ruled out) but there are other threats to basic human needs and capacities protected under human rights, and ecological threats are among the first to qualify in this regard.

Human beings, on account of their biological basis, need certain environmental conditions in order to fulfil whatever interests they may have, and they need such conditions in order to exercise their will, whatever the objects of their will may be. If you live in Beijing, you will experience how important fresh air can be: before you think about exercising your freedom of speech, you need to be able to breathe. Similarly, exercising your right to go from one place to another can be seriously hampered by a lack of fresh air. The same holds for the relatively stable climate that is required for many things that enable civilisation, such as access to natural goods for the production of food and energy. Moreover, one can ask whether human beings may not need some access to the aesthetic qualities of nature in order to flourish or find their place in the totality of nature (e.g. Sandler 2009). It is disputable exactly which goods are necessary for human beings, but whatever the answer to that question is, it should be clear that many environmental goods are implicitly presupposed in all kinds of interests that humans may have, and in all kind of goals they may want to realise. Some authors have therefore argued that certain environmental goods are necessary 'objects of rights', regardless of what human beings may want to realise specifically (Shue 1980); others have called the rights to such goods 'generic rights' (Gewirth 1978) – rights that are implied in all kinds of other rights. If traditional human rights regulations (of the mid-twentieth century) did not focus on such environmental rights, this may have been simply because these goods were not seen as endangered, let alone endangered in the kind of way that was considered a grave concern after the world wars. Of course, like rights generally do, environmental rights offer protection only for things that are within human control; we cannot have a right not to be hit by a meteorite, as such protection is beyond human control.

Environmental rights, then, are generic rights par excellence, since we are to some extent all dependent on environmental goods in order to be able to exercise our will or to realise basic interests. Correspondingly, environmental rights seem to imply the existence of rights that offer protection at a collective level. Fresh air, climate stability and biodiversity are not just goods for me, but goods for all human beings – in fact, they go beyond borders and generations. But even though they are important for collectives of human beings, these environmental rights are not in contradiction with the idea of the human individual's inalienable rights. In fact, they are implied in this idea. Basic environmental goods are necessary for the ability of human beings to exercise their own rights. Once again, it can and should be discussed which environmental goods are so important for human beings that we should take them to have a *right* to these goods. And we will have to discuss which of these goods are so important that their protection may legitimate limitations of the exercise of our freedoms – after all, it is likely that the protection of environmental goods will be in conflict with the exercise of some things that are currently perceived as unquestionable liberties. So, it may be inevitable to restrict our using airplanes, energy or food consumption in order to protect some environmental goods. That will create the necessity of comparing and weighing the relative importance of different right protections. Notwithstanding these open questions, it seems generally plausible that there are some environmental rights. It is not rational to say that we all have a right to freedom of speech while denying that we have a right to fresh air if we know that the exercise of the right to freedom of speech presupposes fresh air (and if we also know that human activity can impair or protect this access to fresh air). The more endangered environmental goods on which protection of human rights depends are, the more urgent the protection of these goods is from a human rights perspective.

The protection of an environment that is necessary for the free activity of human beings is at least implicitly protected by the traditional human rights regimes, and increasingly it is explicitly protected too, as will be discussed in Chapter 5. Some aspects, however, require measures that are different from traditional human rights regulations. These have to do with the *spatial and temporal distance* between actions and human rights violations, the recognition and representation of future rights and rights holders in the present, the *uncertainty* about certain causal relationships and the *kinds of actions* with rights-violating potential – aspects that will be further discussed in the following chapters. These differences mainly result from specific features of modern developments such as industrialisation, globalisation, population growth and modern lifestyles. The environmental effects are often embedded in complex spatiotemporal relationships. The use of energy and accompanying CO_2 emissions in one part of the world will accumulate with those of other parts, and together they may result in climatic changes in yet another part of the world, not now but decennia in the future. Activities such as the production of nuclear waste may have irreversible environmental effects centuries from now. We will not be able to reconstruct the entire network of causes and effects for every action we may do; we can only estimate the long-term effects of our actions at a general level. This means that the links between actions and potential rights violations can be indirect, and there are often significant spatiotemporal gaps between certain actions and effects that are relevant to rights. Furthermore, the kinds of actions at stake here are not the kinds one would traditionally expect to be human rights violations. We are not talking about torture or intentional harm to another person. Most of us do not destroy the environment simply for fun. What is at stake are rather activities such as travelling, cooking, heating, producing industrial goods and agriculture – activities that, if done on a massive scale, may affect the rights of other people. Those that perform these actions will not necessarily think about their detrimental effects, and normally they will not perform these actions with the intention to produce rights-violating effects. They are not torturers, dictators or concentration camp guards, but normal people doing things that normal people do. In fact, if these activities happened at a smaller scale or by other means, perhaps they would not have any significant impact. This means that actions that affect environmental rights are in some regards different from the human rights violations that the drafters the Universal Declaration of Human Rights had in mind. But this does not mean that these actions are not significant from a human rights perspective. All it takes for such actions to be considered relevant is to accept that we should be concerned with the protection of vital human interests or capacities, rather than with merely curbing intentional violations of these.

2.3 Rights of future people?[3]

A specific challenge is related to the long-term effects of our actions. We are engaged in actions that will affect people in the future. In the case of nuclear energy, we have reason to assume that people thousands of years from now might be forced to deal with the waste we produce. That raises the question to what extent actions that will affect future people – people who do not yet exist – can be regulated within the human rights framework at all. Can we violate rights of human beings who do not yet exist?[4] To some extent, we actually can. We cannot humiliate someone who does not exist, we cannot hinder her in exercising her freedom of speech and we cannot harm her – there is just nobody to be harmed, nobody who may want to exercise her freedom of speech. We cannot even know what kinds of activities future people will want to perform and what desires and wishes they may have – perhaps they will not be interested in any of the activities many of us are interested in. And partly we don't have reason to concern ourselves with their specific rights. How they want to organise their societies and their social lives is really not our business – they can figure this out themselves. But nevertheless future people are relevant in human rights terms. We will briefly present two possible lines of argumentation for this.

The first argument will focus merely on the specific nature of human rights. The normative commitment to human rights is based on the assumption that all human beings have dignity, and that the rights that follow from this status have to be respected by all human beings.[5] So it is not enough for one person to respect another's human rights merely on the basis of these rights being prescribed by law – to recognise someone's human rights requires respect for them on the basis of the other person's status as a human being and the dignity involved in this status. But if human rights are based on the dignity of human beings, it is unclear why the same should not apply to future people. On the basis of what kinds of presuppositions would it be plausible to speak about the rights of future people? At least three assumptions are necessary. First, we have to assume that there will be people in the future. If we were to know that the apocalypse would come quite soon, this would limit our duties significantly. But since the world population is growing more than ever, we have reason to assume that there will be (a lot of) people in the future. Second, we have to assume that these future human beings are sufficiently similar to us, that is, that they will share with us relevant basic bio-logical features and will have needs for an ecological environment similar to the environmental needs we have. We don't have to assume that the environmental needs of future people and their respective rights will be fully the same as ours or that the contents of their needs are obvious. But even if humankind may sig-nificantly evolve and transform, we have to assume that these changes will not be so fast that human beings in the centuries to come will become independent of the sort of ecological environment that we depend on. Third, we have to assume that our actions today affect the environmental needs of future people. Given the long-term effects of the environmental changes that we bring about at the moment, we have good reason to assume that this is the case.

This consideration does not imply that future people *now* have rights; it is suffi-cient to assume that people that will exist will be rights holders. Nor does it follow that we have a duty to bring future people into existence. The argument – thus far – only shows that people living now can have duties on the basis of rights that future people will have. To determine the concrete normative consequences of this consideration is not that easy, because we lack information of various sorts, such as how many people there will be, what kind of technologies will emerge, and how climate change and biodiversity will develop concretely. All those things influence our concrete duties, but the relevant point for the moment is that in any case we would – on the basis of the three assumptions mentioned above – have to integrate future people into any human rights protection.

One way to do so is via the second, 'chain of status' argument. The argument builds on two assumptions. First, it observes that members of different generations lead partially overlapping lives: there is no point in time at which one generation stops and the next generation starts. Second, it emphasises that human rights should be conceived of as recognised and protected in response to someone's being human – nothing more, nothing less. Building on these assumptions, the 'chain of status' argument emphasises that the *possibility* of the right kind of protection and recognition within the lifetime of us, currently living people, depends on the same *possibility* for our future contemporaries (those with whom our lives will, at some point, overlap), which in turn depends on the same possibility for *their* future contemporaries, and so on (Bos 2016). This means that we should see to it that the future possibility of the recognition and protection of human rights, beyond our lifetime, is not obstructed by our actions. Our commitment to human rights thus requires us to make sure that human rights institutions are continuously robust, future-proof and resilient in their capacity to recognise and protect human beings as such. Hence, we should oppose environmental developments that undermine this capacity of these institutions within our lifetime and beyond. We need environ-mental conditions in which human rights institutions can exist and function properly.

We are aware that this outline of an argument does not answer all questions of what a human rights regime would look like that takes the rights of future people seriously. In fact, we think that it would need this entire book to sketch out what the right-based ethics of a green future should look like.

3 Criticisms and alternatives

Conceiving of future-oriented environmental duties in terms of rights is not uncontroversial. Since it is impossible to discuss each possible criticism here, we will only address three perspectives: (a) criticisms of rights theories in general; (b) criticisms of the rights of future generations in particular; and (c) non-anthropocentric alternative perspectives.

3.1 Criticisms of rights theories in general

Rights theories are criticised from different backgrounds. Some *communitarians* have argued that an ethics formulated in terms of rights of individuals presupposes a specific 'atomistic' perspective on society (Taylor 1985), according to which human beings are isolated individuals that can autonomously decide whether or not they relate to each other in forms of contractual agreements. Some claim that this atomistic view is a dominant pattern that underlies the modern world and its dominant view on politics as a social contract. They argue that this is an unrealistic and inappropriate account of the human being, because human beings are fundamentally dependent on each other and therefore cannot be conceptualised as isolated individuals. Human beings would not be able to grow up without social relationships, and they would not be able to develop language without a social environment. Some of these criticisms combine the critique of an atomistic anthropology with the further criticism that a rights approach would introduce formal, government-organised social relationships while at the same time destroying traditionally grown organic forms of a social life.

However, we may ask whether this criticism is valid for rights theories in general or only for specific types of rights theories. Some rights theories assume that rights are merely the result of a strategic self-interested calculation according to which it is in the self-interest of all to establish arrangements in which the exercise of our freedom is protected. One can indeed doubt that such a self-interested perspective on rights can really form the basis of a *human* rights approach. Why, from a self-interested perspective, should we respect the rights of all human beings, independent of whether or not the others may form a realistic threat for us? However, if human rights are seen as inalienable, something that belongs to human beings as such, then presumably such rights need another source than just self-interested reflections of individuals. An ethics of rights is relational in the sense that they are providing us with reasons why we should care about each other. Such an ethics just has to assume that it is possible that human beings violate the rights of others and treat each other with disrespect. Therefore, it will argue for the necessity of creating institutions that embody respect for the dignity and rights of others, a 'community of rights' (Gewirth 1996). Furthermore, some rights theories explicitly defend the position that there are positive rights that support the ability to exercise autonomy. This would preclude atomism as described above. So, the criticism of atomism may be valid to the extent that a rights theory would work with the presupposition that human beings are isolated from each other and that rights are conceptualised as fortresses to protect our identity as individuals isolated in such a way. But it is far from obvious that this is a fundamental criticism of a rights approach in general.

A second line of criticism doubts to what extent rights can be a fundamental concept in ethics at all. According to this argument, duties or virtues are much more fundamental than rights. From this perspective, we first would have to assume that human beings see themselves as having duties in general, or that they need the idea of a virtuous life before rights can be elaborated as a meaningful concept. They would assume that it is only possible to determine any rights of human beings when we have already established an overarching view on the duties people have towards one other. To some extent this could be seen as a linguistic question, since, after all, rights and duties are correlated; if persons have rights, then by implication others have corresponding duties. If we have a duty not to kill other people, this duty can also be formulated as a right of other people not to be killed. It may also be the case that rights are a meaningful concept merely within the legal–political realm, but that those rights can only be understood within a broader moral framework where duties and virtues are the more fundamental concepts.

A meaningful moral perspective on rights does indeed presuppose that human beings should consider themselves bound by moral obligations. If we do not have reason to follow moral duties, we do not have decisive reasons to respect the rights of others. But the question is now which status the duties to respect others have within our set of moral duties in general. There are, after all, duties that are independent of any particular rights of others; there may even be an approach of ethics not expressed in terms of respect for others. The more substantial question is therefore whether rights-related duties have some sort of normative priority over duties of other kinds.

Some moral doctrines will, for instance, claim that human beings have religious duties to follow the rule of God, or they might prescribe virtuous behaviour regarding specific attitudes. These duties may be compatible with an ethics of rights to some extent, but it is not clear that all such duties are. God may e.g. prescribe the duties to convert, exclude or even kill as many unbelievers as possible. Or it may be seen as the most fundamental virtue to refrain from action independent of the circumstance and independent of whether or not this non-activity will be harmful for others or will restrain me from fulfilling any perceived duties towards others. An 'ethics of rights' will always claim that rights-related duties deserve normative priority and that the respect we owe to others is of prior importance. Of course, such an ethics will accept that there are limits to what can be expected from us with regard to others. Such an ethics will also accept that rights-based duties cannot be isolated within the moral lives of human beings; it would be psychologically very implausible to assume that we orient our behaviour always by first addressing the question 'What do I owe to other people?' Respect towards others must be part of our attitudes and habits, and we will only be able to treat others with respect if we have general habits of controlling our behaviour, being sensitive to the outside world, etc. For example, a drug-addicted person will have difficulty respecting others when he is caught up pursuing his habit. It may be that the drug addict also has duties of virtue, but even an 'ethics of rights' will require each of us to live a kind of life that makes it realistically possible for us to fulfil our other-regarding duties. What is central, however, is that an 'ethics of rights' will not allow us to overrule rights-related duties by other considerations, moral or otherwise.

But there are of course a variety of discussions around the extent to which an ethics of rights can be seen as complete, whether there can be a comprehensive ethical approach based solely on respect for the rights of others. An ethics of rights would have to ask what kinds of presuppositions are required to make the normative commitment for the respect of human beings intelligible. And it is of course possible that an explanation of those presuppositions would entail a variety of further considerations relevant to notions of duty and virtue. However, to discuss them would go far beyond the scope of this book.

Third, utilitarians among others criticise rights-based ethics for fundamental reasons too. The classic utilitarian will assume that the aggregation of goods should be determinative of our moral duties – so if we act in a way that results in more happiness for more people, this action is better than one from which only a few people benefit. From this perspective, rights seem much too protective of individuals. The reply of a rights ethicist could be that it is correct to assume that goods for different people can and should be aggregated and feed into our moral considerations, but that the protection of fundamental rights of people cannot be outweighed by any aggregated or collective good.

We are fully aware that there are – of course – many more discussions about rights that would be relevant here, but our exploration above may suffice for the purpose of this volume.

3.2 Criticisms of rights for future generations

Not all rights approaches accept that there is an obvious connection between the importance of rights per se and the recognition of rights for future generations. That is to say, there are views on rights that emphasise the legitimacy and scope of rights in terms of agreement and acceptance by individuals in a shared community. There are at least three ways to address criticism of such a connection.

First, human rights were conceived in international agreements in response to the Second World War, and have since developed on the basis of further international negotiation and agreement. Correspondingly, the internationally guiding conception of human rights is at least partially independent of an underlying philosophy or unifying moral view of human rights (Beitz 2003; 2009). Lacking such a theoretical basis, and as long as there is no international agreement on the inclusion of future people, the question would be whether and why we would recognise duties to human rights of future generations. In response, we would emphasise that there is a clear commitment to human rights founded in human dignity in the declarations and the treaties, challenging or denying which would fundamentally alter our modern international commitments – no matter how much they *also* depend on international agreement. Following that, we would restate the two points made above as to why concern for future generations is mandatory in the context of human rights.

Second, philosophically grounded conceptions of rights sometimes fail to include obligations to rights of future people. For instance, some accounts of rights understand rights as agreements between human beings made in order to mutually secure or further their individual freedom or well-being. From this standpoint, the question arises why we should recognise rights of people with whom we will never interact. If our freedom or well-being are not under the control of future people, then why would we recognise rights for them, given that doing so does not help us secure our own freedom and well-being? One can wonder whether it is a plausible account of human rights in the first place to see it as mutually securing our own interests. But even if we would do so, how would it be possible to limit the scope of this application to the current generation? Particularly if we are aware that there is an overlap between generations. Even if the motivation for our engaging in securing rights of individuals is egoistic, would it not be necessary to extend the rights to human beings in general in order to protect rights of individuals? Of course, it may be advantageous for me as an individual to see my own interests and those of my direct social environment, my country, etc. be protected independent of the rights protection of human beings in general. So, I must have reasons to extend respect for rights to human beings in general. But if I do that, it is hard to see how we could argue for a strict discontinuation in the protection of rights between present and future generations.

Third, there is arguably a gap between recognising rights for future people and enforcing corresponding duties. For example, one may recognise rights for future people, or even moral obligations towards future people, but hold that no state has any authority to enforce these obligations – for instance because one thinks that the state is limited to securing the safety of the citizens it represents. This would exclude enforcing rights that concern those outside of it, both in space and time. Alternatively, one may accept that future people have rights, but question one's duty to secure their basic needs, for instance because relevant actors may deny responsibility for the hardships that future people might face. One may argue that one's contribution to any future hardship as an individual, state or generation is quite limited. And that the fact that future generations will face hardship does not suffice to show that one should stop contributing to it, let alone that one should invest in preventing it. However, we would insist that human rights entail a moral commitment to human dignity that should guide, rather than be constructed as a function of, agreement between currently living people on how to secure the freedom and well-being of human beings. If this is the case, the recognition of obligations to respect the dignity of future people should be less controversial, and the political enforcement of such obligations possible.

Apart from these three concerns raised by specific rights approaches, there are general theoretical reasons to doubt that the rights approach is appropriate for dealing with the challenges of future people. Relatedly, there is a set of more practical questions. How should we represent future people in politics and law, if we wish to recognise and enforce rights of future people? How should such representation be aligned with the core human institutions, as well as with more specific ones? How are we to identify what future generations will need environmentally, find out how to secure that, and implement protections of these needs and identify or even sue those who violate rights of future generations? Some of these issues will be addressed in other chapters of this book.

3.3 Non-anthropocentric perspectives

A final group of scholars is critical of human rights approaches, as such scholars consider them too anthropocentric. Those scholars will often view the fact that, traditionally, ethics has centred so much on the human being as one main reason why we face ecological crises. They argue that the ecological system has become unbalanced because we have allowed human beings to fulfil all their interests, rationalised by the view that nature should be used and cultivated. There are a variety of ethical traditions that could be mentioned here. First, some would extend the moral status that we ascribe to human beings to animals as well (Warren 1997; Singer 2009). Some might argue that animals have the same or a comparable status as humans, since they can be harmed by actions. Some conclude from this that the human rights regime should be extended to animal rights, while others consider rights approaches bound to the human species, and reject it for this reason. In the context of this book, these positions are not of prior importance, since we are first and foremost concerned with tackling the already difficult relation between basic human interests and capacities and the future.

More important are positions such as 'deep ecology', bio- or eco-centric approaches, which assume that only a non-anthropocentric position would be able to justify long-term duties regarding the environment (Taylor 1986; Rolston III 1988; Serres 1995; DesJardins 2006; Callicott 2014). On these accounts, only if we understand that nature is not a resource that we can use to our liking, and only if we start to develop some respect for nature in a broader sense, will we have a chance to change our attitudes towards nature and to develop a more sustainable lifestyle. Approaches grounded in deep ecology will, from a practical point of view, consider it insufficient to limit our legitimate use of nature in terms of protection of human beings, and they will, from a philosophical point of view, consider it necessary to purge the bias towards humanity from our moral convictions.

These approaches mean we have to reframe our political and legal orders and remove the specific focus on protection of humankind. It would then be impossible to justify political institutions on the basis of considerations of respect for or recognition of human beings – at least forms of recognition that prioritise human beings over, say, the ecosystem. A deep ecology approach would insist that we have reason to value nature and to protect the integrity of ecological systems and similar goods, and that our political institutions need to be redesigned in ways that incorporate such protection. To us, it seems that non-anthropocentric approaches can still accommodate a position for human beings in nature, and even accept that the protection of some of the vital interests or capacities of human individuals, present and future, can outweigh concerns for other aspects of nature – let alone inspire future-oriented environmental duties. On a more critical note, however, this sort of approach is confronted with at least three questions. First, how are we to explain the kind of fundamental value that is recognised for nature? Since such a justification could not refer to the requirements of human rationality as a justificatory reason (since this would already be problematically biased towards humanity), the intuitive appreciation of nature as absolutely valuable would probably be the only possible ground. However, for those who do not share this intuition – no matter how much they appreciate nature – the question would be why we should embrace this basic intuition about nature as normatively decisive. Second, we need to ask what precisely the object of our respect would be. Nature as such is very unspecific. Would it be the cosmos? Would it be wilderness? Would it be traditional landscapes? Would it be ecosystems? Would it be life? And: life of species or of individual living entities? How can we determine the object of respect? Finally, we wonder whether within such an approach we would have reason to make any distinction between the status of humans and that of other natural entities. If we were to have to value nature or life at some very general level, we should wonder whether there is any specific role for the human being. If that is not the case, then we would wonder what a normative order that realises such a deep ecology ethics would look like.

4 Further questions

We are aware that we have not been able to do justice to the complex debates on our long-term responsibilities regarding future generations, the relationship between human rights and the duty to sustainability, and the criticisms of those ideas and philosophical alternatives. But we have attempted to at least present some reasons why a normative commitment to human rights would, for reasons of consistency, force us to include future people in our normative considerations. If that is correct, it leads to a variety of follow-up questions. We will mention only four of them, with the intention of outlining basic elements of an agenda for future research.

First, we would have to ask about the concrete normative implications of the extension of the idea of human rights to the long-term future. Probably the relevant duties would be to ensure that our ecological system remains in such a state that future human beings will have sufficient opportunities to secure their basic needs and respond to ecological challenges. But how can we determine thresholds that are sufficient to ensure this? How can we weigh our duties to future people against duties we have to our contemporaries? How can we deal with the uncertainties that follow from our ignorance concerning future developments?

Second, on a practical level, we should ask what the extension of the system of legal protection of human rights might look like. This question has various dimensions. Such a system would have to protect rights that are generic, that is, rights that hold not only for certain human beings, but for *all* human beings as such, most of whom are yet to be born. How can human rights institutions deal with this? Probably, we would need new forms of human rights institutions.

Third, effective measures for a sustainable lifestyle would probably require a high level of international collaboration, and probably new and stronger global institutions that have the power to enforce those measures. But the stronger those institutions will be, the more we have to wonder to whom they are accountable. Don't global institutions form a potential obstacle to the implementation of human rights, because they will probably be very bureaucratic and hardly understandable for normal people? How is democratic legitimation possible on such a global scale? And aren't balances of power between different independent states very important to avoid power monopolies that could ultimately become corrupt?

Fourth, the extension of our social, moral, political and legal world into the future is not just a form of broadening its scope. The idea is not just that the social world becomes a bit bigger and that the cake has to be divided among more people. The point is rather that the entire structure of our social world changes, in ways that are more responsive to the conditions of securing human rights into the future. The world will be extended into a particular future, and we have responsibility for the direction this development takes. This responsibility is unavoidable, since we have already established technologies that make our life longer and more comfortable, that have enhanced our reproduction rate and have enabled us to have particular lifestyles. All these effects together have strong and problematic consequences for the future. This fact changes our moral perspective in a fundamental way. We have to see ourselves as responsible for a future that transcends our knowledge and that often even transcends our imagination. We bear responsibilities because our actions affect people that do not yet exist and that we will never know. This is a challenge for the psychology of human action and the very way we think about the place of human beings in the world. It will be necessary to rewrite central elements of philosophical anthropology, ethics and the philosophy of history in light of this insight.

Notes

1 Particularly important for an understanding of the history of the concept of rights are Tuck (1979) and Tierney (1997).
2 It is a difficult task to determine concretely where the limits of our correlative duties will be. We may have basic interests in something but to what extent to these imply duties of others to protect us in realizing those interests? This question is e.g. important when it comes to the question to what extent we have duties to protect people not only against actions from which we know will violate our rights but also against actions where there may be a risk of such a rights violation (for an extensive discussion, see Chapter 3).
3 See for this context, Hiskes (2009); Düwell (2014b); Bos and Düwell (2016a, 2016b); Beyleveld et al. (2015).
4 For an excellent overview, see Beckerman and Pasek (2001).
5 For an overview of concepts of human dignity, see Düwell (2014a); McCrudden (2014).

Bibliography

Beckerman, Wilfred and Joanna Pasek. 2001. *Justice, Posterity, and the Environment*. Oxford: Oxford University Press.

Beitz, Charles. 2003. 'What human rights mean'. *Daedalus* 132(1): 36–46.

Beitz, Charles. 2009. *The Idea of Human Rights*. Oxford: Oxford University Press.

Beyleveld, Deryck. 1992. *The Dialectical Necessity of Morality: An Analysis and Defense of Alan Gewirth's Argument for The Principle of Generic Consistency*. Chicago, IL: The University of Chicago Press.

Beyleveld, Deryck and Gerhard Bos. 2009. 'The foundational role of the principle of instrumental reason in Gewirth's argument for the principle of generic consistency: a response to Andrew Chitty'. *Kings College Law Journal* 20(1): 1–20.

Beyleveld, Deryck, Marcus Düwell and Andreas Spahn. 2015. 'Why and how should we represent future generations in policy making?'. *Jurisprudence* 6(3): 549–566.

Bos, Gerhard. 2016. 'A chain of status: long-term responsibility in the context of human rights'. In Gerhard Bos and Marcus Düwell (eds), *Human Rights and Sustainability*. Abingdon: Routledge, 107–120.

Bos, Gerhard and Marcus Düwell (eds). 2016. *Human Rights and Sustainability*. Abingdon: Routledge.

Buchanan, Allen. 2014. *The Heart of Human Rights*. Oxford: Oxford University Press.

Callicott, J. Baird. 2013. *Thinking Like a Planet: The Land Ethic and the Earth Ethic*. New York: Oxford Scholarship Online. Oxford: Oxford University Press.

Cruft, Rowan, S. Matthew Liao and Massimo Renzo (eds). 2015. *Philosophical Foundations of Human Rights*. Oxford: Oxford University Press.

DesJardins, Joseph R. 2006. *Environmental Ethics: An Introduction to Environmental Philosophy*. Belmont, CA: Thomson Wadworth.

Düwell, Marcus. 2014a. 'Human dignity: concepts, discussions, philosophical perspectives'. In Marcus Düwell, Jens Braarvig, Roger Brownsword and Dietmar Mieth (eds), *Cambridge Handbook on Human Dignity*. Cambridge: Cambridge University Press, 23–52.

Düwell, Marcus. 2014b. 'Human dignity and future generations'. In Marcus Düwell, Jens Braarvig, Roger Brownsword and Dietmar Mieth (eds), *Cambridge Handbook on Human Dignity*. Cambridge: Cambridge University Press, 551–558.

Düwell, Marcus. 2017. 'Transcendental arguments and practical self-understanding: Gewirthian perspectives'. In Jens-Peter Brune, Robert Stern and Micha H. Werner (eds), *Transcendental Arguments in Moral Theory*. Berlin/Boston, MA: De Gruyter, 161–178.

Düwell, Marcus and Gerhard Bos. 2016. 'Human rights and future people – possibilities of argumentation'. *Journal of Human Rights* 15(2): 231–250.

Donnelly, Jack. 2003. *Universal Human Rights in Theory and Practice*, 2nd edn. Ithaca, NY: Cornell University Press.

Dworkin, Richard. 1984. 'Rights as trumps'. In J. Waldron (ed.), *Theories of Rights*. Oxford: Oxford University Press, 153–167.

Forst, Rainer. 2007. *The Right to Justification: Elements of a Constructivist Theory of Justice*. New York: Columbia University Press.

Gewirth, Alan. 1978. *Reason and Morality*. Chicago, IL: The University of Chicago Press.

Gewirth, Alan. 1996. *The Community of Rights*. Chicago, IL: The University of Chicago Press.

Gewirth, Alan. 2001. 'Human rights and future generations'. In M. Boylan (ed.), *Environmental Ethics*. Malden, MA: Wiley Blackwell, 118–122.

Griffin, James. 2008. *On Human Rights*. Oxford: Oxford University Press.

Hart, H. L. A. 1955. 'Are there any natural rights?'. *Philosophical Review* 64(2): 175–191.

Hiskes, Richard P. 2009. *The Human Right to a Green Future: Environmental Rights and Intergenerational Justice*. Cambridge: Cambridge University Press.

Hohfeld, Wesley Newcomb. 1964. *Fundamental Legal Conceptions as Applied in Judicial Reasoning*, 3rd edn. New Haven, CA: Yale University Press.

Hopgood, Stephen. 2013. *The Endtimes of Human Rights*. Ithaca, NY: Cornell University Press.

Kant, Immanuel. 1996 [1797]. *Metaphysics of Morals*. Edited and translated by M. Gregor. Cambridge: Cambridge University Press.

Locke, John. 2016 [1689]. *Second Treatise of Government; And A Letter Concerning Toleration*. Edited by M. Goldie. Oxford: Oxford University Press.

McCrudden, Christopher. 2014. *Understanding Human Dignity*. Oxford: Oxford University Press.

Morsink, Johannes. 2000. *The Universal Declaration of Human Rights. Origins, Drafting, and Intent*. Philadelphia, PA: University of Pennsylvania Press.

Moyn, Samuel. 2012. *The Last Utopia: Human Rights in History*. Cambridge, MA: Harvard University Press.

Nozick, Robert. 1974. *Anarchy, State and Utopia*. New York: Basic Books.

Raz, Joseph. 2010. 'Human rights without foundations'. In Samantha Bessson and John Tasioulas (eds), *The Philosophy of International Law*. Oxford: Oxford University Press, 321–338.

Rolston III, Holmes. 1988. *Environmental Ethics. Duties and Values in the Natural World*. Philadelphia, PA: Temple University Press.

Sandler, Ronald L. 2009. *Character and Environment: A Virtue-Oriented Approach to Environmental Ethics*. New York: Columbia University Press.

Serres, Michel. 1995. *The Natural Contract*. Translated by E. MacArthur and W. Paulson. Ann Arbor, MI: University of Michigan Press.

Shue, Henry. 1980. *Basic Rights. Subsistence, Affluence, and U.S. Foreign Policy*. Princeton, NJ: Princeton University Press.

Singer, Peter. 2009. 'Speciesism and moral status'. *Metaphilosophy* 40(3–4): 567–581.

Taylor, Charles. 1985. 'Atomism'. In *Philosophy and the Human Sciences*. Cambridge: Cambridge University Press, 187–211.

Taylor, Paul W. 1986. *Respect for Nature: A Theory of Environmental Ethics*. Princeton, NJ: Princeton University Press.

Tierney, Brian. 1997. *The Idea of Natural Rights. Studies on Natural Rights, Natural Law, and Church Law 1150–1625*. Grand Rapids, MI: Emory University.

Tuck, Richard. 1979. *Natural Rights Theories. Their Origin and Development*. Cambridge: Cambridge University Press.

Warren, Mary Anne. 1997. *Moral Status. Obligations to Persons and Other Living Things*. Oxford: Oxford University Press.

3

RISK AND RIGHTS

How to deal with risks from a rights-based perspective

Lukas H. Meyer, Fabian Schuppert, Harald Stelzer and Adriana Placani

The presence of risk is indisputable, but how to deal with it less so. Risks are not only an inescapable feature of our everyday lives and decision-making, but they are also central to maybe the largest threat facing us today – climate change. It is no surprise, then, that understanding risks has become a priority in moral philosophy, where risks challenge long-held assumptions. Certainty has been a common, yet seldom acknowledged supposition of many philosophical debates. For this and other reasons, the topic of risk has the potential to expand our current moral thinking. Such expansion should be embraced as it carries with it the potential to offer valuable insights for our decisions and policymaking, where risks and uncertainty are all but certain.

Even our everyday observation reveals that almost any decision we make happens under conditions of uncertainty and comes with certain risks. While we might have a good understanding of what is *very likely* to happen if we choose A or B, we can never be entirely sure of what the *actual outcome* of a particular decision will be. Although we might be confident that the action we choose is safe, there is almost always a small chance of unforeseeable negative consequences. For example, I might think that taking the train is faster than riding my bike, but I cannot know whether that will indeed be the case. Taking the train might also seem reasonably safe, but there nevertheless exists a risk that I will get hurt in a train accident. Despite this widely shared knowledge and feeling that risks lurk around every corner of our life for a long time, many, if not most moral theories simply ignored the issue of risk and uncertainty, focusing on questions that took certainty as a given (e.g. what ought to be done once a bad outcome materialised). However, in recent years risk and uncertainty have come to the forefront of moral philosophy, not just in areas such as climate ethics but also with regard to the very idea of moral theorising (Lockhart 2000; Sepielli 2009).

In this chapter we set out to illustrate how a rights-based ethical framework can help us to deal with issues of risk and uncertainty particularly in the context of climate change. In so doing, we will first introduce important terminological distinctions so as to clarify what we mean when we talk of risk and uncertainty (section 1), before turning our attention to the idea of rights against risking (section 2) as one possible way to deal with risk and uncertainty within a rights-based framework. In section 3 we will discuss alternative ways of dealing with risks from a rights-based perspective before turning our attention to the complex issue of formulating acceptability thresholds – indications of what level of risk it might be acceptable to expose others to (section 4).

1 Terminology and some relevant background

In most everyday decision-making cases we feel so confident about assessing the future consequences of our actions and choices that we would not want to use the term 'risk'. Furthermore, even though we all know that we cannot see into the future, with regards to many decisions we remain pretty sure that we know what will happen if we decide to do something. In other words, we often operate under the assumption that we can reliably predict certain future outcomes. For example, when I purchase a sandwich, I believe that the sandwich is reasonably fresh and that if I eat it I will feel less hungry, even though I don't know for sure whether eating the sandwich is 'safe' (e.g. it could be poisoned or spoilt) or whether eating it will satisfy my hunger. In short, in everyday situations we often take risk and uncertainty to be negligible variables when making decisions. This is particularly true for decisions that affect only the near future, since it is often the case that uncertainty increases the further into the future a predicted outcome lies.[1] Consequently, many normative theories that focus on simple action scenarios with a limited time frame do not take risk and uncertainty into account when making normative judgements about whether a certain action is ethically permissible.

The situation changes when we consider policy-level decision-making about the future. Many threats and problems related to environmental issues, as well as their medium- to long-term development, come with risks and uncertainties that raise important questions for policymaking. In this area, it becomes important to clarify terms such as uncertainty, ignorance, and risk, since they are often confused.

'Risk' describes potential bad outcomes that come about as a result of an action or actions. Often risk is taken to refer to *probabilistic risk*, i.e. potential bad outcomes to which we can assign a probability. Thus, risks are often seen as a function of the probability of a certain outcome coupled with a certain magnitude of negative consequences if that outcome does occur. Consider as an example the following situation in which you need to choose between two risky actions, which we will call A and B: you are hiking in the mountains and encounter a stream which you need to cross in order to continue your journey. You now can either try to jump across the stream in place A where the stream is fairly narrow (this is option A), or you can try to balance across a very narrow tree trunk that lies across the stream in place B. In place B the stream is wider and there are several sharp-edged rocks in the river bed (which is option B). If you choose A and fail you simply get wet (which we assign a disvalue of 10), while if you fall off the tree trunk you will get wet and hurt yourself on the rocks which we assign a disvalue of 20. If the probability for attempting A and B unsuccessfully is the same, say, 35 per cent, then we could calculate the risks involved in options A and B as follows: Risk(A): .35 x 10 = 3.5; Risk(B): .35 x 20 = 7. So, in our example trying to jump across the stream is less risky than trying to balance across the fallen tree trunk. Things may change if jumping has a much higher probability to end in the water (.80 x 10 = 8), or the tree trunk allows an almost safe passage to the other side (.20 x 20=4).

Even though we make such 'back of the envelope' calculations on many occasions, within the literature there are varied alternative functions for calculating risk, and most theorists would in fact reject the formula 'probability x disvalue = risk' as too simplistic and one-dimensional. Consider, for instance, that in most cases risk does not affect all people of a population equally, and that the intensity of outcomes may vary. Moreover, the assessment of risk becomes even more complicated when considering *sequences* of decisions under risk. In such cases, the consequences of what is being done at t1 for t3 depends on what will be decided at the intermediate decision point t2. When forming a decision at t1 one has to make a decision about whether to regard t2 as under one's control, but it is not always clear whether one should regard oneself as in control of one's future actions (Hansson 2013: 18–9). In cases of addiction, for example, a decision to quit a certain substance (at t1) because of health benefits (at t3) may come with the added calculation of the risk that somewhere down the line (at t2) the habit will be renewed because of a weakness of the will. Thus, one might also have to consider the risks of regarding oneself as being in control of one's future actions or decisions.[2] Furthermore, these issues are of relevance to many practical considerations, among them how to deal with climate change, which would likely involve such series of decisions as opposed to just one-off actions.

Moreover, often it is simply impossible to assign numeric values to either the probability of an outcome or the expected disvalue of the outcome, for example, when the outcome concerns the very survival of humankind or the destruction of habitats. For instance, in deciding whether to interfere with ecosystems, we lack the confidence of assigning precise probabilities to the consequences of intervening in the workings of such complex systems. This brings us to the matter of uncertainty, which is different from that of probabilistic risk. As just explained, in cases of probabilistic risk, we have relatively sound knowledge about the probability of the whole spectrum of possible consequences of an action. By contrast, in cases of *uncertainty* (or so-called 'Knightian uncertainty')[3] we possess *only partial or no probabilistic knowledge* (Lempert 2002). While we could still be aware of the possible consequences that an action might produce, we can only attach degrees of probability to these different outcomes, i.e. we can define probability ranges and assess them in terms of degrees of certainty. If we have no knowledge about all potential outcomes of a certain action and *also* no probabilistic knowledge, we are in a situation of *ignorance*.

It is crucial to keep these three concepts separate, as probabilistic risk is very different from uncertainty, while uncertainty in turn allows us to say a lot more about possible scenarios than ignorance. However, within the philosophical and policymaking literature on risk these terms are not always kept strictly apart. While 'risk' is normally used as an umbrella term for probabilistic risk, uncertainty and ignorance, the use of the three defining terms isn't consistent. For the purposes of this chapter, we will keep these terms distinct. We use the term 'risk' as an umbrella term, speak of probabilistic risk when we mean a risk for which we know both all the possible outcomes and can assign probabilities to them, and use 'uncertainty' and 'ignorance' for specific cases that fit the definitions above.

Policy debates and public discussions on the impact of large-scale interventions into the environment attest to how crucial it is to understand both the difference between probabilistic risk, uncertainty and ignorance, and the kind of epistemo-logical conditions that operate in the definition of these concepts. Take the example of the production, use and consumption of genetically modified organisms (GMOs) in foods, such as genetically modified corn and soy. While advocates of GMO foods argue that several studies have shown GMOs to be non-hazardous for humans and other organisms, GMO critics emphasise the uncertainties concerning the long-term and cumulative effects of widespread GMO food production, use and consumption. Within this debate, advocates and critics often seem to operate with different con-ceptions of what counts as proof for a technology to be considered safe, objection-ably risky, or simply still too uncertain. Similar problems beset much of the debate around anthropogenic climate change and its relation to issues of social, global and intergenerational justice. In this chapter, we focus on the latter in order to highlight the challenges of probabilistic risks, uncertainties and ignorance.

In the context of climate change, our knowledge is limited, meaning that we often deal with cases of uncertainty and ignorance. The many distinctions in levels in the reports of the Intergovernmental Penal for Climate Change (IPCC) make clear that it is crucial not to treat all uncertainties as equal. The IPCC specifies both (qualitative) levels of confidence and, where possible, probabilistically quantified levels of likelihood. These levels are expressed in terms ranging, in the case of confidence, from 'very low' to 'very high', and, in the case of likelihood, from 'virtually certain' to 'exceptionally unlikely'. The terms used to express levels of likelihood correspond to specific percentage ranges (e.g. 'very likely' indicates 90–100 per cent probability), making them effectively technical terms. A finding, then, might be expressed as follows:

> Relative to 1850–1900, global surface temperature change for the end of the 21st century (2081–2100) is projected to likely exceed 1.5°C for RCP4.5, RCP6.0 and RCP8.5 (high confidence). Warming is likely to exceed 2°C for RCP6.0 and RCP8.5 (high confidence), more likely than not to exceed 2°C for RCP4.5 (medium confidence), but unlikely to exceed 2°C for RCP2.6 (medium confidence).[4]

These assessments are in turn based on evidence and agreement, which are qualified in summary as limited, medium or robust (evidence) and low, medium or high (agreement), respectively.[5] While nearly all IPCC findings and projections involve some degree of uncertainty, in some cases researchers are quite unsure about what will happen, while in other cases the likelihood of an event can be determined with considerable precision. This means that observations such as those claiming that climate scientists 'do not even agree' on what will occur if the Greenland ice sheet melts, or that we 'cannot even be sure' that temperatures will continue to rise, should not give rise to claims that we have no reason to believe that there is solid likelihood and significant confidence about such matters.

Still, while scientific proof for climate change is robust, the issue involves a wide range of uncertainties, including the strength and the dynamics of the relationship between emissions and temperature increases (climate sensitivity), and the effect of temperature increases on the distribution and quality of particular weather patterns (Weitzman 2011). Moreover, the climate system is so complex that it is extremely difficult to develop accurate models and scenarios about the degree to which changes related to one variable might affect others.[6] Probabilistic risk, uncertainty and ignorance therefore become key variables for any kind of sound normative analysis of what we should do. If climate change develops roughly according to our most reliable scientific models, then significant losses in well-being and other negative consequences are likely to occur in the future. Rising sea levels, which may make low-lying coastal areas and islands uninhabitable, and increased frequencies of heat waves, storms, floods and droughts, which could lead to shortages of water or food, are among these possible consequences. Moreover, so-called 'tipping points', after which certain processes become virtually irreversible and a radical change occurs, should significantly influence our approach to risk-taking and climate change mitigation, even though the exact nature of these tipping points is uncertain as well (Lenton et al. 2008).

The situation is even more complex: even if we knew all the environmental effects of climate change, their impact on social, economic and political systems depends on many different factors, such as the set-up of these systems, their vulnerability to climate change events, and their resilience to climate change-induced consequences. Also, the consequences of large-scale adaptation measures can be fairly uncertain. This also holds for the living conditions of future generations: we do not know how many people will live in the future and what their technological capacities will be. Thus, when we think of how we should respond to the challenges of anthropogenic climate change, we cannot do so without considering the uncertainties involved and the risks at hand.

If we aim to make morally permissible choices, for instance by taking the requirements of global and intergenerational justice into account, we furthermore run into a host of complex philosophical problems. These include issues such as the non-identity problem, which seems to suggest that in many cases we can't make future people worse off because the existence of these particular future people depends on our actions (Parfit 2010). It seems difficult to claim that a future person's life will be worsened by our present choices because if we were to take a different course of action, then that particular person may well not exist at all. According to this argument, if we were to continue business as usual instead of bringing about a low-carbon society, those who would bear the costs of a continuance of our lifestyle could not be considered worse off as they would not even come into existence if we had adopted the low-emission policies.[7] In addition, there is disagreement concerning what exactly global and intergenerational justice prescribes and which moral theory should inform our normative assessments.[8] However, while some might want to label these disagreements as uncertainties also, this kind of dispute is of a different sort. Analysing and interpreting such normative uncertainty and the accompanying disagreements is a central task of philosophers, given that the practice of doing philosophy involves scrutinising the reasoning underlying our moral commitments in order to ensure conformity with reason.

Also, even though we will have to provide more philosophical analysis of many of the issues related to climate change, normative philosophical research is well advanced in terms of contending with anthropogenic climate change (Kolstad et al. 2014). This is evinced by a shared understanding of many of the relevant disagreements, for example, the just distribution of benefits and burdens in climate change mitigation (see, e.g., Page 2008; Caney 2010; Meyer and Sanklecha 2017), the normative significance of currently living people's legitimate expectations (see, e.g., Meyer and Sanklecha 2014), and the moral permissibility of climate engineering (see, e.g., Stelzer and Schuppert 2016).

Notwithstanding the foregoing, any exhaustive enumeration or deep exploration of the many philosophical debates surrounding climate change is neither feasible nor needed for our purposes. In turn, for the remainder of this chapter, we will focus on how a rights-based account could and should respond to the issue of risk in the context of global climate change in part through an analysis of the respective strengths and weaknesses of existing theories.

2 Rights against risking

Rights-based theories can respond to the issue of risk in several ways. A particularly prominent strategy is to invoke the idea of a right against risking; in other words: rights not to be exposed to risk (Oberdiek 2009, 2012; Steigleder 2016). However, before we deal with the idea of a right against risking, let us briefly explain why it makes sense to use a rights-based framework in situations of risk even in the face of rival approaches, such as intergenerational cost–benefit analyses.

A (human or basic) rights approach contrasts sharply with the dominant cost–benefit analysis approach, which tries to calculate the economic costs of negative outcomes, such as death, injury, malnutrition, water stress or illness, and weigh these costs against the opportunity costs of reducing the risks at hand (Bell 2011: 100). In situations of uncertainty, however, it sometimes becomes extremely difficult to adequately apply cost–benefit analyses, cost-effectiveness analyses and other economic decision-making tools. In the case of climate change we have to rely on climate models that give us some information of possible developments based on our limited understanding of the complex climate system and against the background of certain assumptions or so-called 'scenarios'.[9] Integrated assessment models (IAMs) are used in order to represent the effects of certain human activities, especially economic activities, on the natural system and on other human activities (Heal and Kriström 2002). These models are based on a framework of expected utility: they assume that a social planner will choose an optimal policy to maximise the discounted stream of benefits and costs over long periods of time.[10] But if future impacts are discounted at relatively high rates, if the benefits of mitigation and adaptation are evaluated based on incomplete information or questionable criteria (see Roberts and Reich 2002 for a discussion of, among others, the Disability-Adjusted Life Year (DALY) index used by the WHO), and if the costs of mitigation and adaptation do not properly account for technological change and learning, then results from IAMs cannot properly deliver optimal decisions nor adequate estimates for benefits and/or costs of climate policy (Füssel 2007; Lempert and Collins 2007; Ackerman et al. 2009). From a rights-based normative approach it is possible not only to expose the considerable internal deficits of such models, but also to reject their underlying assumption that utility should be the baseline for our moral considerations and decisions.

First, even if we were to have sufficient information about the probability of different outcomes, this would not automatically enable the attribution of monetary values to all benefits and burdens, including human life, physical security, subsistence and health. It seems at least questionable whether judgements about these impacts can be quantitatively calculated and, therefore, whether they can be considered as reducible to economic calculations (Shue 1999: 47; Jamieson 2010). Neither the risk of a rights violation nor the actual prospective rights violation itself can be quantitatively expressed in terms of (monetary) costs. Therefore, a different scale is needed in order to weigh one risk of a rights violation against another.

Second, when approaching the issue from a rights-sensitive point of view, the aim of policy decisions is not merely to secure the most beneficial outcome in terms of aggregative well-being. Rather, in the context of severe risks, the aim of policymaking includes, fundamentally, the protection of basic rights. Thus, the normative weight of a risk of rights violations could be assessed by focusing on comparing policy outcomes in terms of their expected rights violations. Seeing rights as more than mere constraints upon acceptable courses of action can open up the evaluation of policy options with respect to their protection of human rights. While some have argued that concerns such as the fulfilment of basic human interests and/or capabilities should be central, using rights as a currency has the advantage of giving a strong interpretation of normative individualism. This is important as it is not sufficient to merely maximise overall well-being; we must also consider how well-being is distributed, which goes beyond an aggregative function only. Additionally, a rights-based approach connects nicely to the need for institutional arrangements for the protection of rights. Henry Shue has argued for a social guarantee against standard threats (1980: 13). Human rights generate 'a duty to create [or] to preserve effective institutions for the enjoyment of what people have rights to enjoy' (Shue 1980: 17). Furthermore, Simon Caney recognises a duty to promote and preserve effective institutions 'that ensure that persons can enjoy their human rights' (2007: 287). For Shue, such a duty does not exist with respect to all possible violations of human rights, but only against predictable remediable threats (1980: 33). As Bell showed, anthropogenic climate change can be seen as such a threat and would create a duty to promote effective institutions for the protection of basic human rights against the threat posed by severe consequences (2011: 111).

In light of the limitations of cost–benefit approaches and IAMs, some theorists have argued that a better way to think about risk is by assuming a general right against risking. The underlying thought is that all such forms of risk imposition are either some kind of objectionable harm or that all risk impositions are normatively objectionable as they undermine a person's autonomy or reduce (quantitatively and/or qualitatively) a person's set of options. Proponents of a general right against risking have argued that the right could be defended instrumentally (Perry 2014), for instance by referring to the positive effects on society that the widespread recognition of such a right could have (McCarthy 1997). However, on closer inspection, all of these justifications face some problems, especially due to their potential for being overly restrictive.

Whether all risks are harms is far from a straightforward matter since harm is commonly defined as something that makes a person, in a normatively relevant sense, worse off. Given that not every risk materialises, it seems unclear why the mere existence of a small risk should count as harm, especially since many risks are such that they are not directly imposed on a particular person, but on a population or space as a whole (as in the case of me cycling to work). By using my bicycle, I impose a risk of collision on others: I might collide with them if they move at the same time and in the same space as I do. However, this seems trivial and hardly normatively relevant even though the risks are many – just think about everything that could possibly happen while riding your bike – and the damage that may result severe – people could get killed. This clearly indicates that there must be a difference, at least in many cases, between the risks we impose and the normative evaluation of the harm that might result from our action. So, what could make the imposition of a risk morally impermissible or blameworthy?

A first answer to this question is offered by John Oberdiek (2009) who claims that the imposition of risk forecloses formerly safe possibilities available to other persons. In turn, the curtailment of (safe) alternatives constitutes a diminution of autonomy. Oberdiek employs Joseph Raz's view that autonomy 'is exercised through choice' and 'requires not merely the presence of options but of acceptable ones' (Raz 1986: 398). This seems a highly relevant position for the case of climate change, given that the latter can be expected to lead to higher rates of insecurity regarding the protection of basic rights and to the foreclosure of options. For instance, people may no longer be able to live on land owned by their families for generations, or at least they might not be able to do so without incurring high costs or risks. Furthermore, the increased possibility of future harms may interfere with the autonomy of future people because it will make certain actions and policies necessary and others impossible. In the case of climate change, certain strategies may reduce or foreclose the options of future people, thus violating their right to autonomous self-determination (Ott 2012; Smith 2012) or leading to morally tragic situations in which agents cannot help but act in ways that are morally reprehensible in some sense (Gardiner 2010).

However, there is an enormous difference between the claim that certain forms of risk imposition can undermine people's autonomy and the claim that *any* risk imposition undermines another person's autonomy and that, hence, every person should be considered to have a general right against risking. The latter theory seems to imply either an unconvincingly strong set of conditions for autonomy (i.e. even things I am not and cannot be aware of can undermine my autonomy simply by imposing a minuscule risk on me) or a very particular understanding of what counts as risk imposition (one that already distinguishes between normatively relevant and irrelevant cases) (see Ferretti 2016 for similar points). The idea that a risk imposition changes a person's opportunity sets and thus infringes a person's right to be left alone, as well as to free and independent choice, which is sometimes considered the basis for a right against risking, is similarly overly restrictive. This is because such a claim seems to imply that, for instance, a highly qualified person who applies for a job and thereby increases the risk of failure for all other applicants, infringes the others' rights against risking. This would be a bizarre implication: the idea that anybody applying for a job is performing a potentially morally objectionable act appears to get things wrong.

Therefore, even though for a rights-based approach it might seem initially plausible that there is a general right against risking, on closer inspection it is clear that a more nuanced approach is needed. One way of incorporating the idea of a general right against risking into a more nuanced account is suggested by Klaus Steigleder (2016). Steigleder claims that while a right against risking exists, some risks are connected to activities and things that are fundamental to a person leading a decent life. In other words, there is not just a right against risking, but also a right to impose certain risks.

Another solution is put forth by Sven Ove Hansson (2013), who claims that while each and every person might have a *pro tanto* (that is: defeasible) claim not to be put at risk, what ultimately counts in a normative respect is a societal risk contract in which the members of a society decide on the risks that may be imposed on other members. In so doing, risk is democratised, and nobody should find themselves exposed to unacceptable risk. Hansson's contractual approach to risk does not require one to hold that all people have a general right against being exposed to risk. In fact, Hansson's societal decision-making mechanism would also be compatible with many other rights-based perspectives on dealing with risk, which we consider below.

3 Dealing with risks in a rights-based framework

As discussed above, when it comes to risks associated with anthropogenic climate change, one way of approaching the issue from a philosophical point of view is to think primarily about the rights that people might have against being put at risk. Yet another way is to take as a starting point the duty of currently living people to create institutions for the protection of the interests and rights of future generations. No matter from which side one comes to the problem, the key normative issue to consider first is the difference between actual rights violations and the imposition of risks of rights violations as these are clearly not the same.

This can be clarified again by the example of climate change. Although we have strong reasons to believe that climate change imposes significant risks on human rights, we cannot say that by emitting greenhouse gases we violate the human rights to life, health or subsistence. Rather, what we can say is that by emitting these gases we increase the risk that these rights will be violated. Even though it is very likely that future people will claim that we harmed them if we continue business-as-usual policies, it is an open question whether we harm future people by imposing risks of harm to them and, *a fortiori*, whether, by doing so, we can be said to wrong them. We need to ask whether the imposition of risks by causing climate change constitutes a harm and/or a rights violation and if not, whether it constitutes some other kind of moral wrong that makes the corresponding actions (or omissions) blameworthy or impermissible. To come closer in answering these important questions, we can look at different situations brought about by our risky actions.

Ordinarily, to harm a person means that that person's well-being is negatively affected in a normatively significant way, or that her interests are set back by certain action(s). However, when we talk about the imposition of risks of harm, we do not yet know whether the harm will actually materialise. For instance, in the case of climate change, we impose huge risks of harm onto future people, but we cannot know whether these harms will actually materialise. Yet imposing a risk on some-one seems to be of moral relevance – at least in certain cases – even if the risks imposed do not materialise and nobody is actually harmed. Even in such instances we may still have wronged or harmed other people by putting their interests at risk. This indicates that the moral significance of risking cannot rest – at least not exclusively – on the possible harmful outcome of the risky action, but may also be based on some nonmaterial form of harm constituted by the very imposition of risks, which must be directly linked to the nature of the action itself.

For an illustration of this point, consider the following example (which follows Thomson 1986): person A points a gun at person B, unlocks it and pulls the trigger. Neither A nor B know whether the gun is loaded, and nothing happens. In this case, we might still think that A acted wrongly, even though B was not physically harmed. Moreover, even though B did not sustain any injuries, we might consider B to have been harmed. Of course, in this example harm could be related to B's psychological stress caused by A's risky action. A's pulling the trigger might not only cause B to feel threatened for a second, but could lead to a psychological trauma with far-reaching consequences for B's life, a drawback often experienced by victims of crime. Even in the absence of direct physical harm, it seems plausible that we should regard the threat in terms of its possible psychological consequences as a form of harm. This is relevant in the context of climate change because living under a permanent threat of floods, droughts or other severe weather events could negatively influence the psychological well-being of many people in the future even if the harms were never to materialise during their lifetime or in their region.

However, one might even argue that the harms of risk imposition are independent of the potentially harmed person's knowledge. Even if B did not notice that A had picked up a gun, aimed it at him and pulled the trigger, B's ignorance would, arguably, not mean that he was not wronged or not harmed. From such a perspective, escaping any injury (physical or psychological) threatened by a risk imposition does not entail that one has escaped harm and/or that no wrong was committed. Rather, the risk imposition itself can constitute a harm as well as a wrong. The difficulty is how to cash out this supposed insight in normative terms, since we need a good account of what exactly makes certain forms of risk imposition wrong and/or harmful.

One way to develop such an account is to start by looking at the preferences of those exposed to risk. According to preference-based accounts, what makes the imposition of risk objectionable is that it is, in many cases, not preferred by those being put at risk (Finkelstein 2003). In our example, if B had a choice, then even in those cases where she would remain ignorant of the risky actions, B would prefer not to be exposed to the risk of A pulling the trigger. A version of such an account would speak of B having a legitimate interest not to be exposed to the risk. The interests of a person include all those things in which that person has a stake, and any setback to these interests can be seen as harmful (Feinberg 1984). Of course, there are cases in which we accept the risks that others impose on us because of the positive effects of their risky actions. One example that illustrates this is driving cars. Even people who normally don't use cars may have an interest in others using cars, given that the economy and many services depend on such forms of mobility. The possibility that the risks involved in a certain action are outweighed by the benefits flowing from the same action is a challenge for preference-based positions, among others, because all things considered we may prefer the risky action (even if it is conducted by others) and we may even have a legitimate interest in its performance.

An alternative way of arguing for the wrongfulness and/or harmfulness of risk impositions is to argue that people are caught in a lock-in, that is, a situation in which they can't really choose an action that doesn't follow the already established path. This argument rests on valuing autonomy, and is part of Oberdiek's (2009) account of a right against risking (see above). To illustrate this idea, take the following example: by using certain climate engineering techniques (i.e. intentional large-scale interventions into the climate system of the Earth with the aim of reducing climate change), one generation would be choosing a specific climate path for future people, a path that may be irreversible or changeable only with considerable high costs (Jamieson 1996). For example, we may prevent the Earth from heating by injecting certain gases into the lower stratosphere and thus cause the atmosphere to reflect more sunlight back into space. However, this process would have to be extended for a long period of time (Vaughan and Lenton 2011). This would create a permanent threat: the already accumulated carbon dioxide in the atmosphere would only be masked and not reduced, and the failure to maintain the aerosol counter-forcing could result in abrupt and potentially very damaging warming, depending on the time and scale of deployment (Ross and Matthews 2009).

Even though these accounts differ in how they analyse the consequences of risking as harmful to the victims, many of them locate the wrongness of the risk imposition in the act of risking itself. At least in cases where intentionality is present, the moral significance of risk imposition could be traced back to the expression of a lack of respect for the person being put at risk. In these cases, it can be argued that what is impinged is a person's interest in dignity (Placani 2017). If one sees dignity as a first-order interest, then risks stand to negatively impact agents' vital interests, as has been argued by Stephen Perry (2003: 1306).[11] For Perry, primary interests are 'life, health, dignity, the physical integrity of the body, autonomy and freedom of movement, the interest in not experiencing severe pain, the interest in not experiencing severe mental or emotional distress, and certain kinds of property interest' (2014: 54). These interests are always vital, but they develop a new sense of relevance in the context of climate change because they are under threat from it.

Another possible way to explain what is morally objectionable in cases involving risk is to refer to a duty of care that seems to apply to us with regard to the possible influence of our actions on others. In many cases of otherwise permissible actions, the risk imposed by an action makes that action wrong or, at least, creates the need for further justification. Such an account can make sense of why, under normal conditions, it is permissible to drive a car, while at the same time it is impermissible and blameworthy to operate the same car under the influence of alcohol. In the context of climate change, the concept of a duty of care can also do important normative work. Here, we deal with actions (such as polluting activities) that – at least at the collective level – can be expected to have consequences that will lead to setbacks to future people's interests in the long run. What seems to make these actions morally questionable is that we go ahead in performing them, even though, for all we know, future people may well end up materially harmed by their consequences. From such a perspective, what we are to be blamed for seems to be one or more of the following: we do not take these aspects of our actions to be conclusive normative reasons against so acting; we neglect alternative options available to us (e.g. mitigation); we give priority to certain current interests and, thereby, discount the interests of others and/or the interests of future generations.

The above discussion considered some prominent rights-based theoretical approaches of conceptualising risk and its justifiable imposition. It can be argued that none of the accounts presented provide unassailable ways of handling the difficulties that risk poses to our moral intuitions and commitments. Unfortunately, matters are far from becoming simpler when the conversation shifts to the complex plane of policymaking.

4 The precautionary principle and acceptability thresholds

Neither the possibility of our actions' negative influence (that is, the risk of harm) nor a certain duty of care can be taken as sufficient reasons against the imposition of risks. Unfortunately, in the context of policy decisions the issue is much more complex, as can be shown by reference to the precautionary principle. When managing risks in the context of international environmental politics, the precautionary principle is probably the most widespread idea that governments rely upon. In its most famous formulation, this principle expresses a demand to take precautionary measures against serious and plausible threats of harm to human health or the environment, even if some of the relevant cause and effect relationships are not fully scientifically established (Wingspread Statement 1998; Rio Declaration Principle: 15). Even though the application of the principle to climate change seems well founded, there exist several problems. The practical relevance of the principle is contested, especially since at the national level the precautionary principle is interpreted in various forms with different degrees of stringency (Feintuck 2005). The precautionary principle also faces the challenge of a denial of responsibility and of resulting political inertia owing to risks being the outcomes of cumulative processes and without an accurate understanding of the chains of causality being available.

In addition to these more practical implications at the policy level, there are also some basic problems with the principle itself, which are similar to the problems of a rights-based approach. A strong version of the precautionary principle can be interpreted to exclude all policies and actions that could create further threats to basic human interests or the environment (Sunstein 2005). Such a strict interpretation would prohibit a wide range of possible responses to climate change, as most of them include the imposition of such risks. Even though one of the key benefits of using a precautionary approach to environmental governance is that it establishes a justificatory logic that forces policies to make the case for being compatible with fulfilling our duties to future generations, the precautionary governance can only be effective and helpful if it goes hand in hand with the establishment of clear risk thresholds, since taking a zero-risk approach to technological and political change is simply unfeasible. More generally, despite cases in which it is evident that imposing risks on others is impermissible, or at least culpable or blameworthy (for a normative differentiation, see Oberdiek 2012), it often does seem permissible to impose certain risks on others or on ourselves. To completely abstain from risk would make social life impossible as risky actions are an essential part of our everyday lives.

Furthermore, even for very risky policies the application of the precautionary principle is ambiguous. Consider the case of climate engineering by injecting hydrogen sulphide or sulphur dioxide into the lower stratosphere (Elliottt 2010; Hartzell-Nichols 2012). The severe risks to humans and ecosystems and the 'unknown unkowns' involved in such a practice seem to speak against this option, and from a precautionary perspective we would normally not be willing to take such risks (Gardiner 2006). However, not taking action due to serious and plausible threats of harm to human health or the environment is in tension with the possibility to use such techniques as a precautionary measure to prevent severe consequences of climate change and associated human suffering (Carr et al. 2013; for a discussion of such arguments, see Morrow (2014)).

First, this gives rise to the question of whether a policy that secures certain interests or rights while putting other interests or rights at risk would ever be ethically acceptable – and, if so, under what circumstances. Given that it is often possible to minimise risks only at considerable cost, we need to investigate under what conditions the imposition of risk can be justified. In many cases the acceptance of risks will depend on the evaluation of the interests or rights that are under threat of being violated and the interests or rights being secured by carrying out certain risk-imposing actions, as well as available alternative actions and policies.

Second, the foregoing means that even if the harm materialises we may still have not acted morally wrongly. For instance, actions that have prevented basic interests of currently living people from being violated or that will create great benefits for future people may provide adequate compensation for harms resulting from these actions. This may be true for adaptation measures securing basic interests of future people while at the same time imposing risks of harm. Certain climate engineering proposals may be used as examples of such 'wrongless harmdoing', as they may help to deal with climate change-induced consequences even though, at the same time, they could also lead to harms in other parts of the world or in a more distant future. In all these cases of wrongless harmdoing the harm that materialises could be excused by the avoidance of other harms.

A rights-based perspective can help with these problems in the case of risk imposition by developing certain principles that can distinguish between acceptable and unacceptable, permissible and impermissible risk impositions.[12] In other words, what is needed is an account of acceptability thresholds for risks and the identification of the kinds of criteria that should be used in assessing the moral permissibility of risk impositions. For instance, if we were convinced that any action we chose carried certain risks, then we would need clear and informative (normatively well-grounded) criteria for establishing what kinds of risks and risk-taking would be deemed acceptable and unacceptable in such circumstances. However, there are difficult problems connected to the idea of establishing acceptability thresholds. Here we will focus on two. First, from a rights-based perspective, advancing thresholds would need to take rights seriously, while at the same time leaving room for policies that might lead to risks of rights violations. Second, a threshold solution raises the issue of context sensitivity, as in the case of so-called 'lesser evil situations' (i.e. situations in which, under normal circumstances, none of the available options would be deemed morally acceptable, but one option nonetheless seems less bad than the other available options).

The first of these problems concerns establishing an acceptability threshold that is neither too restrictive (e.g. by declaring all options that might potentially lead to the loss of a future life morally impermissible), too permissive (e.g. by declaring that as long as humanity continues to exist everything goes), nor too biased (e.g. by discounting either present or future well-being, leading to intergenerational imbalance). While using a human rights framework seems to imply that all human rights violations should be regarded as unacceptable, the issue is more complex when it comes to assessing the permissibility of imposing the risk of rights violations on others. Risk is a matter of degrees, which makes absolute risk minimisation unfeasible, especially since risk is often the flip side of positively perceived uncertainties such as 'opportunities' or 'prospects'.

The second problem concerns fears of establishing moral slippery slopes if we want our acceptability threshold to be context-sensitive. In principle, normative accounts of moral permissibility can take one of two routes. They may establish strict immutable thresholds based on established moral principles (e.g. human rights protection); however, in many real-world decision-making scenarios the threshold will prove irrelevant. In many cases, the question is not whether human rights might be violated, but whose rights and what rights might be violated by whom, and under which circumstances. As a second option, normative accounts of moral permissibility may establish context-sensitive thresholds. The danger, however, is that such accounts stand to oversimplify complex decision-making scenarios in order to advance lesser evil arguments, which benefit particular sets of interests at the expense of others. Neither way of conceptualising acceptability thresholds is thus without problems. However, if we want respect for human rights and other moral principles to influence decision-making in complex real-world scenarios, it seems advisable to explore the prospect of a risk-sensitive rights-based framework, which allows for a degree of context-sensitivity while keeping a lid on hasty lesser evil arguments.

Furthermore, it can be argued that the determination of acceptability thresholds should be based on a multidimensional metric (Peterson 2012; Stelzer and Schuppert 2016). That is to say, we should be sensitive to the different values that can be affected by particular instances of risk-taking, such as rights violations, well-being, fairness and equality, which all can be understood both intragenerationally and intergenerationally. Moreover, one's framework should be sensitive to different kinds of risks since irreversible pervasive risks ought, most likely, to be treated differently from recoverable isolated risks, even though the latter might come with huge negative utility. Based on the complexity of issues involved under non-ideal real-world circumstances, there might not be a single morally best choice, but rather a range of choices none of which obviously superior to the others. In cases such as this, the available options should be carefully compared and weighed. Such weighing generates many new problems, based on questions of potential harms and benefits involved, the list of rights presupposed, their commensurability and relevance/order. The determination of the normative weight of a risk of a rights violation will depend on basic criteria like the quality of the right and the quantity of the rights violation, i.e. the number of people affected by the risk of a rights violation as well as the number of rights that will possibly be violated.

As a rule of thumb a human rights-based account of the sort discussed above would hold the following premises to be relevant for arriving at ethically justifiable choices: (a) all people matter, both intra- and intergenerationally; (b) currently living people have a demanding duty not to cause predictable and avoidable future harm; (c) while risk impositions might be unavoidable, the nature of possible harms, the probability of their materialisation and the distribution of these harms as well as the existence of other available options matter for assessing whether such risk impositions can be justified. In other words, if one causes harm to others or imposes a risk of harm onto others, one needs to give solid reasons why doing so should be considered morally permissible.

5 Conclusion

The preceding sketched out some key considerations that must govern a rights-based framework able to handle the challenges posed by risks. For the governance level, a rights-based approach can only provide rough guidance because in non-ideal real-world circumstances policymakers' options will often involve certain uncertainties and risks. Risk governance, irrespective of the level at which it operates, needs to be context-sensitive. That is to say, when dealing with complex environmental problems it seems naive to assume that we could settle for one-size-fits-all approaches. Moreover, the risks we deal with are typically part of complex and overlapping 'risk-scapes', which means that in most cases the point of risk governance is not to aim for the complete avoidance of certain risks (which is often an unhelpful illusion), but the careful balancing and controlling of a myriad of risk potentials.

It should be evident by now that risks and uncertainties pose considerable difficulties both for moral theories and, *a fortiori*, for policymaking. A rights-based approach can address the complexity of decisions under risk and uncertainty by taking into account the many dimensions according to which the decision situations and the likely or possible outcomes of the available policy options should be assessed. There is little doubt that the development of a plausible rights-based account will face considerable difficulties in explicating justifiable criteria for weighing up the differing concerns and determining what we have called acceptability thresholds for the imposition of risks or rights violations. In times of anthropogenic climate change, when all available options come with considerable risks for the violation of rights of many people, we simply cannot afford to ignore the ethics of risk and the normative issues surrounding decision-making under uncertainty.

Notes

1 Note that many predictions are more likely to be true concerning the further future than the more immediate future. For example, the prediction that some policy will have changed or that certain resources will have been exhausted is more likely to be true in the further future.
2 Control is a particularly thorny philosophical topic. However, delving into the complexities surrounding this issue is beyond the scope of this chapter.
3 The distinction between risk and uncertainty is attributed to Frank Knight (1921).

4 IPCC (2014): summary for policymakers: 10; RPCs (representative concentration pathways) are projections about 'concentration' of greenhouse gases in the atmosphere under different scenarios.

5 Confidence levels are a combination of level of agreement and evidence, see IPCC (2014): summary for policymakers: 2. For more detail, see Mastrandrea et al. (2010).

6 One key issue in the context of climate change is that the existing uncertainties do not allow us to make predictions (in the proper sense of the term) as that would require us to have probabilistic knowledge about all possible outcomes, something that isn't the case for most climate change related phenomena. The issue of predictions and scenarios will be developed in more detail in Chapter 4.

7 However, see Meyer (2015: sec. 3.1) for a review of responses to the non-identity problem.

8 For an overview of normative theories of intergenerational justice and their implications see, e.g., Gosseries and Meyer (2009).

9 Questions surrounding scenarios will be discussed in more detail in Chapter 4.

10 'Discounting' refers to the fact that the value of a particular benefit is higher the closer to the present it may be had (a benefit of €10 now has more value than €10 in ten years' time; e.g., because of investment opportunities). 'Discount rates' determine the relative value of present compared to future benefits. This concept of discounting and its significance are discussed in detail in Chapter 6.

11 The idea of a lack of respect can also explain what is wrong in cases of blameworthy unintentional risk imposition, at least as long as the creation of the risk was at least reasonably foreseeable, meaning that the person imposing the risk acted recklessly.

12 For recent work on this issue, see Ferretti (2016), Hansson (2003), Stelzer and Schuppert (2016) and Lenman (2008).

Bibliography

Ackerman, Frank, Stephen J. DeCanio, Richard B. Howarth and Kristan Sheeran. 2009. 'Limitations of integrated assessment models of climate change'. *Climatic Change* 95(3): 297–315.

Bell, Derek. 2011. 'Does anthropogenic climate change violate human rights?' *Critical Review of International Social and Political Philosophy* 14: 99–124.

Caney, Simon. 2007. 'Justice, borders and the cosmopolitan ideal: a reply to two critics'. *Journal of Global Ethics* 3(2): 269–276.

Caney, Simon. 2010. 'Climate change and the duties of the advantaged'. *Critical Review of International Social and Political Philosophy* 13: 203–228.

Carr, Wylie A., Christopher J. Preston, Laurie Yung, Bronislaw Szerszynski, David W. Keith and Ashley M. Mercer. 2013. 'Public engagement on solar radiation management and why it needs to happen now'. *Climatic Change* 121: 567–577.

Elliott, Kevin C. 2010. 'Geoengineering and the precautionary principle'. *International Journal of Applied Philosophy* 24(2): 237–253.

Feinberg, Joel. 1984. *Harm to Others: The Moral Limits of the Criminal Law, Vol. 1.* New York: Oxford University Press.

Feintuck, Mike. 2005. 'Precautionary maybe, but what's the principle? The precautionary principle, the regulation of risk, and the public domain'. *Journal of Law and Society* 32(3): 371–398.

Ferretti, Maria. 2016. 'Risk imposition and freedom'. *Politics, Philosophy and Economics* 15: 261–279.

Finkelstein, Claire. 2003. 'Is risk a harm?' *University of Pennsylvania Law Review* 15: 963–994.

Füssel, Hans-Martin. 2007. 'Adaptation planning for climate change: concepts, assessment approaches and key lessons'. *Sustainability Science* 2(2): 265–275.

Gardiner, Stephen. 2006. 'Protecting future generations: intergenerational buck-passing, theoretical ineptitude and a brief for a global core precautionary principle'. In J. C. Tremmel (ed.), *Handbook of Intergenerational Justice*. Cheltenham: Edward Elgar, 148–169.

Gardiner, Stephen, Simon Caney, Dale Jamieson and Henry Shue (eds). 2010. *Climate Ethics: Essential Readings*. Oxford: Oxford University Press.

Gosseries, Axel and Lukas H. Meyer (eds). 2009. *Intergenerational Justice*. Oxford: Oxford University Press.

Hansson, Sven Ove. 2003. 'Ethical criteria of risk acceptance'. *Erkenntnis* 59(3): 291–309.

Hansson, Sven Ove. 2013. *The Ethics of Risk: Ethical Analysis in an Uncertain World*. Basingstoke: Palgrave Macmillan.

Hartzell-Nichols, Lauren. 2012. 'Precaution and solar radiation management'. *Ethics, Policy and Environment* 15(2): 158–171.

Heal, Geoffrey and Bengt Kriström. 2002. 'Uncertainty and climate change'. *Environmental and Resource Economics* 22(1): 3–39.

Intergovernmental Panel on Climate Change (IPCC). 2014: *Climate Change 2014: Synthesis Report. Contribution of Working Groups I, II and III to the Fifth Assessment Report of the Intergovernmental Panel on Climate Change* [core writing team, R. K. Pachauri and L. A. Meyer (eds)]. Geneva: IPPC, 151.

Jackson, Frank. 1991. 'Decision–theoretic consequentialism and the nearest and dearest objection'. *Ethics: An International Journal of Social, Political and Legal Philosophy* 101(3): 461–482.

Jamieson, Dale. 1996. 'Ethics and intentional climate change'. *Climatic Change* 33(3): 323–336.

Jamieson, Dale. 2010. 'Climate change, responsibility, and justice'. *Science and Engineering Ethics* 16(3): 431–445.

Knight, F. H. 1921. *Risk, Uncertainty, and Profit*. Boston, MA: Houghton Mifflin.

Kolstad, Charles, Kevin Urama, John Broome, Annegrete Bruvoll, Micheline Cariño Olvera, Don Fullerton, Christian Gollier, William Michael Hanemann, Rashid Hassan, Frank Jotzo, Mizan R. Khan, Lukas Meyer and Luis Mundaca. 2014. 'Social, Economic and Ethical Concepts and Methods'. In *Climate Change 2014: Mitigation of Climate Change*. Contribution of Working Group III to the Fifth Assessment Report of the IPPC. Cambridge and New York: Cambridge University Press.

Lempert, Robert J. 2002. 'A new decision science for complex systems'. *Proceedings of the National Academy of Sciences of the United States of America* 99: 7309–7313.

Lempert, Robert J. and M. T. Collins. 2007. 'Managing the risk of uncertain threshold responses: comparison of robust, optimum and precautionary approaches'. *Risk Analysis* 27(4): 1009–1026.

Lenman, James. 2008. 'Contractualism and risk imposition'. *Politics, Philosophy and Economics* 7: 99–122.

Lenton, Timothy M., Hermann Held, Elmar Kriegler, Jim W. Hall, Wolfgang Lucht, Stefan Rahmstorf and Hans Joachim Schellnhuber. 2008. 'Tipping elements in the Earth's climate system'. *Proceedings of the National Academy of Sciences* 105: 1786–1793.

Lockhart, Ted. 2000. *Moral Uncertainty and Its Consequences*. New York: Oxford University Press.

McCarthy, David. 1997. 'Rights, explanation, and risks'. *Ethics* 107(2): 205–225.

Mastrandrea, M. D., C. B. Field, T. F. Stocker, O. Edenhofer, K. L. Ebi, D. J. Frame, H. Held, E. Kriegler, K. J. Mach, P. R. Matschoss, G.-K. Plattner, G. W. Yohe and F. W. Zwiers, 2010. *Guidance Note for Lead Authors of the IPCC Fifth Assessment Report on Consistent Treatment of Uncertainties*. Geneva: IPPC.

Meyer, Lukas H. 2015. 'Intergenerational justice'. In E. N. Zalta (ed.), *The Stanford Encyclopedia of Philosophy*. Available at: http://plato.stanford.edu/archives/fall2015/entries/justice-intergenerational (last accessed 1 August 2016)

Meyer, Lukas H. and Dominic Roser. 2010. 'Climate justice and historical emissions'. *Critical Review of International Social and Political Philosophy* 13(1): 229–253.

Meyer, Lukas H. and Pranay Sanklecha. 2014. 'How legitimate expectations matter in climate justice'. *Politics, Philosophy and Economics* 13: 369–393.

Meyer, Lukas H. and Pranay Sanklecha (eds). 2017. *Climate Justice and Historical Emissions*. Cambridge: Cambridge University Press.

Morrow, David R. (2014). 'Starting a flood to stop a fire? Some moral constraints on solar radiation management'. *Ethics, Policy and Environment* 17(2): 123–138. DOI: doi:10.1080/21550085.2014.926056

Oberdiek, John. 2009. 'Towards a right against risking'. *Law and Philosophy* 28: 367–392.

Oberdiek, John. 2012. 'The moral significance of risking'. *Legal Theory* 18: 339–356.

Ott, Konrad. 2012. 'Might solar radiation management constitute a dilemma?'. In C. J. Preston (ed.), *Engineering the Climate: The Ethics of Solar Ration Management*. Plymouth: Lexington Books, 33–42.

Page, Edward A. 2008. 'Distributing the burdens of climate change'. *Environmental Politics* 17: 556–575.

Parfit, Derek. 2010. 'Energy policy and the further future: the identity problem'. In Stephen Gardiner et al. (eds), *Climate Ethics: Essential Readings*. Oxford: Oxford University Press, 112–121.

Perry, Stephen R. 2003. 'Harm, history and counterfactuals'. *San Diego Law Review* 40(4): 1283–1313.

Perry, Stephen R. 2014. 'Torts, rights, and risk'. In J. Oberdiek (ed.), *Philosophical Foundations of Tort Law*. Oxford: Oxford University Press.

Peterson, Martin. 2012. 'Multi-dimensional consequentialism'. *Ratio* 25: 177–194.

Placani, Adriana. 2017. 'When the risk of harm harms'. *Law and Philosophy* 36(1): 77–100.

Raz, Joseph. 1986. *The Morality of Freedom*. Oxford and New York: Clarendon Press.

Roberts, Marc and Michael J. Reich. 2002. 'Ethical analysis in public health'. *The Lancet* 359: 1055–1059.

Ross, Andrew and H. Damon Matthews. 2009. 'Climate engineering and the risk of rapid climate change'. *Environmental Research Letters* 4. http://dx.doi.org/10.1088/1748-9326/4/4/045103

Sepielli, Andrew. 2009. 'What to do when you don't know what to do'. *Oxford Studies in Metaethics* 4: 5–28.

Shue, Henry. 1980. *Basic Rights: Subsistence, Affluence, and U.S. Foreign Policy*. Princeton, NJ: Princeton University Press.

Shue, Henry. 1999. 'Global environment and international inequality'. *International Affairs* 75(3): 531–545.

Smart, John, Jamieson Carswell and Bernard Williams. 1973. *Utilitarianism: For and Against*. Cambridge and New York: Cambridge University Press.

Smith, Patrick Taylor. 2012. 'Domination and the ethics of solar radiation management'. In C. J. Preston (ed.), *Engineering the Climate: The Ethics of Solar Ration Management*. Plymouth: Lexington Books, 43–61.

Steigleder, Klaus. 2016. 'Climate risks, climate economics, and the foundations of a rights-based risk ethics'. *Journal of Human Rights* 15: 251–271.

Stelzer, Harald and Fabian Schuppert. 2016. 'How much risk ought we to take? Exploring the possibilities of risk-sensitive consequentialism in the context of climate engineering'. *Environmental Values* 25: 69–90.

Sunstein, Cass R. 2005. *Laws of Fear: Beyond the Precautionary Principle*. Cambridge: Cambridge University Press.

Thomson, Judith Jarvis. 1986. *Rights, Restitution, And Risk*. Cambridge, MA: Harvard University Press.

Vaughan, Naomi E. and Timothy M. Lenton. 2011. 'A review of climate geoengineering proposals'. *Climatic Change* 109(3): 745–790.

Weitzman, Martin L. 2011. 'Fat-tailed uncertainty in the economics of catastrophic climate change'. *Review of Environmental Economics and Policy* 5(2): 275–292.

4

LOOKING INTO THE FUTURE

Finding suitable models and scenarios

Joachim H. Spangenberg

1 Introduction

As made clear in the previous chapter, we are, on the whole, not sure what will happen in the future. In some cases, we are least able to estimate how likely a certain development is; in others, we can't even do as much as that.[1] As has become clear in Chapter 3, one of the main challenges in the context of climate change is that we are often unable to make actual predictions, since predictions require probabilistic knowledge about all possible outcomes, which isn't available for most of the phenomena driven by climate change or biodiversity loss. Moreover, as we actively shape the future with our decisions, the situation of future generations will inevitably depend on our current choices. The fact that our decisions, whether we like it or not, shape the living conditions of future generations constitutes a responsibility of current decision makers, a duty to pay adequate attention to the impacts their decisions have not only immediately, but also for the generations to come. Given our lack of reliable knowledge about the future, this is a major challenge to all decision makers.

However, we have to make decisions nonetheless, and in order to do so in a responsible way, we need to form an idea of what might happen as a consequence. Therefore, we need to have a way to think about how the future might change if we were to make a particular decision, without having to involve questions of how likely it is that this will happen.

In order to make the best decisions possible, it is vital to distinguish properly between what can be predicted with certainty and when we can merely compare plausible options in what is referred to as 'scenarios'. While in situations of certainty or statistically normal distributed risk predictions can be made, in cases of uncertainty and ignorance we have to compare different plausible but not necessarily probable options, asking 'what would happen if ...?' This is where scenarios come in, storylines often supported by modelling which offer potential answers to this question. Unfortunately, both academic literature, and press releases and media coverage often lack a clear distinction between predictions, projections, probabilistic forecasts and scenarios. Predictions are often referred to as 'scenarios', while certain scenarios, such as economic growth forecasts, are habitually presented as (probabilistic) predictions. Of course, as the world consists of different systems with different degrees of predictability, predictions and scenarios will ultimately need to come together to guide our decisions.

This chapter aims to clarify the different strategies used in dealing with uncertainties. In particular, it will focus on scenarios as a heuristic device. We will argue that if done properly, the combination of models and scenarios can support decision-making under uncertainty with improved information. To substantiate this argument, however, we first have to clarify what are scenarios, and then what are the suitable models, and what makes them 'suitable' as a basis for decision-making. From this basis, we will draw some conclusions regarding how these tools can help taking better informed and thus potentially more responsible decisions.

2 What are 'scenarios'?

Scenarios are explorative tools. Unlike predictions, they do not claim to outline the future that will *be*, but describe a future which *might* become reality. These futures must be *possible* and inherently *plausible*, but not necessarily *probable*. A scenario may aim to explore what possible future states may arise from certain policies or decisions – in this case, the type of scenario-making is called 'forecasting'. Alternatively, the scenario may take its start from a given future state that is deemed desirable, and try to see what policies or decisions may be required to bring about this situation – a procedure known as 'backcasting'. In forecasting, scenarios can be based on ongoing trends, but also on unexpected events which change the development path. Such events can be external (shocks or wild cards), but they can also result from the inherent dynamics of the social and environmental system that have been previously overlooked (Spangenberg et al. 2012). In backcasting scenarios, a guiding vision is developed at the intersection of the possible and the desirable, and the events are policy interventions or behavioural changes that help to orient the development towards that vision.

- Whether a view of the future is a scenario or a prediction depends not on the kind of forecast undertaken, but on the context in which the forecast is embedded. In science parlance, this is described as a 'system', a term referring to any set of things within a common frame (the system boundary) that is ruled by a given set of interactions (the system rules). To draw an analogy with games: dice, cards, tables and players would be system elements, the system rules are the rules of the respective game and a general code of conduct (don't cheat, for instance), while the house or online environment would represent the system border. Applying the terminology to the whole of the outside world, three systems have to be distinguished (Sayer 2000; Spash 2012): The *'real-world system'* or *'the reality'* is the object we would like to know more about. However, this system is not accessible to direct human observation since our perception is limited by the senses and instruments we have and interpreted by our brain, often unconsciously (as critical realism postulates and environmental sociology shows). Nonetheless 'the reality' makes itself felt in cases when our observation is confronted with unexpected experiences in a way that cannot be overlooked: then the prevailing construction of the following two systems must be considered falsified.

- The *'mental model'* we apply in the analysis of our experiences is the often unconscious model of the world and its functioning the analyst holds (and as a scientist, should reflect and make explicit). This world view is the basis of her interpretation of experiences and observations, and shapes the recommendations derived from them. Mental models are described in qualitative narratives or storylines.
- *Computer models* are the tools used to quantify a selected set of the expectations raised by the mental models. They are limited by the system margins and the relatively simple descriptions of a limited number of interactions within the system.

Surprisingly, most public trust lies in the latter, most simplified models. In order for computer models to be reliable, though, the mental model – although already a simplification – must first capture the major behavioural characteristics of 'reality' so that it can derive workable strategies. Only then the technical tools can be developed or existing ones adapted, attempting to enable them to express the main characteristics of the mental model, many of them qualitative in kind, and derive quantitative functions complementing and illustrating the qualitative mental models. As the mental model, expressed in scenario narratives, can accommodate qualitative aspects in a way no computer model can, the mental model narrative is the matrix in which diverse and complementary computer models can be embedded, illustrating and quantifying specific aspects of the scenario (Alcamo 2001). As both mental models and even more so computer models are simpler than the reality they describe, we should assess how the simplifications that are inherent to the model development process (and that indeed is, to a certain degree, its aim) impact the recommendations derived.

3 System complexity: what makes useful models and scenarios?

As scenarios and models are simplified descriptions of reality, they are bound to fail when it comes to describing those aspects of reality they did not capture. Which aspects those are, how decisive they are for the model functioning and ultimately whether the recommendations derived are achieving their intended aims when applied in reality or turn out to be ineffective or even counterproductive, depends on the model. If it captures the process dynamics of the *real world*, the chance is good that its results will offer workable insights into which measures have to be taken to reach a policy objective such as ending the loss of biodiversity, overcoming poverty and unemployment, or mitigating climate change.

Systems theory can help to distinguish suitable and inadequate approaches by identifying the assumptions and simplifications at hand and demonstrating their impacts on the model outcome (Holling 2001). The key means in this respect is a comparative analysis of the complexity of the respective systems; if the level of complexity of 'real world' systems and those used to emulate their behaviour diverges, the dynamics and direction of the system's development may not be reproduced by the model. A mental model assuming that it is always sunny in the Caribbean summer may lead to packing a holiday wardrobe with nothing suitable for when rainstorms and hurricanes hit. Drawing conclusions from zoo observations regarding animal behaviour can turn into a disaster when applied to freely roaming animals in the savannah: oversimplification can render models useless or even dangerous as policy and planning tools.

3.1 Levels of complexity

One way of identifying such complexity discrepancies is to analyse the character-istics of a system and its behaviour. On the next pages, we will shortly explain some elements of system theory that are relevant for our topic.

Returning briefly to the analogy with games, we can see that the system rules (the rules of the respective game and a general code of conduct) determine the complexity of the game – Go, for instance, has simple system elements but the rules make it one of the most complex games. In analogy, systems to which the same set of rules applies are of comparable complexity. This helps distinguishing systems which are more or less deterministic, and thus *predictable* from those which can accommodate the *unpredictability* of the real world. On the basis of Allen (2001), we define five distinct rules, which, if they all apply, signal maximum determination. The fewer of these rules apply, the less deterministic the system.[2] The *five system rules* are, simply expressed:

1. It is possible to distinguish between 'the *system*' and 'its *environment*'. Defining the border line is crucial as what the system can explain is only what is inside; for instance, when economists regret that their predictions (which in fact have been scenarios) did not correctly predict real-world developments, repeatedly explaining that with unforeseen 'external factors' they essentially indicate that they have drawn the border line in the wrong place, excluding factors decisive for the functioning of the system.

2. All *system components* can be recognised and distinguished, which means it is possible to describe and at best understand their interaction. For instance, an economic model not able to distinguish investment and savings would be rather useless, so these factors are always distinguished. However, recognising their interaction does not explain whether savings drive investment or vice

versa – their different interpretation of the empirical findings based on their respective world views has led to a deep disagreement about the character of the real world between neoclassical and Keynesian economists, unresolved for at least 40 years.

3. The *active system elements* are all identical, or at least the range of their behaviour is normally distributed around the average. In an economic system, for instance, consumers and producers are key active system elements. Microeconomics tries to understand their interaction by analysing the interplay between 'representative agents' – one consumer representing all consumers and one producer representing all producers. To be able to do so, one must assume that all consumers and all producers are identical regarding their behaviour in the situation analysed. The result is a deterministic development, with at most a random variation around the predicted outcome. In a similar vein, agent-based modelling uses identical agents (but usually defines more than two groups of agents) to analyse the interaction mechanisms of societies.

4. The individual behaviour of the system elements can be described by *average interaction parameters* which characterise the system behaviour. This implies that producers, consumers and others always follow the same set of behavioural rules and norms (with some stochastic variation); they are extremely stubborn, do not learn or change their behaviour towards others for any other reason, at least not as groups (this is not a statement about individual behaviour and learning).

5. The system develops towards a *stationary equilibrium*, which permits defining fixed relations of system variables. If this is the case, the future is predictable as the development trajectory of the system is defined and unchangeable.

The complexity assessment of a system will, in turn, allow us to assess whether particular policy arguments are based on 'mental models' corresponding to the level of system complexity to which they are applied: *the real world*.

3.2 What about reality?

In the context of real-world policymaking, we face complex and hardly deterministic systems – everybody knows that the future development of the economy, society or environment cannot be predicted (even the weather report fails from time to time). However, the unpredictable evolution of nature and the human-made systems society and economy differs due to their different level of complexity.

Natural systems develop through the evolution of their biological system elements (e.g. plant and animal species) and adaptation of their physical elements (e.g. a stream finding a new course after a landslide) in unpredictable ways. The feedback loops inherent to any system (A influences B which in turn influences A again) shape the development of the internal structure of the system elements in this evolutionary process, which in turn influences the processes and the structures on the system level, which in turn changes the context of the system elements and thus their behaviour, and so forth: evolution acts not only on the system level, but also on the level of system elements (individuals, species, ecosystems, etc.).

In social and economic systems where the system elements are humans, additional complexity arises from the fact that individual behavioural change is not necessarily driven by the change jointly experienced by the individual, but can also be based on rather unrelated objectives and motivations (e.g. belief systems, ideals and ideologies). Humans adapt their behaviour not only due to learning processes, local system processes or external influences (such as TV news), but also as anticipatory reactions, i.e. as adaptations to expected future developments (which can of course be based on misjudgements due to the unpredictability of the system development). While the human capability to change behaviour as a reaction to the (local) state of the system creates a dynamics within the system, which leads to comparably fast system adaptation, this adaptation is not always targeted as different expectation can easily lead to inhomogeneous reactions amongst the human agents, i.e. the system elements.

For instance, since the mid-nineteenth century, the suffragettes' movement organised women in campaigns for universal suffrage. Getting organised changed the self-perception of women, strengthened their position and encouraged them to make themselves heard. In a lengthy process they finally won what they had been fighting for: equal rights to vote and to stand for election for men and women, a change to the structures and processes of the political system. This strengthened the role of women in society, and without it the emancipation movements (in the West from the 1960s onwards) would have hardly been possible – the system evolution went on.

The evolutionary dynamics can be described as the combination of the unpredictable process of random change (in biology, mutation; in economics, innovation) and the deterministic process of selection. In our example, the spontaneous self-organised women's movements' activities were the unpredictable innovation, while the power brokers' institutional resistance led to different kinds and levels of delay and, as a response, of militancy in different countries (universal suffrage was introduced in New Zealand 1881, Finland 1907, Argentina 1911, Uruguay 1918, the UK 1928, Greece 1952, Switzerland 1971, Liechtenstein 1984), but always ended with a legal guaranty of voting rights irrespective of age, wealth, sex or race.

In systems parlance, selection results in directed development while the presence of the innovation/mutation introduces irreducible uncertainty. Therefore, the development is not predictable, even if the relevant structures and starting conditions are known. The trends (and thus the probability of sudden shifts) can be changed by external influences (gradually, or suddenly by shocks, including non-linearities caused by thresholds and delays), and by internal structural change (gradually or suddenly), driven by interventions resulting from any kind of internal process. If the experiences of individual system elements have been positive, changes can spread rapidly through the whole population of system elements as a result of positive feedback to success, leading to imitation. This is true regardless whether the behaviour of the system elements is consciously oriented towards a specific target or not, as it is the case in 'natural' systems, i.e. the bio-geosphere as the example of a monkey population demonstrates: some individuals learned by incident that washing the fruit in salty water makes them more tasty, and the whole group adopted that behaviour.

Such evolving dynamic systems are capable of passive adaptation to changes in their environment (which on the system level appears as a kind of passive learning behaviour), a behaviour in line with rules 1–3 (clear system border, distinguishable system elements, identity of active system elements). However, if the system consists of elements with no behavioural restrictions - the system elements can change their behaviour as the suffragettes did, rule 3 does no longer apply. Thus in complex, dynamic evolving systems in general, and in society in particular, only rules 1 and 2 apply.

So, in a nutshell, we have seen that the world we live in, its social, economic and environmental components are complex evolving systems. They are undergoing permanent change, slow at times, but with possible sudden accelerations known as environmental or economic crises. We can now use the tool of system rule analysis, introduced in the previous section, to compare the real-world system complexity with the one of the models used to describe and analyse it. This allows some conclusions regarding the appropriateness of the tools applied to understand reality.

3.3 Current models between theory and reality

The trouble with future-related policies, including climate policies, is that they are frequently based on computer models in which most or even all of these rules apply (clear system border, distinguishable system elements, identity of active system elements, standard interaction of elements, stationary equilibrium) – in other words, based on models which are deterministic, predictable systems. This is in stark contrast to what we have just seen: that in reality the relevant system (our world in all its aspects) is a far more complex and far less predictable evolving system where only rules 1 and 2 apply. Computer models of such complex adaptive systems have been developed for instance in the research of artificial life; however, thus far the application of such models has been limited to simple, usually small-scale systems. In any case, if reflecting nature's level of complexity, they unavoidably also share nature's characteristic of unpredictability which makes them appear less attractive to many economists, planners and politicians.

Systems where rules 1–3 apply (clear system border, distinguishable system elements, identity of active system elements) are closer to observations of 'real-world' systems than dynamic or deterministic models where 4 resp. all five rules apply. Nevertheless, the fact that the elements of such systems cannot change their behaviour as a response to local system conditions means that such models are out of step with the observed behaviour of and within actual natural and social systems. More recently, agent-based modelling (models using not just one 'representative agent' as described before, but a multiplicity of agents, i.e. many interacting consumers, producers, traders or banks) has been used to emulate many characteristics of these kinds of systems. This is a promising way forward, particularly when applied in a non-constant environment, e.g. in a system dynamics context. However, attempts to further enhance the complexity of models in this manner are not only still rare but also insufficient since all agents of one type are modelled as having a standardised behaviour, making the system confirm to rule 3, one rule too many as compared to the real world.

Even worse, neoclassical economics and its partial or global equilibrium models still perceive the economy as a predetermined system on its way to a clear-cut and predictable future state (or even having reached it) (see Chapter 8). The predictability resulting from applying rules 4 and 5 (standard interaction of elements, stationary equilibrium) permits scholars to derive what they consider 'rational management decisions' by allowing comparison between the known system state before and the predictable one after a certain action is taken. For instance, there are many insects damaging plants, and if you treat them with insecticides, the insects are gone and the harvest is safe. The evolution of resistance (insensitivity to the specific insecticide) is not taken into account, nor are the damages to the natural enemies of the pests, which limit the damage but suffer from the insecticides (Spangenberg et al. 2015). Theories based on the assumption of equilibria and predictability (e.g. normative decision theory, cost–benefit analysis, continual dose–response curves) are mental models easily translated into technical tools like computer models – which is what makes them popular with decision makers despite their mismatch with reality. Such models are necessarily based on the cause–effect relationship used in programming (and random relations with known probability distributions in fuzzy models) – that is how programming works. In the limited time periods of relative system stability, trend extrapolations and probabilistic predictions may be produce valid results (i.e. in these situations the uncertain and unknown factors play a marginal role, risk dominates uncertainty and ignorance – see Chapter 3). However, as this stability is always relative, structural change happens at varying speeds and abrupt changes remain possible, with unknown probability, these models do not properly reflect the dynamics of the more complex natural or social systems. They are not able to integrate all the relevant systemic factors that are playing a role in real environments, economies and societies, and thus lead to wrong predictions and potentially dangerous recommendations. One example is the suggestions of the Millennium Ecosystem Assessment MA that the precautionary principle might (only) be applied 'in instances where knowledge of costs and benefits is incomplete [and] the costs associated with ecosystem changes may be high or the changes irreversible' (MA Millennium Ecosystem Assessment: vi). In plain language, this is the recommendation to base decisions primarily on cost–benefit-analyses (CBA) which assume the predictability of future cost trends, and only in specific cases base decisions on precaution – which as we have seen in the previous chapter is the most appropriate approach in situations of uncertainty and ignorance typical for the development of complex systems.

This is not to say that models based on highly deterministic systems (in which rules 1 to 4 or 5 apply: not only clear system border and distinguishable system elements, but also identity of active system elements, standard interaction of elements, and stationary equilibrium) have no use whatever, although modelling is only possible for certain system elements and a limited set of system processes. For instance, so-called 'system dynamics models' presume unchanged behaviour of the system elements and structures, making the results predictable if system structure and starting points are known (rules 1–4 apply). Examples include complex geo-physical systems like the Special Report on Emissions Scenarios (SRES) simulation runs used by the IPCC (IPCC et al. 2000), biodiversity models taking a certain climate development as given, or land use models with input from climate and from socio-economic scenarios (e.g. Spangenberg et al. 2012), or economic models based on simplified assumptions regarding consumer behaviour. While they cannot predict the future development of an evolving and thus unpredictable system, they can still help to understand some system processes. For instance, they may be useful in the context of specific research questions, when not the system development as such, but the outcome of a certain behavioural pattern in a constant environment is the objective of the analysis. But since such models neglect important characteristics of natural and social systems, they are insufficiently complex for supporting real-world decisions.

3.4 Back to the real world

Nature, society and the economy are complex evolving systems characterised by system learning (all three) plus, for human systems, by learning and anticipation of the agents which are the system elements. We will now take a closer look at these human-made systems and their dynamics.

In these systems, the elements (individuals, groups, households, companies) can act consciously, based on reflections about the future internal and external development (for instance climate change and its impacts). However, humans rarely do so; most human behaviour is not based on reflection but on habits and routines carried out without reflection – a psychological necessity given how many decisions we have to take every day (Kumar and Kumar 2008). It is usually only in situations when routines fail that humans reflect about a new way, leaving the trodden path, for instance to adapt to or to mitigate anticipated system developments like climate change (selling the house near to the coastline, reducing energy consumption). With these changes of behaviour, humans are more or less consciously influencing the development of the socio-economic system and its influence on its environment. In particular the (subjective) expectation of negative outcomes (which may be right or wrong, or different for different population groups) gives reasons for intervention, altering the framework gradually, as reflexive actors try to direct the system towards a more desired state (in this case, attempting to encourage climate policies on the system level and behavioural change on the individual level).

However, such a change is not a one-off process. The behavioural patterns of system elements/agents are not only dependent on the individual characteristics of the agents and their common explorative behaviour, but are also influenced over time by behaviour-shaping mechanisms such as experiences, social practices, routines, habits, knowledge and technologies (Shove and Walker 2010; Shove et al. 2012). The resulting dynamics cause an ongoing development process of behavioural patterns of systems and their elements (the now independent agents), changing the system and its environment, thus enforcing renewed adaptation, i.e. evolutionary processes. Recognition and anticipation are key factors accelerating the system evolution, making the socio-cultural evolution much faster than the still ongoing biological evolution processes.

The more trial-and-error is replaced by or at least embedded into anticipatory problem-solving strategies, the more effective and efficient the capability of the system to react and adapt becomes (Hornung 1985). In the social domain, these processes have a significant influence on leading principles and norms, and deliberate interventions by self-conscious and reflexive system elements – that is, by stakeholders, individually or collectively – shape the behaviour of the system.

However, anticipation has its limits in complex evolving systems: adaptation to expected future states can be fatal if the expectation is wrong as the system develops in an unforeseen way. This is always possible and a reason for caution when using models and scenarios, as the system behaviour is unpredictable and will most probably deviate from what models suggest. One reason is that the system processes are influenced by non-linear cause–effect relations. Take for instance threshold phenomena: for a long time, adding a drop of water to a bucket will raise the level in a pretty foreseeable way, but at a certain point it will be the drop that makes the bucket flow over. Losing 20 or 30 per cent of insects may be something nature can compensate, but when 70 to 80 per cent of insects are lost (measured as biomass, Hallmann et al. 2017), there are good reasons to worry when e.g. pollination will collapse and with it the majority of fruit and vegetable production. Delays, acting as a kind of buffer, lead to time lags between causation and impact: there is no immediately visible damage from emitting greenhouse gases, but it manifests itself after years and decades. The unpleasant result is that stopping the pressures, for instance completely ending greenhouse gas emissions now, does not stop the warming driven by last decades' emissions – it will be effective only after the delay period, and thus with a significant time lag.

As a result, a certain pressure may have a small or no impact for a considerable amount of time (the drop in the bucket), but can have immediate and significant impacts at other times (the overflow), for instance once a threshold (like the bucket being full) has been passed – which, due to time lags, can happen even after the pressure has ended. This way, even rather small changes on the lower level can trigger dynamic processes which lead to significant changes on the higher level (the 'butterfly effect').

Overlapping positive (self-enhancing) and negative (breaking) feedback loops make systems even more volatile and their behaviour less predictable. For instance, a negative feedback loop is that if during a pest infestation the number of crop damaging organisms is rapidly increasing, in rather short time the number of predators feeding on them also goes up. This in turn reduces the number of pest organisms and limits the damage (this is the biological pest control on which organic agriculture rests and which is suppressed by spraying insecticides which also affect the biocontrol organisms). A positive feedback loop is that globally permafrost soils tend to thaw due to climate change, in this process releasing methane, a potent greenhouse gas. On sea, the continental shelves hold significant amounts of methane hydrate – a substance storing methane in crystalline water, known only since 1971 – and could release enormous amounts of greenhouse gases as soon as the ocean warming reaches the sea floor.

As a result of different decision options of the agents/system elements and the role of randomness, evolving systems do not have one predetermined future, but a wealth of possible futures. They can switch from one development trajectory to another, but not every transition is possible, and those which are possible occur with different frequencies. As a result, the future development path is not completely open, but influenced by past constellations and transition frequencies. For instance, a climate disaster is no fate, but the risk of it is the result of past decisions pro-fossil fuels when other options were available but were dropped, and now their decisions' consequences are unfolding according to the laws of nature governing our environment.

The current path towards disaster can be left, but that requires significant efforts (including reducing resource consumption and switching to renewables), and not every transition is possible: for a transition to a bioeconomy, there is not enough biomass on earth, and for unchanged consumption patterns and permanent economic growth, sufficient resources are missing regarding both sinks and sources. While returning to Stone Age consumption levels may be desirable for environmental reasons, for social reasons revitalising Stone Age life styles is no option (aside from the fact that there are probably not enough caves for nine billion humans).

In some sense, it is like climbing uphill out of a frozen valley, where a disaster looms at the bottom: the faster and deeper one has been going down, the steeper the valley walls (the structures) and the more slippery the ground (our habits and routines), the more difficult it will be to resist gravity, and escape. For instance, in the history of habitation, a shift of means has been rare (from cave via hut to house), but in transport there have been more options used – hence renovating the transport system appears to be easier than restructuring the way people are accommodated.

However, it is not possible to derive probabilities for future transitions from the ones observed, for instance in the transport sector, as the probabilities evolve with the evolution of the system. Therefore, relying on model runs when planning policies always implies the risk – indeed the probability – of unexpected developments; models can neither foresee them nor help preparing for them. In particular the frequent use of IA (Integrated Assessment) models (which integrate CGE (Computable Global Equilibrium) economic and biophysical models, most often in an intransparent way, but the former always built on assumption 1 to 5) as the basis for future projections and the reliance of decision-making on such models is a reason for concern; partial equilibrium models suffer from similar concerns.

4 Decisions for transitions

As we have seen, decisions are necessary to shift from one system trajectory to another; some such shifts are possible, but not all, and each is associated with different kinds and levels of difficulty. The existing computer models are of limited help in identifying the optimal transition pathways – but decisions must be taken, on as good an information basis as possible, supported by new tools and decision-making mechanisms.

4.1 Decision support in complex evolving systems: the task of scenarios

In this situation, the *scenarios* introduced in section 2 are a key tool to explore the futures of a system, each illustrating one of many possible '*system biographies*'. A key scenario component is its narrative, a plausible, fact based and coherent storyline, describing the assumptions made, and thus suitable for comparing the outcomes of different policies. To be useful, scenarios must be inherently consistent and plausible, reflect the dynamics of the system, confirm to the known facts, correspond to past experience and on this basis describe possible developments of the system, even if they cannot quantify their probability. All of these criteria can be fulfilled based on informed qualitative and fact-based reasoning, preferably combined with brainstorming and participatory processes and with specific elements illustrated by model runs.

Being plausible implies that the assumptions made represent real-world possibilities (although they do not have to be the most probable ones). Fact based means that the available scientific and non-scientific information is taken into account, i.e. that the storyline is not counterfactual. Finally, coherent requires that the storyline is free of inherent contradictions; for instance, a scenario representing neoliberal or sustainability policies must make assumptions in line with the respective political orientation in economic, social, environmental, taxation, trade, defence and all other policy domains covered by the scenario. Of course, what is plausible in the real world is a subjective assessment, based on the mental model of reality its authors hold. As a storyline, it can and should incorporate qualitative factors, surprises and results from social and cultural science research computer models cannot accommodate. Such narratives can be complemented by computer modelling results, but also by graphs, rich pictures (Bell et al. 2016) and other visualisations.

In terms of the system rules, narratives can describe mental models based on rules 1 and 2 (clear system border, distinguishable system elements), reflecting the complexity of reality, while computer models at least need to apply rule 3 (identity of active system elements), frequently also rule 4 (standard interaction of elements) and in economics and related disciplines all too often rule 5 as well (stationary equilibrium). Since all computer models are insufficiently complex, the narratives are the centre piece of scenarios describing the irreversible process of system development (including non-linearities, thresholds, delays etc. as described above) in a qualitative or semi-quantitative manner, e.g. by using ordinal scales (classes like bad–medium–good, or absent–scarce–available–abundant–plentiful), capturing as much of the system complexity as possible.

In such scenarios, a diversity of models can be run to illustrate different aspects of the storyline, but with a clear hierarchy: modelling results cannot stand by themselves, they have to be interpreted and if necessary modified against the background of the narrative to reconcile them with the factors the narrative includes, but the respective model could not take into account (Alcamo 2001). The quantitative 'hard figures' from the models have to be considered 'soft results' which acquire relevant meaning only in the process of their contextual interpretation (Spangenberg 2005; Settele et al. 2012). Scenarios which reverse this hierarchy fail in accommodating the complexity levels necessary for solid policy support. Each scenario corresponds to one development trajectory or system biography, and vice versa. Each bifurcation constitutes a new scenario (which can also be described as a 'sub-scenario', thus creating a hierarchy of scenario families). However, as the totality of possible futures is far beyond any given analytical capacity, in reality a choice must be made which scenarios to analyse. Here more subjective elements are important: which scenario is considered the most plausible, the probable, the most positive or negative (worst-case analysis), the most interesting, etc. Subjective choice and informed reasoning are also the basis of complex scenarios such as the MA Millennium Ecosystem Assessment (2005) which analysed the threats to and the expected development of global biodiversity, or the scenarios of the Intergovernmental Panel on Climate Change (IPCC) (Field et al. 2014).

The pattern of extended periods of relative stability followed by abrupt changes leading to a new system configuration described above (Holling 2001) characterises our situation as one where there is nearly always a probability of gradual change (which is the issue of politics and media, and to a certain degree accessible to models), but at the same time the possibility of abrupt change (which is most often not taken into account; its description denunciated as 'fearmongering' and 'unscientific'). However, scenario narratives can do better than the political discourse: they are not restricted to gradual, smooth developments, as most computer models are. Whereas incremental change is usually chosen as the basis for scenarios, they can readily be extended to accommodate shocks, events that are possible in reality and that lead to unexpected midway changes of the course taken by the system as a whole (its development trajectory) creating a new system biography (Spangenberg et al. 2012).

For instance, no economic model foresaw the collapse of the financial markets, but some economists working with plausible reasoning instead of complex models had long warned against the upcoming disaster (Cooper 2015).[3] Climate scientists developed scenarios describing the 'shock event' of a collapse of the Gulf Stream when models were still weak and empirical evidence was not yet available, assessing the impacts on livelihoods and biodiversity with interdisciplinary colleagues (Settele et al. 2012). Models can help assess some aspects of the impacts a pandemic might have (like the amount of vaccines to stockpile), but disaster prevention and mitigation must take social dynamics into account – while models might easily fail this task, narratives can do so.

Although the probability of scenarios cannot be quantified, they can help deriving interventions that reduce this unknown probability – sustainable strategies are those which sustain system functions under a maximum diversity of possible futures. To be effective, interventions must take the diverse rationalities of different agents into account, and so must the scenarios on which they are based. If done properly, the combination of models and scenarios can support decision-making under uncertainty with improved information. Unexpected events, shocks, bifurcations and other unpredictable events are then included in the narrative and implemented as externally set starting points for the models to emulate the system behaviour in this specific situation, providing an information basis for decision-making. To make the decision support as robust as it can possibly be, in any case the criteria of plausibility, fact conformity and coherence have to be maintained, in the core narrative itself as well as in the additional assumptions made regarding shocks and other events not occurring on a development path based on gradual change.

4.2 Decision-making in post-normal situations

The call for scientific support, scenarios and models frequently arises in situations where stakes are high, decisions are urgent, scientific knowledge is uncertain and values are disputed – in short, in *post-normal* situations, to use the term coined by Funtowicz and Ravetz (2003).

Already in situations described as 'normal' (Kuhn 1962), i.e. in the quasi-stable state of the system, the objective must be evidence evaluation at the science–policy interface to generate the best possible information basis corresponding to a high level of certainty regarding the outcomes of any measure taken.

However, while in particular in the current age of 'alternative facts', 'fake news' and 'post-truth' it is of utmost importance that politics insists on taking scientifically informed decisions, the frequent call for 'science-based' or, even worse, 'evidence-based decision-making' is misguiding as it overlooks the different functional logic in the scientific and the political subsystems of our societies. Scientific results are not only always open to falsification, but also often based on disciplinary mental models less complex than those of political analysis, let alone the real world. Furthermore, the traditional scientific paradigms apply the quality criteria of the respective scientific communities by vigorously trying to avoid 'type 2 errors', i.e. not to endorse statements which later turn out to be false. This necessarily goes at the expense of creating 'type 1 errors', in other words rejecting right statements due to a yet insufficient level of evidence – the higher the threshold for acceptance, the more frequently early detection of dangerous phenomena will fail. However, for decision makers and the public at large it is important to balance the risk of falling victim to either error (differences regarding the right balance are a bone of contention between the USA insisting on scientific proofs of risks and the EU emphasising the precautionary principle). So, science, models and scenarios are indispensable, but insufficient.

Even in the 'normal' political process, politics is always decision-making under incomplete and uncertain information, values are disputed and stakes of 'being wrong' are (perceived as) high, regarding both type 1 and type 2 errors (Giampietro et al. 2006). Nonetheless, policy action is still needed, despite the fact that in any situation science may fail to identify relevant pressures or suggests precautionary measures that in retrospect turn out to have been unnecessary.

Unlike this quasi-stable situation perceived as 'normal', the (normal) dynamic state of the system corresponds to 'post-normal' situations characterised by a level of irreducible uncertainty beyond the 'normal' situation of politics and science. In the economic system, the global financial crisis (2007–2009) was the symptom of such a post-normal situation, which in many aspects still lingers on. In the political sphere, the rise of populism, nationalism and neofascism has falsified the assumptions about the functioning of the political system in many Western democracies and created a post-normal situation of 'fake news' and 'alternative facts' hardened into public beliefs in the online echo chambers. Climate change and biodiversity loss are altering the functioning of the biosphere, and thus the conditions under which human civilisations emerged – another dimension of the current multiple post-normal situation. In such post-normal situations, the standard approach of causality analysis fails, as it is not capable of capturing all the relevant system characteristics including non-linearities and conditions of uncertainty and ignorance. Not surprisingly for a dynamic phase of the system, in a considerable amount of cases our understanding of the system is not sufficient to determine the identity, role and contribution of the direct drivers of system change, let alone those of the indirect drivers behind them.

With the failure of prediction, the effectiveness of decisions can no longer be taken for granted. In this situation, legitimacy begins to play a greater role (allowing for improved decisions as much as for collective errors). Thus, discursive processes have been suggested to derive some provisional and 'negotiated' positions or 'shared truths', and to avoid 'negotiated nonsense' (EEA 2004). Examples of such shared truths emerging from extensive consultations with experts, stakeholders, civil society and governments are the climate assessments by the IPCC, and the biodiversity assessments by the Intergovernmental Science–Policy Platform on Biodiversity and Ecosystem Services (IPBES). They are typical for what Funtowicz and Ravetz (2003) call an 'extended peer community', paying respect to the fact that in a knowledge society knowledge ownership is no longer a privilege of science, and that different kinds of knowledge are complementary rather than of different quality.

The necessary level of precaution or precautionary prevention depends on the quality of the information available, which in turn is influenced by the kind and the state of the system and the variety of contributors within and beyond the scientific community. Science has always been transformation science, monitoring and analysing change. With scenarios and the warning signals they provide it turns into transformative science, contributing to the sustainability transition by advocating a transformation (and in the process, transforming itself). Science has become part of a broader coalition attempting to modify the currently dominant development trajectory, and for policies that (hopefully) push the system in the desired direction (it should however not be ignored that there are also scientists, dominant in certain disciplines, who are vocal advocates against any structural change of the status quo). Participation can improve knowledge quality (for the assessment and management of knowledge quality, see, e.g., O'Connor 2002; Van der Sluijs 2002; 2006), and it can be combined with scenario development. Scenarios, then, are no truth machines, but helpful devices to explore different development options, and participation helps to merge competence and legitimacy.

5 Concluding remarks

If we want to act responsibly towards the future and care about future generations, it is of crucial importance to reflect on the way we look towards a future we do not and cannot know – larger-scale predictions are impossible. This chapter has discussed different ways of dealing with this lack of knowledge. We distinguished two ways of looking to the future: on the one hand, we have an approach trying to 'calculate' the future within simplistic mental models that can easily be translated into computer models. However, computers are only able to integrate a set of parameters and their interactions that have already been identified as relevant systemic factors. Changing structures and relations do not occur, and evolution does not happen. Consequently, those models have difficulties in understanding the complexity of the real world, they are promising us a level of scientific certainty that we don't have due to the complexities in times of climate change and other ecological, social and political challenges. In light of this, most predictions and forecasts published today should be considered to be scenarios. Doing so would imply the need to reveal their assumptions to permit comparisons with alternative scenarios based on the same historical data, but invoking different assumptions (often corresponding to deterministic mental models and narratives).

On the other hand, we have approaches that try to take the uncertainty of the future seriously. They work under the assumption that we have to understand ecological and societal processes in their complexity as evolving systems and that we have to be open for permanent processes of reconsideration of the parameters that we are working with. They use scenario narratives to explore possible futures, forgo attempts at predicting and using computer models as a secondary information source, illustrating aspects of the narratives. For the future, it will be of crucial importance to develop this direction further. We have to get better at dealing with an uncertain future and to develop an understanding of the complex processes that will shape it. In any case, scholars should be aware that even if their mental model and their tools have been demonstrated to be applicable at a certain point in time, they may be invalidated soon by a change of structure or dynamics evolving in the 'natural' or social system under observation. Recognising the indeterminacy of the future is the condition for any successful attempt at shaping it, hopefully for the better.

Notes

1 For an explanation of the relevant notions of risk, uncertainty and ignorance, see Chapter 3.
2 These five rules can be aggregated to a smaller number and otherwise rephrased (see, e.g., Bossel 1999), without changing their distinctive function for different levels of complexity. The formulation of Allen (2001) has been chosen since the way it is phrased provides a good opportunity to assess economic systems and mental and technical models.
3 See: www.intheblack.com/articles/2015/07/07/6-economists-who-predicted-the-global-financial-crisis-and-why-we-should-listen-to-them-from-now-on (last accessed 9 April 2018). From Germany, Jörg Huffschmid could be added to the list.

Bibliography

Alcamo, Joseph. 2001. *Scenarios as Tools for International Environmental Assessments. EEA Expert Corner Report Prospects and Scenarios No. 5. Expert Corner Reports. European Environment Agency.* Luxembourg: Office for the Official Publications of the European Communities.

Allen, Peter M. 2001. 'The dynamics of knowledge and ignorance: learning the new systems science'. In H. M. W. Matthies and J. Kriz (eds), *Integrative Systems Approaches to Natural and Social Dynamics.* Berlin, Heidelberg, New York: Springer, 3–30.

Bell, Simon, Tessa Berg and Stephen Morse. 2016. 'Rich pictures: sustainable development and stakeholders – the benefits of content analysis'. *Sustainable Development* 24(2): 136–148.

Bossel, Hartmut. 1999. *Indicators for Sustainable Development: Theory, Method, Applications.* Winnipeg, MB: IISD International Institute for Sustainable Development.

Cooper, Cameron. 2015. '6 Economists who predicted the global financial crisis'. *Intheblack*, 7 July. Available at: www.intheblack.com/articles/2015/07/07/6-economists-who-predicted-the-global-financial-crisis-and-why-we-should-listen-to-them-from-now-on (last accessed 9 April 2018)

European Environment Agency (EEA). 2004. *A Framework for Evaluating Complex Scientific Evidence on Environment Factors in Disease Causation.* Background paper No. 3 from the EEA for the EU Environment and Health Strategy. Copenhagen: EEA.

Field, Christopher, Vincente Barros, Katharine Mach and Michael Mastrandrea (eds). 2014. *IPCC AR5 Climate Change 2014: Impacts, Adaptation, and Vulnerability.* New York: Cambridge University Press.

Funtowicz, Silvio and Jerome Ravetz. 2003. 'Post-normal science'. *Internet Encyclopaedia of Ecological Economics.* Available at: www.ecoeco.org/publica/encyc_entries/PstNormSc.pdf (last accessed 3 February 2004)

Giampietro, Mario, Kozo Mayumi and Giuseppe Munda. 2006. 'Integrated assessment and energy analysis: quality assurance in multi-criteria analysis of sustainability'. *Energy* 31(1): 59–68.

Hallmann, Casper, Martin Sorg, Eelke Jongejans, Henk Siepel, Nick Hofland, Heinz Schwan, Werner Stenmans, Andreas Müller, Hubert Sumser, Thomas Hörren, Dave Goulson and Hans de Kroon. 2017. 'More than 75 percent decline over 27 years in total flying insect biomass in protected areas'. *PLoS ONE* 12(10). doi:0185809.

Holling, Crawford Stanley. 2001. 'Understanding the complexity of economic, ecological, and social systems'. *Ecosystems* 4(5): 390–405.

Hornung, Bernd. 1985. *Grundlagen einer problemfunktionalistischen Systemtheorie gesellschaftlicher Entwicklung. Sozialwissenschaftliche Theoriekonstruktion mit qualitativen, computergestützten Verfahren.* Frankfurt, Bern, New York, Paris: Peter Lang.

Intergovernmental Panel on Climate Change (IPCC). 2007. *Synthesis Report.* Gland: IPCC.

IPCC, World Meteorological Organization (WMO), United Nations Environment Programme (UNEP). 2000. *IPCC Special Report: Emission Scenarios.* New York, Nairobi: IPCC, UNEP.

Kuhn, Thomas. 1962. *The Structure of Scientific Revolutions*. Chicago, IL: The University of Chicago Press.

Kumar, Manasi and Pushpam Kumar. 2008. 'Valuation of ecosystem services: a psycho-cultural perspective'. *Ecological Economics* 64(4): 808–819.

MA Millennium Ecosystem Assessment. 2005. *Synthesis Report: Ecosystems and Human Well-Being*. Washington, D.C., MD: Island Press, vi.

O'Connor, Martin. 2002. 'Social costs and sustainability'. In Daniel Bromley and Jouni Paavola (eds), *Economics, Ethics and Environmental Policy: Contested Choices*. Oxford: Blackwell, 181–202.

Sayer, Andrew. 2000. *Realism and Social Science*. London: Sage.

Settele, Joseph, Timothy Carter, Ingolf Kühn, Joachim Spangenberg and Martin Sykes. 2012. 'Scenarios as a tool for large-scale ecological research: experiences and legacy of the alarm project'. *Global Ecology and Biogeography* 21: 1–4.

Shove, Elizabeth, Mikar Pantzar and Matt Watson. 2012. *The Dynamics of Social Practice: Everyday Life and How It Changes*. London: Sage.

Shove, Elizabeth and Gordon Walker. 2010. 'Governing transitions in the sustainability of everyday life'. *Research Policy* 39(4): 471–476.

Showstack, Randy. 2014. 'Sector of West Antarctic ice sheet in "irreversible retreat"'. *EOS: Transactions American Geophysical Union* 95(20): 168–168.

Spangenberg, Joachim H. 2005. 'Will the information society be sustainable? Towards criteria and indicators for a sustainable knowledge society'. *International Journal of Innovation and Sustainable Development* 1(1–2): 85–102.

Spangenberg, Joachim H., Alberte Bondeau, Timothy Carter, Stefan Fronzek, Jill Jaeger, Kirsti Jylhä, Ingolf Kühn, Ines Omann, Alex Paul, Isabelle Reginster, Mark Rounsevell, Oliver Schweiger, Andrea Stocker, Martin Sykes and Joseph Settele. 2012. 'Scenarios for investigating risks to biodiversity'. *Global Ecology and Biogeography* 21: 5–18.

Spangenberg, Joachim H., Jean-Marc Douguet, Josef Settele and Kong Luen Heong. 2015. 'Locked into continuous insecticide spraying in rice. Developing an integrated ecological and socio-political DPSRI analysis'. *Journal of Ecological Modelling* 295: 188–195.

Spash, Clive. 2012. 'New foundations for ecological economics'. *Ecological Economics* 77: 36–47.

Van der Sluijs, Jeroen (ed.). 2002. *Management of Uncertainty in Science for Sustainability*. Utrecht, Copernicus Institute: Utrecht University.

Van der Sluijs, Jeroen. 2006. 'Uncertainty, assumptions, and value commitments in the knowledge base of complex environmental systems'. In Ângela Guimarães Pereira, Sofia Guedes Vaz and Sylvia Tognetti (eds), *Interfaces between Science and Society*. London: Greenleaf, 46–57.

5

PATHWAYS FOR FUTURE GENERATIONS IN EXISTING LEGAL HUMAN RIGHTS PROVISIONS

Elina Pirjatanniemi

1 Introduction

Human rights comprise a powerful message for humankind. As expressed in the preamble to the Universal Declaration of Human Rights[1] (hereafter: UDHR), the recognition of the inherent dignity and of equal and inalienable rights of all members of the human family is the foundation of freedom, justice and peace in the world. Importantly, equal and inalienable rights are not restricted to the present generation only. On the contrary, the UDHR emphasises the dignity and rights of all members of the human family.[2] It is possible to argue that this reference has a temporal dimension that brings all generations, past, present and future, within the scope of the UDHR.[3]

The realities of the international legal order are to some extent different from this normative starting point. Human rights protection is primarily based on agreements between states. Legally binding treaties, such as the 1966 International Covenant on Civil and Political Rights[4] (ICCPR) or the 1950 European Convention on Human Rights[5] (ECHR), include detailed provisions regarding the temporal application of the treaties. Seen from a legal perspective, this is fully understandable. States, the duty-bearers, need to know what their commitments are, and they have to agree to them. Once the treaty has been signed and accepted in accordance with the procedures required by the treaty at hand, the state is under an obligation to perform it in good faith. It is, however, important to notice that human rights treaties are legal agreements and as such, they can be amended. Some human rights treaties even explicitly allow withdrawal. For example, the Convention on the Rights of the Child[6] (CRC) provides the states with an option to denounce the Convention. In case the treaty is silent on this point, the situation is different. The Human Rights Committee, the organ monitoring the implementation of the ICCPR, has taken the view that the ICCPR and its sister Covenant, the International Covenant on Economic, Social and Cultural Rights (ICESCR) cannot be withdrawn from. This interpretation was confirmed in 1997, when North Korea sought to denounce the ICCPR. As these Covenants were meant to codify in treaty form the UDHR, according to the Committee they did not have the temporary character typical to treaties.[7]

The possibility of amending a treaty or withdrawing from it seems to indicate that human rights are negotiable. Nevertheless, this is not the case. Even if treaties between states are in practice the most important source for legal obligations, they are not the only mechanism by which legal obligations are created. There is, for example, a growing consensus that most of the rights listed in the UDHR have become part of general public international law with the implication that all states have to respect these rights.[8] *First of all*, it is possible to defend a position according to which some of the rights enumerated in the UDHR have acquired a status of customary international law.[9] This refers to a body of international norms that have been established via consistent and identifiable state practice and further backed up by a belief that this very practice is legally binding. For example, the prohibition of torture is widely perceived as having the status of customary law.[10] *Second*, human rights may also constitute general principles of law, which form, alongside treaties and customary law, a valid source of international law. General principles of law are legal principles that are common to all, or almost all, legal systems. Some of the rights enshrined in the UDHR are thus seen as fundamental principles, which are recognised by all states.[11]

Even if we are able to convincingly argue that at least some human rights reach beyond treaty obligations, we still face the problem of identifying the rights belonging to this category. This task is challenging as such, and the temporal aspect linked to future generations' rights naturally increases the difficulty. All in all, it can be argued that the more nuanced and contested obligations we are discussing, the more unlikely it is that they will be accepted as binding without reference to specific and explicit treaty obligations.

Alongside the debate on the origin of legally binding human rights norms, it is important to take into account the distinction between *peremptory norms (jus cogens)* and *dispositive norms (jus dispositivum)*. Whereas the latter can be subject to modifications, the former operates in an absolute and unconditional way. Consequently, a peremptory norm cannot be put aside by treaties or customary rules not endowed with the same normative force.[12] Prohibition of slavery, genocide, torture and the prohibition of *refoulement*, that is, of returning a person to a territory where he or she runs a risk of torture or of being ill-treated, are examples of peremptory norms the status of which is widely accepted in the international community.[13]

From the perspective of future generations, also the category of peremptory norms remains ill defined. Some of the prohibitions mentioned above, such as the one concerning genocide, do include elements that could be used to defend the position that future generations are right-holders in international law. For example, the crime of genocide contains an intention to destroy a group by killing members of the group or by deliberately inflicting on the group conditions of life calculated to bring about its physical destruction in whole or in part or by imposing measures intended to prevent births within the group.[14] Accordingly, the prohibition of genocide aims to protect not only persons belonging to the present generation, but also future generations.[15]

This brief discussion on the origin of legal obligations intends to show that the rights of future generations, as legal entitlements, are primarily in the hands of states. This limitation nevertheless characterises public international law in general and has nothing to do with the concept of rights of future generations per se. Legal order may be dependent on the will of the sovereign, but this limitation can also be seen as an asset: legal norms and their interpretations can be changed. The development within human right law bares evidence on that. Even the fiercest critics of the international human rights jurisprudence tend to admit that human rights law has shown incredible ability to adjust itself to new circumstances. This phenomenon is, in fact, well exemplified by the way that environmental concerns have been integrated into the body of human rights law.

The aim of this chapter is to introduce the state of the art regarding the relationship between human rights and duties to protect the environment for the sake of future people. After these introductory remarks, I will develop some arguments in favour of the legal rights of future generations. In addition, the question of the operationalisation of the rights is examined. The chapter concludes with a discussion on the limits and possibilities of law in protecting the rights of future generations.

2 Human rights and the environment – the state of the art

The UDHR was drafted in the aftermath of the Second World War. Quite understandably, environmental concerns were not the focus of attention during the postwar era. If the UDHR were written today, it would nevertheless be unthinkable to leave aside the relationship between human rights and the environment.

As with the UDHR, most of the early human rights instruments are silent on environmental issues. Environmental awareness simply came at a later date. Consequently, the ICCPR and the ICESCR do not include any specific provisions regarding the environment. The same is true of the early regional human rights treaties, that is, the ECHR and the 1969 Inter-American Convention on Human Rights[16] (IACHR).

Concerns about the degradation of the environment grew in the late 1960s and early 1970s. One of the milestones in this respect was the United Nations Conference on the Human Environment held at Stockholm in 1972. The Conference adopted a Declaration including common principles to inspire and guide the peoples of the world in the preservation and enhancement of the human environment.[17] According to Principle 1 of the Stockholm Declaration, human beings have the fundamental right to freedom, equality and adequate conditions of life, in an environment of a quality that permits a life of dignity and well-being. In addition, humans bear a solemn responsibility to protect and improve the environment for present and future generations.

The groundbreaking significance of the Stockholm Declaration is not dimin-
ished by the fact that it represents soft law, meaning that its importance is of a
moral and political, rather than of a legal, character.[18] It is fair to argue that the
Declaration opened up the international debate on the consequences of environmental degradation for future generations, which is also the debate that this book is
addressing. It is indeed noteworthy that the idea of responsibility towards future
generations appears in the first international document linking human rights to the
environment.

The development after the Stockholm Conference was partly positive, partly
not. The follow-up conference held in 1992 in Rio de Janeiro re-emphasised the
relevance of environmental and developmental needs of future generations.[19] At
the same time it loosened itself from the more rights-based approach adopted in
Stockholm. Focus was directed towards the achievement of sustainable development, whereby environmental protection was understood to constitute an integral
part of the development process. This was a step back according to those who had
hoped for a more robust approach to environmental rights.[20] From an environmental rights perspective, the strong focus on sustainable development is not a
problem as such. The problem is the watering down of the meaning of sustainable
development. It is apparent that in the post-Rio period the environmental
dimension has not been given as much attention as the economic dimension of
sustainable development.[21] At the same time, to merge development and environment as the concept of sustainability does was most likely the only politically
viable step available in the early 1990s.

In retrospect, it can be concluded that the debate on environmental rights did go
on even after the conferences in Stockholm and Rio de Janeiro. The content of
these rights nevertheless remained unclear and even contested, and the importance
of environmental rights was mainly supported by non-binding soft law documents.
Occasional references to environmental issues nevertheless started to appear in
legally binding instruments drafted after Stockholm. For example, according to
Article 24 of the 1989 CRC, states shall, inter alia, take appropriate measures to
combat disease and malnutrition through the provision of adequate nutritious foods
and clean drinking water, taking into consideration the dangers and risks of environmental pollution. Article 11 in the Additional Protocol to the American Convention
on Human Rights in the Area of Economic, Social and Cultural Rights from 1988,
better known as the Protocol of San Salvador,[22] went even further. It states that
everyone shall have the right to live in a healthy environment and to have access to
basic public services. In addition, the Protocol stipulates that states shall promote
the protection, preservation and improvement of the environment. The most
recent of the regional human rights treaties, the 1981 African Charter on Human
and Peoples' Rights[23] (ACHPR), also contains a specific provision on the environment. According to Article 24 of the Charter 'All peoples shall have the right to
a general satisfactory environment favourable to their development'. Despite these
notable exceptions, existing human rights treaties are silent on environmental
concerns. It is especially unfortunate that UN human rights treaties, with their goal

of universal coverage, have not provided any stronger linkage between human rights and the environment. However, human rights treaty bodies and particularly regional human rights courts have been rather innovative in interpreting the human rights provisions so as to protect environmental interests. For example, the European Court of Human Rights (ECtHR) has developed extensive case law on environmental issues by dynamic interpretation of the ECHR.[24] Other regional courts have interesting case law as well, and UN treaty body jurisprudence also finds novel ways to protect the environment via human rights provisions.[25] In this context, it is also important to notice that one of the most important recent achievements in the field of environmental protection, that is, the Paris Agreement on Climate Change,[26] emphasises the relationship between human rights and the environment. The Agreement acknowledges in the preamble 'that climate change is a common concern of humankind' and states should, when taking action in order to address climate change, 'respect, promote and consider their respective obligations on human rights'. Notably, the preamble also explicitly highlights the relevance of intergenerational equity.

Numerous difficult questions still wait for answers, but it is clear that the linkage between human rights and the environment is widely recognised. As already mentioned, the regional human rights courts have impressively taken into account environmental considerations. The same holds true, although to a lesser extent, for human rights treaty bodies. Activities of the UN in general cannot be neglected either, even if the legal breakthrough in the form of legally binding agreement on the right to environment has not yet materialised. Finally, a growing number of states have included specific environmental provisions in their constitutions.[27] This development is likely to have, and already has, implications at regional and international levels.

Seen from a legal perspective, discussions regarding the relationship between human rights and the environment seem to concentrate on two key questions. *First*, environmental degradation and nuisances of different sorts can have a negative impact on the enjoyment of several substantive human rights. In the gravest form, environmental problems threaten the very basis for life. Even less dramatic scenarios can constitute an impediment for the enjoyment of one's property, private life or one's right to health. *Second*, environmental concerns activate a discussion about the ways we make decisions regarding the environment. In this respect, environmental issues coincide with the general efforts to strengthen people's participation already imbedded in human rights law. The following two sections focus on these two dimensions of the relationship between human rights and the environment.

3 Environmental obligations towards future generations?

Efforts to formulate a specific human right to a healthy environment have been many, but so far the endeavours have not been very successful. Even if the right has established its position in many national constitutions, it has been difficult to reach a consensus on an international formulation of it. Regarding international human rights, the development can rather be explained as a *greening* of existing human rights. Instead of creating a specific right to a healthy environment, established human rights are interpreted so as to indirectly support the protection of the environment, via the rights of individuals.

It is a notorious fact that environmental degradation can have an impact on the enjoyment of several human rights. As stated earlier, the state of the environment has nevertheless been, with the exception of the African Charter, a marginal issue in the texts of the human rights treaties. Having said that, it is vital to emphasise that there is now a growing body of case law opening up the human rights regime to environmental considerations. This, however, does not yet mean that the rights of future generations are taken into consideration. The greening of the human rights regime only indicates that environmental dimensions are seen as relevant, but it is not the same as to extend rights to apply to future people. The inclusion of future generations requires more than environmental awareness, but this awareness is a necessary condition for a broader understanding on the concept of rights-holders.

The greening of existing human rights is a logical consequence of the nature of human rights treaties. A human rights treaty is designed to be dynamic. It is, as famously stated by the ECtHR in the *Tyrer* case: 'a living instrument which . . . must be interpreted in the light of present-day conditions'.[28]

It is possible to find natural linkages to the environment in most of the human right provisions. However, it is inevitable that some provisions have been more frequently referred to than others. As the UN Independent Expert on human rights and the environment, John H. Knox, puts it: '[S]ome human rights are more susceptible than others to certain types of environmental harm'.[29]

Environmental concerns have often entered into the system via the right to life, right to health, prohibition of inhuman and degrading treatment, right to private life and the right to property. It is beyond the scope of this chapter to provide detailed insight into the environmental dimensions of all these rights. As the focus of our interest is on the rights of future generations, I have chosen to exemplify the mechanism via right to life, which is the prerequisite for the enjoyment for other rights.

On a general level, the link between environmental conditions and the right to life is obvious. Without access to such environmental goods as air, water, soil and flora and fauna, our living conditions are seriously hampered. It is equally apparent that environmental degradation has consequences on the essential interests of future generations. Another question is, however, whether future generations' right to life can be operationalised within the context of a legal order.

As a starting point it is crucial to note that the concept of right to life have been given diverse constructions in different regional systems. It is nevertheless clear that the right to life, being a precondition for the enjoyment of other rights, creates far-reaching obligations for states. *First*, states have the obligation to respect the right, and not to deprive anyone of life arbitrarily. *Second*, states also have the duty to prevent situations that might imperil the right to life. It is noteworthy, that this duty, or rather, positive obligation, is not limitless. In the case law of the ECtHR it has been established that this duty 'must be interpreted in a way which does not impose an impossible or disproportionate burden on the authorities'.[30]

As an example, we can refer to the case of *Osman* v. *United Kingdom*. This particular case concerned the killing of a schoolboy's father, Mr Osman, by a teacher who had been involved in a series of increasingly serious incidents and who had been suspended. When assessing the limits of the positive obligation to protect the right to life, the Court held that it must be established that the authorities knew or ought to have known of the existence of a real and immediate risk to the life of an identified individual or individuals. In addition, it must be established that the authorities failed to take measures within the scope of their powers which, judged rationally, might have been expected to avoid the risk.

As far as future generations are concerned, the interpretation above includes several challenges. In order to have a duty to take measures, it must be established that the authorities either knew or they ought to have known about the risk to life. Knowledge of the risk is nevertheless not enough. In addition, there are limits as regards the temporal aspect of the risk. The farther away the risk is in time, the more difficult it is to argue that the state has a positive obligation to act. The level of protection is naturally to be determined in accordance with the magnitude of the risk involved, but in order to come within the scope of the right to life the risk must reach a certain level of certainty.

Even if these impediments could be overridden, the most difficult obstacle still remains. Human rights violations are violations with specific addressees. A violation must, in other words, have a causal link to a specific individual or individuals. Human rights instruments do not primarily protect life as such, but the life of a particular identifiable person.

There are, however, some interesting openings that could be utilised in order to anchor the rights of future generations in the human rights regime. Regarding the example here, the right to life, the right of future generations can be linked to the concept of *human dignity*.

The concept of human dignity is especially interesting in the context of future generations, because it seems to be timeless. It embodies the basic status of a human being, which means that it is fully plausible to argue that generations to come will also have an intrinsic worth. In other words, respect for human dignity requires that we recognise and respect the intrinsic worth of future generations and since future generations cannot stand up for their rights themselves we would need representatives to defend their rights (see Chapter 6).

A second possible avenue to argue for the rights of future generations is linked to the discussion concerning the *rights of indigenous peoples*. Their position is equivalent with that of future generations in at least two ways. *First*, the enjoyment of indigenous people's rights has a robust collective emphasis. Their rights are enjoyed in community with others. This dimension is obviously present in the enjoyment of rights in general, but it is especially tangible regarding indigenous communities. *Second*, protection of the rights of indigenous peoples is geared towards future. This is manifested, for example, in Article 11 of the 2007 United Nations Declaration of the Rights of Indigenous Peoples, which emphasises that:

> Indigenous peoples have the right to practise and revitalize their cultural traditions and customs. This includes the right to maintain, protect and develop the past, present and future manifestations of their cultures, such as archaeological and historical sites, artefacts, designs, ceremonies, technologies and visual and performing arts and literature.[31]

Human rights treaty bodies and the non-European regional human rights organs have presented noteworthy viewpoints about the object of protection in the indigenous context. For example, in the case concerning the Yanomami Indians, the Inter-American Commission on Human Rights strongly emphasised the importance of the preservation and strengthening of the cultural heritage of indigenous peoples.[32] The conflict had its origin in the construction of the Trans-Amazonian highway that goes through the territory where the Indians live. The project had significant consequences for the indigenous community. It had caused the break-up of their age-old social organisation and introduced prostitution among the women. In addition, the massive penetration of outsiders into the area had resulted in many deaths, caused by a variety of epidemics. The Commission stated that the Brazilian government had failed to protect the cultural heritage of this indigenous group and found the government in violation of their right to life, liberty and personal security; the right to residence and movement and the right to the preservation of health and to well-being.[33]

Indigenous populations have a special connection to nature, which means that they depend on a healthy environment more than the general population. This particular connection can thus be seen as a limitation as far as other groups' rights are concerned. Future communities are not necessarily indigenous. On the other hand, other groups can make similar claims to the protection of environmental resources, such as water, food, shelter and cultural enrichment. The fact that human rights organs have demonstrated a willingness to recognise these factors in the indigenous context indicate that similar arguments could be made by non-indigenous claimants who are able to establish a comparable dependence on the environment under threat.[34] This, for its part, supports the idea of the rights of future generations. Without efficient measures to combat such environmental threats as the climate change, future generations will be put in a vulnerable position, which is analogous to the fate of indigenous peoples.

To conclude, the human rights framework does include interpretative openings that can be used in order to enhance the rights of future generations. The intrinsic worth of all human beings – past, present and future – seems to require that states take into consideration at least such future consequences of their actions that they know, or ought to know. The development as regards the rights of indigenous peoples also gives argumentative tools to those promoting the rights of future generations. The question remains, however, how the operationalising of the rights could be done in practice. This directs our attention towards participation, to which this chapter now turns.

4 Empowerment through participation

Whereas it has been difficult to formulate a feasible definition on the legal right to a healthy environment, the position of environmental procedural rights is already generally acknowledged. It is widely accepted that environmental issues are best handled with the participation of all concerned citizens. Broad participation not only strengthens the democracy, but it also improves the quality of the decisions and supports their legitimacy.

Efficient participation presupposes information regarding the environment, and access to judicial and administrative proceedings. These three pillars, the *right to participation*, the *right to information* and the *right to access to justice*, are recognised by many human rights instruments and environmental agreements. However, the most important legal instrument in this respect is the 1998 Aarhus Convention on Access to Information, Public Participation in Decision-making and Access to Justice in Environmental Matters (Aarhus Convention).[35] It includes the most elaborated provisions on participation, information and access to justice and it has also given guidance and inspiration for regional human rights courts.

The relevance of the Aarhus Convention in the context of future generations' rights resides in its ability to go beyond the individualistic bias characteristic to the human rights regime. In contrast with most of the human rights instruments, the Aarhus Convention recognises the *actio popularis* claims. These are made by a person or a group in the interest of the public order and thus they differ from a typical human rights claim, where the claimant must be individually suffering from a violation. Suffice to say, the former type of claims must be possible if the rights of future generations are to be operationalised.

As far as the concept of a 'victim' is concerned, regional human rights systems have chosen slightly different solutions. In general, human rights instruments require individualisation of the violation. The ECtHR takes the most stringent approach. According to Article 34 of the ECHR, every natural person as well as every non-governmental organisation (NGO) or group of individuals can apply to the Court. All claimants, individuals or groups, must nevertheless fulfil the requirements of victim status. This means that the claimant must personally suffer from violation of his/her rights, as enumerated in the Convention. In order to put forward a successful case on, for example, excessive airport noise, one must show that the nuisance has an impact on one's right to enjoy the right to private life. Therefore, those natural or legal persons, whose rights are not affected, cannot apply to the Court. In environmental cases, this is not necessarily a dilemma, as many of them have an impact on a larger group of persons and an NGO can represent such a group. Moreover, the Court has also recognised the status of a potential victim. This refers to natural or legal persons who can demonstrate that they have a serious and imminent risk of being directly affected by an alleged legal situation in a given country. Furthermore, a natural or legal person might be recognised as an indirect victim, that is, having a close connection to a direct victim, who may be deceased or minor. However, the ECtHR has so far not explicitly accepted *actio popularis* claims, which alleges general human rights violations unconnected to any specific victim applicant.

Unlike its European counterpart, the Inter-American system has a more positive approach towards *actio popularis*. Pursuant to Article 44 of the IACHR, victims, other persons or group of persons as well as any NGO have standing before the Inter-American Commission. It is noteworthy, that claimants can act on behalf of others and thus do not have to suffer from violations themselves. However, they need to be able to identify the victims.

The African system is clearly in favour of *actio popularis*. The most significant case regarding the protection of the environment, the *Ogoni* case, was in fact brought before the African Commission by human rights NGOs. Interestingly, the existence of this possibility was seen as an asset by the Commission:

> The Commission thanks the two human rights NGOs who brought the matter under its purview: the Social and Economic Rights Action Center (Nigeria) and the Center for Economic and Social Rights (USA). Such is a demonstration of the usefulness to the Commission and individuals of *actio popularis*, which is wisely allowed under the African Charter.[36]

For the purposes of this chapter it is interesting to note that the African Commission has accepted not only individualised victims, but also hypothetical and collectively defined groups as victims.

A more elaborate analysis on the provisions concerning the concept of victim in international human rights law is beyond the scope of this chapter. As can be seen above, the current European approach is the most conservative: an application to the Court is not possible on behalf of the general public. The other regional systems are more flexible, but it is nevertheless unlikely that an abstract claim on behalf of future generations would be successful. Their rights and interests are simply too abstract for the legal regimes to cope with. In addition, there would be enormous problems with evidence, which is an important practical question that must nonetheless be left aside here.

At the same time, we know that future generations will be the victims of the decisions, or non-decisions, of their predecessors. Without *actio popularis* in relation to environmental damage it is very difficult to make claims on behalf of those who will suffer in the future. It is precisely here that the Aarhus Convention becomes especially interesting. Namely, Article 9(3) of the Aarhus Convention provides for standing to 'members of the public' to challenge environmental decisions. This opening is significant, even if the wording of the Article is somewhat diluted. According to the Article:

> each Party shall ensure that, where they meet the criteria, if any, laid down in its national law, members of the public have access to administrative or judicial

procedures to challenge acts and omissions by private persons and public authorities which contravene provisions of its national law relating to the environment.

The final word as regards standing is left to the states. The approach represented by the Aarhus Convention is in any case important as the Convention is used as a model, also by the ECtHR, for procedural rules concerning environmental decision-making. The presumption according to which members of the general public can be seen as guardians of the environment is a powerful message, even if more is needed before we can efficiently act on behalf of future generations.

5 Law and its limits and possibilities

International human rights law has its obvious limits in advancing the rights of future generations. The obstacles discussed above are, however, not insurmountable. The art of lawyering does not have to be conservative. Lawyers can, if they wish, be part of the progressive development of the law instead of simply acting as external spectators of it. If we want to take the rights of future generations seriously, we must be prepared to broaden our understanding of the concept of rights. Obviously, we must remember that legal thinking is dependent on traditions. It is not possible to create, in a convincing way, concepts that are very isolated from the legal tradition. Neither it is possible to push forward extremely radical interpretations: legal thinking develops in small steps.

The seeds of change are nevertheless out there. We can identify progressive judgments here and there. Human rights courts have interpreted human rights provisions in a dynamic manner and showed willingness to adjust their content to present-day conditions. In addition, human rights courts and treaty bodies have in their jurisprudence emphasised the importance of proper environmental legislation on a national level and required appropriate national proceedings in environmental matters. By doing so, they give indirect support to environmental values.

In order to make the rights of future generations operational, at least four obstacles must be removed. *First*, the human rights community should consider the possibility of giving more room to group-based rights. *Second*, there is a need to reinterpret the principles concerning what kind of likelihood is required of a legally relevant violation. In other words, the system should become more adaptable to precaution. *Third*, the concept of victim must be broadened to also include anonymous groups of victims. *Finally*, we, the present generation, must understand our role as a guardian of the environment for succeeding generations. In the legal world, this role can be best played by *actio popularis*.

Notes

1 General Assembly Resolution 217 A (III), Official Records of the session of the General Assembly, Part I, 21 September 1948, Resolutions (UN Doc.A/810): 71–77.
2 Ibid.

3 See also Weiss (1992: 21).

4 International Covenant on Civil and Political Rights, 999 UNTS 171.

5 European Convention on Human Rights (ETS no. 5) as amended by the provisions of Protocol No. 14 (CETS no. 194).

6 Convention of the Rights of the Child, 1577 UNTS 3.

7 CCPR General Comment No. 26: Continuity of Obligations, Adopted at the 61st Session of the Human Rights Committee, on 8 December 1997 CCPR/C/21/Rev.1/ Add.8/Rev.1, General Comment 26.

8 De Schutter (2012: 41–47).

9 De Schutter (2012: 41–43).

10 Hannum (1995/1996: 340–351).

11 De Schutter (2012: 43–44).

12 See Orakhelashvili (2006: 67–72).

13 De Schutter (2012: 50–53).

14 See Art. II, Convention on the Prevention and Punishment of the Crime of Genocide, 1021 UNTS 277.

15 See also Weiss (1992: 203)

16 American Convention on Human Rights: 'Pact of San José, Costa Rica', 1144 UNTS 123.

17 Stockholm Declaration on the Human Environment, in Report of the United Nations Conference on the Human Environment, UN Doc.A/CONF.48/14, at 2 and Corr.1 (1972).

18 See Koivurova (2014: 59); Dupuy (1990: 422).

19 United Nations Conference on Environment and Development: Rio Declaration on Environment and Development, UN Doc.A/CONF.151/5/Rev.1, 13 June 1992.

20 Francioni (2010: 44–45).

21 Koivurova (2014: 45).

22 Protocol of San Salvador, Additional Protocol to the American Convention on Human Rights in the Area of Economic, Social, and Cultural Rights, OAS Treaty Series No. 69 (1989).

23 African (Banjul) Charter on Human and Peoples' Rights, Adopted 27 June 1981, OAU Doc. CAB/LEG/67/3 rev. 5.

24 For an overview of the development, see San José (2005).

25 See *Report of the Independent Expert* (30 December 2013).

26 Conference of the Parties, United Nations Framework Convention on Climate Change, Report of the Conference of the Parties on Its 21st Session, held in Paris from 30 November to 13 December 2015 – Addendum – Part Two: Action Taken by the Conference of the Parties at Its 21st Session, Dec. 1/CP.21, UN Doc. FCCC/CP/ 2015/10/Add.1 (29 January 2015) ('Adoption of the Paris Agreement'). The Agreement is included as an annex to this document ('Paris Agreement').

27 See further, Shelton (2010: 89–120).

28 ECtHR, *Tyrer* v. *the United Kingdom*, Judgment 25 April 1978, para. 31. The judgments of the ECtHR are available at: https://hudoc.echr.coe.int (last accessed 10 April 2018)

29 See *Report of the Independent Expert* (24 December 2012).

30 ECtHR, *Osman* v. *the United Kingdom*, Judgment 28 October 1998, para. 116.

31 United Nations Declaration on the Rights of Indigenous Peoples (A/RES/61/295), 13 September 2007.

32 Resolution No. 12/85, Case 7615, Indios Yanomami Chile Resolution No. 10/85, Case 8095, Edgardo Condeza Vaccaro.

33 Ibid.

34 Doelle (2004: 208).

35 Convention on Access to Information, Public Participation in Decision-Making and Access to Justice in Environmental Matters 2161 UNTS 447.

36 *Social and Economic Rights Action Center and the Center for Economic and Social Rights* v. *Nigeria*, No. 155/96, 2001, para. 49.

Bibliography

De Schutter, Olivier. 2012. 'The status of human rights in international law'. In Catarina Krause and Martin Scheinin (eds), *International Protection of Human Rights: A Textbook*, 2nd rev. edn. Turku: Åbo Akademi University Institute for Human Rights, 39–58.

Doelle, Meihard. 2004. 'Climate change and human rights: the role of the international human rights in motivating states to take climate change seriously'. *Macquarie Journal of International and Comparative Environmental Law* 1: 179–216.

Dupuy, Pierre. 1990. 'Soft law and international law of the environment'. *Michigan Journal of International Law* 12(2): 420–435.

Francioni, Francesco. 2010. 'International human rights in an environmental horizon'. *European Journal of International Law* 21(1): 41–55.

Hannum, Hurst. 1995/1996. 'The status of the universal declaration of human rights in national and international law'. *Georgia Journal of International and Comparative Law* 25: 287–397.

International Covenant on Civil and Political Rights (CCPR) General Comment No. 26: Continuity of Obligations, Adopted at the 61st Session of the Human Rights Committee, 8 December 1997. CCPR/C/21/Rev.1/Add.8/Rev.1.

Koivurova, Timo. 2014. *Introduction to International Environmental Law*. Abingdon: Routledge.

Knox, John H. 2012. *Report of the Independent Expert on the Issue of Human Rights Obligations Relating to the Enjoyment of a Safe, Clean, Healthy and Sustainable Development*, 24 December. A/HRC/22/43.

Knox, John H. 2013. *Report of the Independent Expert on the Issue of Human Rights Obligations Relating to the Enjoyment of a Safe, Clean, Healthy and Sustainable Environment*, 30 December. A/HRC/25/53.

Orakhelashvili, Alexander. 2006. *Peremptory Norms in International Law*. Oxford: Oxford University Press.

San José, Daniel García. 2005. 'Environmental protection and the European Convention on Human Rights'. Strasbourg: Council of Europe Publishing. Available at: www.echr.coe.int/LibraryDocs/DG2/HRFILES/DG2-EN-HRFILES-21(2005).pdf (last accessed 30 November 2017)

Shelton, Dinah. 2010. 'Developing substantive environmental rights'. *Journal of Human Rights and the Environment* 1(1): 89–120.

Weiss, Edith Brown. 1990. 'Our rights and obligations to future generations for the environment'. *American Journal of International Law* 84: 198–207

Weiss, Edith Brown. 1992. 'In fairness to future generations and sustainable development'. *American University International Law Review* 8(1): 19–26.

Cases

Case 7615, Inter-American Commission on Human Rights, Annual Report 1984–1985

Osman *v.* the United Kingdom, Application No. 23452/94, Judgment 28 October 1998

Social and Economic Rights Action Center and the Center for Economic and Social Rights *v.* Nigeria, No. 155/96

Tyrer *v.* the United Kingdom, Application No. 5856/72, Judgment 25 April 1978

6

POLITICAL REPRESENTATION OF FUTURE GENERATIONS[1]

Danielle Zwarthoed

1 Introduction

A quite straightforward way to secure future generations' interests seems to be to include them in the decision-making process. In representative democracies, this amounts to representing them in the same way as presently living citizens are represented in the decision-making process. But future people do not exist yet. How could we represent them? Such a proposal raises practical questions, such as: how many representatives should there be for future people? How would they be selected? But it also raises deeper ethical issues. This chapter aims to provide an overview of the political and philosophical debates on the representation of future generations. But first, a couple of clarifications are in order.

First, on representation. Future people may be represented at various stages of the decision-making process: at the legislative stage, at the executive stage and at the judicial stage. This chapter attempts to consider all of these because, depending on particular institutions, one stage might have more importance than others. On representation more generally, not all accounts of representation fit with future people as representees. Accounts that require representees to be there will not be compatible with the idea of representing future generations. Hence this chapter will consider whether and how we should broaden the understanding of political representation.

Second, on future generations. In the public debate, future generations often refer to young generations, that is, already existing or soon to come children and young people. This is especially striking in debates on the pension system. But this chapter will rather focus on distant future generations, that is, unborn future generations, because their representation raises specific issues.

The chapter is structured as follows. First, it provides the main philosophical arguments in favour of the representation of future generations and discusses potential major objections. Second, it describes existing concrete proposals that have been made in the literature. An appendix provides a detailed overview of the existing models of representation of future generations as well as a discussion of the concrete attempts to implement representation of future generations at the international level.

2 Why should future generations be represented?

The political representation of future generations is far from uncontroversial. Interference with the existing democratic institutions, proliferation of bureaucracy, trade-offs between present and future needs, and even the costs of such institutions are among the arguments opponents can advance against the official representation of future generations. This section aims to discuss the philosophical issues at stake in this discussion.

2.1 Two normative justifications for the political representation of future generations: justice and democracy

It is important to distinguish between requirements of justice and requirements of democracy. Both democracy and justice raise substantial issues in political philosophy and have led to a significant body of literature. I have no space to properly address these issues and this literature here. I shall thus stick to slightly simplified accounts that should help to cover some of the important issues political representation of future generations raises. Democracy, in a simple and straightforward under-standing, characterises a political system combining majority rule, universal suffrage and free voting (Van Parijs 1996: 2). Justice (i.e. distributive justice) refers to the (morally) right distribution of benefits and burdens within a society, both within and across generations. Political representation for future generations might actually be justified from each of these perspectives. The justice-based justification amounts to the claim that representation of future interests is instrumental to the achieve-ment of intergenerational justice. The democracy-based justification amounts to the claim that all interests should be taken into account in the democratic process, including the interests of future people.[2]

(i) Intergenerational justice

Suppose considerations of distributive justice do apply to relations between gen-erations. There are many accounts of intergenerational justice and there is no space here for an extensive discussion of the various merits of each of these. Some sug-gested accounts are sufficientarian and hold that each generation should have access to a sufficient level of advantages. Egalitarian accounts hold that each generation should have access to an equal level of advantages. These advantages can be assessed in various ways, such as resources or primary goods, productive opportunities, capabilities, democratic capacities (Thompson 2010) or welfare.[3]

Rawls's account of intergenerational justice is a well-known example, but any account that is sufficiently demanding for 'business as usual' to be problematic should do. According to Rawls (1999: section 44, 2001: section 49), intergenerational savings should be such that:

1. As long as a society has not reached the material wealth needed to secure just institution (the accumulation stage) and the fundamental political and social liberties, savings are compulsory.
2. Once a society is wealthy enough to secure just institutions (the steady-state stage), savings are no longer compulsory, though they are permitted.

The capital to be accumulated and preserved consists in the material conditions for just institutions. It comprises natural resources and environmental goods, machinery and means of production, technologies and knowledge, investments in education and healthcare, a set of well-functioning political institutions as well as a social security scheme and cultural heritage.

It is beyond the scope of this chapter to diagnose whether and to what extent current economic, social and environmental policies violate our criterion of inter-generational justice. But suppose the way our institutions currently operate is likely to inflict serious harms to future generations. Even if scientific progress allows us to predict more and more accurately the effects of our actions and policy choices on the environment, health and wealth of future people, implementing policies that would prevent future injustices seems politically unfeasible, given the characteristic short-termism of current political and economic system. Democracy, at least as it is organised now, tends to be 'presentist' (Thompson 2010; Caney 2016). The inadequacy of democratic institutions to face a society's obligations towards future people is due to the fact that decision makers are mainly accountable to present voters and interest groups (Thompson 2010). Whatever discourse they may have on the importance of future generations, they are constrained by the electoral cycle. Decision makers have few incentives to sacrifice their current constituents' interests for the sake of future people. As the Brundtland Report puts it: 'We act as we do because we can get away with it: future generations do not vote; they have no political or financial power; they cannot challenge our decisions' (WCDE 1987).

Additional factors worsen the inability of current democratic systems to fulfil intergenerational obligations: the dispersion of causes and effects and the fragmen-tation of agency in the case of challenges such as climate change (Gardiner 2013), the contemporary consumerist culture, the rising age of the median voter (Van Parijs 1998: 296), epistemic and motivational factors such as uncertainty, procras-tination and overestimation of our capabilities (Caney 2016: 143–145), national sovereignty as an obstacle to international cooperation to deal with issues such as climate change and lobbyism of short-termist interest groups such as fossil fuels and automobile industrials (e.g. Crowley 2013).

There are at least two methods to secure long-termism in democratic institu-tions. The first one is to change behaviours through education, for instance:

environmental education. But this is quite difficult, since we tend to be very weakly motivated to care for distant faceless future people (Birnbacher 2009). Future people can neither threaten us nor trigger our sympathy (see Chapter 9).

The second method does not rely on future-friendly attitudes, but calls for institutional design. This is what Van Parijs terms the 'Rawls–Machiavelli program' (Van Parijs 1998). It is 'Rawlsian' in that the guiding objective of institutional design is a publicly justifiable conception of distributive justice, and 'Machiavellian' in that it assumes individuals are only moved by their own private passions and interests. Institutions would be designed in such a way that they generate the right outcome in terms of intergenerational justice, and this without any transformation of the attitudes of possibly selfish and short-termist citizens. The new incentive structure would shape individual behaviours and actions exactly in the same way as their lacking sense of (intergenerational) justice would do.

Institutional options to secure future generations' interests include many proposals.[4] Different proposals address different sources of short-termism (MacKenzie 2016a): constitutional provisions (e.g. Gosseries 2008b); alternative indicators such as generational accounting (Kotlikoff 1993) or ecological footprint (Ponthière 2013); alternative franchise systems such as granting children the right to vote (this right being exercised by parents or guardians) (e.g. Van Parijs 1998: 308–314; Hinrichs 2007) or age-differentiated voting rights (Van Parijs 1998: 301–308; Wallimann-Helmer 2015); economic incentive schemes (e.g. tying the long-term outcomes of decision makers' decisions to their pension plans (Wolfe 2008)). Caney has proposed a 'five-fold package' combining several long-termist reforms with a parliamentary committee inspired by the Finnish Committee for the future (see Appendix A2(i)) (Caney 2016).

Political representation of future generations would secure future people's interests by shifting the current balance of power, which leads to overdiscounting the future. Giving a voice to guardians of future people's interests should mitigate the negative consequences of short-termist policymaking. Even if future generations' interests sometimes coincide incidentally with other groups' interests – parents, environmentalists, the young, the world poor – it is not necessarily the case, given the broad range of political issues that may affect the future. Moreover, even if citizens and legislators are in fact willing to fulfil at least their minimal obligations to their descendants, they might be victims of misperceptions or self-serving biases. Representatives of future generations are therefore perhaps the only group that could point out the effects of public policies on future people's interests to the public and the officials' attention. They could unite the various efforts for safeguarding future people's interests. Representatives or guardians for future generations could secure the coherence of policy decisions with expert evidence on what is the most likely to secure future people's interests (Van Parijs 1998: 321).

These discussions suggest that current democratic systems negatively affect the fundamental interests of future people, which are the interests that a theory of intergenerational justice aims to define and secure. On an interest-based account of rights, these interests ground rights when they are important enough to create obligations for others. In that sense, future generations have rights (e.g. Caney 2005) (rights of future generations and related conceptual issues are addressed in Chapters 2 and 3). If political representation is a reliable means to secure future generations' rights, theories of intergenerational justice may derive a right to be represented for future people from these other rights.

It is important to understand that the justice-based argument in favour of representation of future generations does only justify such representation in so far as it increases the likeliness that resources and institutional goods will be distributed fairly between generations. According to the justice-based argument, representation of future generations is merely instrumental to the realisation if intergenerational justice. It must thus be efficient in achieving this goal. If it is not, or if its costs outreach its benefits, it must be abandoned. Some have pointed out that altering the democratic process by modifying the composition of either representative bodies or the electorate itself for the sake of promoting certain desirable outcomes is problematic (e.g. Wallimann-Helmer 2015: 72).

(ii) Democratic inclusiveness

But there is another, normative reason, for granting future people a voice in the democratic process. The core idea here is that the democratic decision-making process is legitimate only if it gives a voice to representatives of future interests. The democracy-based argument requires the redistribution of political power and the inclusion of future people in the demos because such inclusiveness is implied by a normative commitment to democracy.

Future people and the all-affected interests principle

One possible rationale for the claim that future people should be given a voice through representatives in democratic decisions for democracy to be legitimate is that future people will be affected by today's decisions. This rationale broadly corresponds to the all-affected interests principle: those whose interests are affected by the collective decisions to be made ought to have the right to take part in the democratic decision-making process. Here is a definition: 'All-affected interests principle: all those who have interests that will probably be affected by any possible decision under any possible political agenda should have the right to participate in the decision-making process' (Goodin 2007).

Many political decisions are likely to affect future people, at least if we understand 'affect' in a causal way (Beckman 2013: 779).[5] A decision causally affects a person if this decision can have as an effect – be it intended or not – a change in what this person has an interest in (interests may be framed in terms of needs, well-being, opportunities, rights, burdens, etc.). The claim that the legitimacy of the involvement of future people in the democratic process arises out of the fact that our decisions will impact them in the future appears in many contributions advocating the representation of future generations (Kavka and Warren 1983: 22; Dobson 1996: 132).

The absence of future people does not seem a good reason for excluding them from the democratic process. We know too well how dangerous it can be to exclude particular constituencies on arbitrary grounds. Nowadays, it seems plausible that the exclusion of women, blacks or Jews from the decision-making process was, to say the least, a deep injustice, among other reasons because their interests were significantly affected by the decisions others made. As Goodin puts it, 'the whole thrust of modern democratic theory is to reject arbitrary delimitation of the subjects whose interests are to be politically considerable' (1996: 837). If legitimate democratic institutions grant the right to participate to those whose interests are being affected, and if future generations' interests are affected in this way, in order to secure the legitimate character of our democratic institutions, we ought to include future people in the decision-making process, and this could be done through representatives.

But this conclusion leaves many questions unanswered. First, since future people outnumber present people, following the rule 'one voice, one vote' might give an excessive priority to the future over the present (Bergström 2005). We thus need further normative developments to justify giving future people's voices a lesser influence on decisions while still granting them the right to participate according to the all-affected interests principle. Second, one may ask what sort of influence future people should have. An alternative way to apply the all-affected interests principle is not to expand the demos, but to limit the decision power of the actual demos, for example by granting representatives of future people a veto right.

Future people and deliberative democracy

The all-affected interests principle provides a justification for including representatives of future people in the decision-making process. But another reason for including representatives of future people in democratic decisions is related to the ideal of deliberative democracy. We could thus distinguish between aggregative and deliberative democracy as well as between their rationale for representing future people's interests. Theories of aggregative democracy take individual votes as given and attempt to determine how they should be aggregated in a collective decision-making procedure so that the outcome of this procedure is as representative as possible of the set of individual votes. Theories of deliberative democracy consider the decision-making process as a way to form and transform conflicting individual preferences so that they become more compatible with ethical principles or general policy considerations everyone can accept. In order to be legitimate, democratic decisions should be the outcome of a discursive process where the affected individuals (or their representatives) have an equal opportunity to defend their position and the obligation to provide justifications for these positions that others can accept. Because an open and free public deliberation is likely to improve the quality of the final collective decision, deliberation has a legitimising force (Ekeli 2009). Deliberative democracy theorists argue that the outcome of such process can be expected to be more rational and impartial than the mere aggregation of votes.

This is because of three mechanisms. First, as everyone should have the opportunity to participate in public deliberations (either directly or through representatives), the basis of information of decisions can be expanded and hence the epistemic quality of the final decision improved.[6] Public deliberation exposes presently living citizens to a variety of perspectives and helps them to imagine what future generations' interests could be (Karnein 2016: 96). Second, the open deliberation prevents concentrations of power. Every proposal is open to public criticism and examinations. Third, having to justify publicly one's position induces one to internalise others' perspectives and makes others' reasons one's own reasons. Each participant will have to internalise others' claims and opinions in order to convince them. Each participant must appeal to publicly acceptable arguments instead of self-interested reasons. We can anticipate that these mechanisms will occur because of the very analytics of interpersonal communication rather than because of speculative empirical hypotheses (Goodin 1996).

Deliberative democracy may require the involvement of representatives for future people in the deliberative process for three reasons. First, deliberative democrats are committed to the all-affected interests principle (Ekeli 2005). Second, since the legitimacy of deliberative democracy itself depends on the epistemic quality of deliberation as well as on its ability to induce participants to adopt a more impartial perspective, representatives of future generations should participate because their presence could improve the epistemic quality of deliberation by providing arguments, information, proposals and perspectives that are different from those that representatives of present people are interested in (Ekeli 2005; Niemeyer and Jennstål 2016). Third, the very fact that representatives of present people know they will have to justify their views to representatives of future people should induce them to take future people's interests into account in their proposals, and thus to 'internalise' their interests.[7] It should even induce them to be more impartial, since, according to the 'law of large number' (Goodin 1996), the broader the public one has to justify one's view to, the more likely one will take into account the general interest rather than particular, group or individual interests.

(iii) The respective institutional implications of justice-based and democracy-based accounts

The justice-based and democracy-based justifications for representation of future generations will use different criteria to assess devices to represent future generations. They will thus advocate different kinds of institutions. Intergenerational justice wants representation of future generations to be efficient in achieving a just distribution of advantages between generations. Lawmaking competence should be ascribed to future people's representatives only to the extent that it is needed by justice. If an advisory commission secures the same outcome, then it is fine from the viewpoint of intergenerational justice. The democratic legitimacy rationale does not claim future generations should have access to their fair share of economic and social advantages, but to their fair share of power (even if there is arguably a connection between both). Therefore, once it is recognised that future people can be affected by current decisions, or that their participation to public deliberation through representatives enhances the quality of deliberation and therefore its legitimising force, they ought to be included in decision-making processes through representatives. This might imply representatives of future people should have lawmaking competency exactly like representatives of present people have. Deliberative democracy might require all modes of inclusion of future people to favour an open and free deliberation, such as a right to delay decisions (to trigger deliberation) or citizens' assemblies and juries.

2.2 Objections to the political representation of future generations

To provide a fully convincing case for the representation of future generations, one must address potential objections to it.

Objection 1: Inflation of representation

The objection may be stated as follows. If we accept that future generations should be represented, why shouldn't the decision-making process also include other constituencies beside future generations, such as children, foreigners, past citizens, animals, trees, stones? If we decide to include future generations in the demos, we might be opening Pandora's box.

But the underlying intuition conflates the normative justification for giving future people representatives (which are not arbitrary and do not all extend to other constituencies such as animals or foreigners) and the practical issues representing future people may raise (Dobson 2005: 35). Future people will be many. But it remains possible to conceive appropriate institutional tools to include them without threatening the functioning of democracies. Note this objection could be understood as contesting the use of representation as a good tool to represent future generations, by comparing future generations with other constituencies which, despite the fact that they are not directly represented, still have their interests taken into account in one way or another.[8]

Objection 2: No representation without accountability

Even if future people can be said to have interests in a meaningful sense, one may doubt these interests can be represented. This is because political representation involves a specific relationship between the representative and the constituent. First, the constituent selects (through elections for instance) the representative. Second, the constituent communicates her will and her interests to the representative, so that the representative can adequately represent her. Third, the constituent monitors the representative's actions. Future people can do none of these. Therefore, future generations cannot be politically represented, at least not in the usual sense of the term.

This objection could be addressed by broadening our understanding of the necessary conditions for representation to be meaningful. For example, Feinberg argues that the sole requisite for a person to have rights and hence to be represented in some way is to have interests (see Kavka and Warren 1983: 24; Dobson 1996: 132). According to Feinberg, neither the temporal remoteness of future people, nor the indeterminacy of their identity precludes the fact that they have interests, a fact that follows merely from their being humans (1980: 66). Let us add that, if representatives of future generations know that future generations will have interests and have some clues about what these interests require in terms of political action, they nevertheless cannot exactly follow their constituents' instructions. Hence, they should act as trustees rather than as delegates. Instead of acting according to the preferences the constituents express (as a delegate does), a trustee follows her own well-considered judgement about how to act in the best interests of her constituent (Dovi 2014).

But a potential objector might have two further concerns. First, what is in the best interests of people living in the (distant) future is highly uncertain. Second, how could representatives for future people be held accountable to their constituents (Wolfe 2008: 1923)?

The issue of uncertainty can be partly met if we grant the reasonably probable claim that there are some basic human interests people living even in very different circumstances from ours would still have. For instance, they should have the same physiological need for fresh air, clean water or food with adequate nutritional quality (Kavka and Warren 1983: 25; Ekeli 2006: 396–398). Furthermore, in so far as our own preferences and values inescapably shape the preferences and values of the next generation (through education and the continuation of political, moral and cultural institutions), there is an extent to which one can predict the values and preferences the (closer) next generations are likely to develop.

The issue of accountability assumes that the interests of the representative necessary conflict with the interests of the constituent.[9] The representative may seek political power or economic gains. Hence the constituent must be able to control the representative through various institutional devices: electoral mandates that are limited in time, transparency requirements, and so on, whereas future people are obviously unable to control their representatives. But is it really the case that the interests of the representatives necessarily diverge from the interests of the constituents? If not, actual monitoring of representatives would be unnecessary. We might, as suggested by Jane Mansbridge, opt for a 'selection model' of political representation instead of a 'sanction model'. Mansbridge discusses both models in the context of classical representation of present people, but the discussion can be fruitfully applied to the issue of the representation of future people. The 'sanction model' is about control, the constituents invigilating regularly their representatives after they have elected them (Mansbridge 2009: 2). The 'selection model' involves devoting more resources and attention to the selection of an adequate representative, that is, a representative whose motivations and objectives are in line with the constituent's ones (Mansbridge 2009: 4).[10] Real-world cases where the selection model prevails include the selection of judges, academic faculty, nannies, etc. In these cases, a lot of resources and time are devoted to check the reputation of competency and honesty of the representative, as well as her intrinsic motivation to act in the best interests of her constituents. The selection model avoids the accountability problem by securing from the very beginning the alignments of objectives between the representative's actions and future people's interests. Indeed, real experiments as well as proposals for representing future generations have often involved criteria to select these representatives that were proxies for these representatives' self-motivation. The Israeli commissioner for future generations had to be an expert in fields relevant for defending future generations' interests. The Hungarian Ombudsmen for Future Generations must have a degree in law and demonstrate excellent academic achievements in the environmental field (these real-world examples are presented in details in Appendix A2(iii)). In order to avoid conflicts of interests, they should not have any other professional occupation or political office.

Objection 3: Moral consideration better than political representation

Another possible objection is that representation of future generations is not needed because we or at least some social groups (environmental lobbies, green political parties, parents, private companies) do already take care of them. However, it is probably not sufficient to protect future people's interests (Kavka and Warren 1983: 36). A more subtle version of this objection is termed the 'Münchhausen problem of motivation' (Jensen 2015): if it is true that presently living people do not take future people's interests sufficiently into account, then, in so far as presently living people are also the ones who will select and act as representatives for future people, we cannot really trust them to achieve this task well; if, on the other hand, if presently living people already care enough for future generations, then extra representation of future generations is not really necessary. In addition, representation of future generations may have undesirable democratic costs that should encourage us to look for other alternatives to better take future generations' interests into consideration (Jensen 2015).

The 'Münchhausen problem of motivation' assumes that the process of representing future generation does not affect the attitudes of presently living people. Either we care for future people or we do not, and representing future people will not change anything. Challenging this assumption allows us to address the objection. Some contributions in the literature suggest representing future generations may affect citizens' perspectives and motivations in such a way that they come to consider future people's interests as their own; and this wouldn't have occurred had future people's interests not been explicitly represented in the decision-making process.[11] Including representatives of future people in public institutions induces citizens and lawmakers to frame policy issues differently. In that sense, including representatives of future people in the deliberation might be seen as an 'educative process' (Ekeli 2005: 448). Hence representation of future generations is not 'representation' in the narrow sense outlined above. It rather amounts to the 'incorporation' of future people's interests in policymaking. Consider the proposal Goodin (1996) makes for representing nature and animals. Goodin suggests that nature and animals' interests are 'encapsulated' in the interests of citizens who have sympathy for them, in the same way as children's interests are encapsulated in their parents' ones. This line of reasoning also applies to future generations. Therefore, as Goodin puts it, the whole point of the democratic process is to design democratic institutions in such a way that citizens come to internalise others' interests, especially the interests of the voiceless animals, children and future generations. Goodin argues deliberative practices are more likely to induce the decision-making process to take into account such encapsulated interests. If we apply this line of reasoning to our issue, this means that representation of future generations, along with deliberative processes, may be part of the devices that encapsulate future people's interests in ours.[12]

3 Towards new proposals

As we have seen, future people cannot be represented in the same way as present people are: it is impossible to enfranchise unborn people. Therefore, various proposals have to be made in order to overcome this difficulty. A first family of proposals consists in reserving some seats in legislative assemblies for representatives of future generation. A second category of proposals suggests creating a special agency. Before discussing these proposals in detail, it is worth outlining the features all should have:

(i)   A broad mandate (Gosseries 2008b) – future generations' interests do not consist only in environmental interests. Representatives should be able to deal with all intergenerational issues such as the future of the welfare state, investment in education and technologies, the maintenance of democratic institutions, the preservation of minority languages.

(ii) Knowledge and expertise – even if future generations' interests are partly unknown, there are means to predict some of them. Representatives of future generations should have the concrete means to assess these interests as adequately as possible.

(iii) Motivation – the selection procedure of future representatives should ensure that these representatives really care about future people's interests.

(iv) Pluralism and argumentative quality of the debates – the institution representing future generations should be able to deal openly with competing views of what ought to be done for the future.

(v)   Independence – representatives of future generations should be capable of resisting pressure from short-termist entities (such as lobbies and interest groups, other elected officials).

(vi) Balance between present and future – institutions representing future generations' interests should be included in the existing democratic institutions in such a way that an adequate balance between present and future interests can be achieved.

(vii) Compatibility with fundamental rights – representation of future generations should be compatible with presently living citizens' fundamental rights.

3.1 Reserving seats in assemblies for representatives of future generations

In what follows I shall refer to future people's representatives by F-representatives and to present people's representatives by P-representatives; (F = future; P = present).

(i) Dobson's proposal: the environmental lobby as proxy electorate and representatives

Dobson (1996) has been one of the first to discuss the possibility of reserving some seats in legislative assemblies for F-representatives. F-representatives would be democratically elected, exactly like P-representatives. However, voters as well as candidates would be drawn from a group of citizens who have a strong concern for environmental sustainability. Environmental activism and lobbyism would thus be a proxy for the interests of future people. The successful F-candidates would sit alongside democratically P-representatives and have the same lawmaking competence. Dobson does not specify how many seats however (which leaves the question of whether F-representatives' power would be well balanced with P-representatives' power unanswered). Plurality of views among F-candidates would be secured to a certain extent, because groups who campaign for environmental sustainability may still hold different conceptions of it (from the Brundtland sustainability view to deep ecology). Dobson also considers depriving the F-electorate from its right to vote for P-representatives in order to avoid violation of the one-person, one-vote principle, which embodies democratic equality.

An objection to Dobson's proposal is that the environmental lobby does not have sufficiently diverse perspectives to be a satisfactory electorate to represent future generations (Ekeli 2005: 435–437; 2009: 446). According to Ekeli, the debate about what is in the best interest of future people ought to be left open. Indeed, it seems there is a trade-off here between two of the requirements outlined above, that is, between pluralism and motivation. Environmental activists are surely motivated to secure future people's interests. However, restricting future-oriented policies to their perspective undermines pluralism. How could we select representatives that still care about future people without endorsing a very specific view of posterity's interests?

(ii) Ekeli's proposal: a double vote to make future people imaginatively present

Ekeli (2005) also proposes reserving some seats in legislative assemblies for representatives of future generations (he suggests 5 per cent of the seats). F-representatives would also have lawmaking competence. Moreover, a qualified majority of F-representatives would have the right to require delaying the enactment of a law, if this law is estimated harmful for future generations. The delay would be either for two years or until a new election. F-representatives would be democratically elected, not by a proxy electorate, but by all citizens. In other words, each citizen would have two votes, one for a P-representative and one for a F-representative. F-representatives would thus be accountable to citizens exactly like P-representatives. F-candidates would be drawn from F-political parties, that is, political parties created with the goal of protecting future generations. F-candidates would campaign exactly like traditional P-candidates, with a programme, etc. F-parties would include more than environmental parties. Hence Ekeli's proposal leaves more room for divergent interpretations of our duties to future people than Dobson's one. A problem is that traditional P-parties might profit from this absence of constraint to create pseudo F-parties in order to get additional voices in the assembly. Therefore, Ekeli proposes that some legal norms should constrain the creation of F-parties. Ordinary P-parties should not be authorised to create F-parties. Neither should interest groups whose members have short-term interests (such as companies, lobbies, employers' organisation or trade unions). These norms would be enforced by constitutional or supreme courts.

Ekeli takes inspiration from deliberative democracy to defend this model. Even if this model is not the definitive answer to democratic short-termism, it has the advantage to encourage debates and information sharing about future issues, among citizens as well as among legislators. The model is designed with this deliberative purpose. For example, by slowing down decisions, F-representatives can create public awareness and debate about intergenerational issues.

A possible objection to the model is that it gives too much power to courts, which would have the final say on who is entitled to represent posterity. Another objection is that there is no guarantee that citizens will be less short-termist while selecting F-representatives than when selecting P-representatives. That is, even if courts make sure only F-candidates who really care about future people's interests can campaign, citizens may still vote for the F-party which endorses the view of posterity's interest that would involve less sacrifice of their short-term interests. Nevertheless, unless presently living people are consciously and fully selfish, the double vote might still at least partly work in performing an educational function. Biases may be overcome by changing the way political issues are framed, that is, by making vivid the distinction between present people's interests and future people's interests.

(iii) A specialised second chamber of randomly selected citizens

Thompson's (2010) proposal is modelled on the Tribune of the Plebs in the Ancient Roman Republic. The Tribune of the Plebs did not participate in ordinary politics, but was missioned to defend the rights and interests of the plebs when these were at stake. It could 'intercede in judicial proceedings', veto laws and force legislators to consider its proposals. To represent future generations, Thompson prefers a citizens' assembly to a special commission, because ordinary present citizens are more likely to resemble ordinary future citizens than members of a special commission. Those citizens could be chosen randomly, that is, by sortation.[13] Such a body should be established at the national and international levels. Thompson outlines powers we might consider attributing to this assembly without further specification. The assembly might be authorised to suspend temporarily the enactment of a law that could harm future generations. It might require posterity impact statements, as well as a democratic deficit impact statement, from the government. It might also establish age-differentiated political rights, a contingency trust fund to compensate future damages, or call for constitutional conventions. It could enter into agreements with other citizens assemblies representing future generations in other countries.

Why use randomly selected citizens as representatives for future generations? First, their social diversity would reflect the diversity of descendants' interests. Second, random citizens' career prospects are not tied to what short-termist electors might think of them. Third, 'lottocracy' proposals are often complemented by carefully designed deliberative procedures in order to render decisions as impartial as possible. Some real-world experiments seem to confirm the capacity of citizens' assemblies to take into account sustainability issues. For example, the citizen jury missioned in the French region of Poitou-Charentes claimed it was necessary to take into account future generations' interests, and it made concrete proposals on climate change and energy independence.[14]

However, some could worry that, contrary to special commissioners, citizens might lack the specific expertise needed to represent future generations' interests adequately. Second, one could wonder why random citizens would specifically care about the future. In fact, successful examples of randomly selected citizens' assemblies should not hide less convincing experiments. For example, in the US state of Maryland, in 2002, five of the 18 participants in the citizens' jury missioned to make recommendations on climate policies opposed a veto to the adhesion of the United States to the Kyoto protocol.[15,16]

(iv) Submajority rules (Ekeli)

A submajority rule authorises a minority to change a decision regardless of how other votes are distributed. Ekeli's (2009) proposal does not involve the selection of specific representatives for future citizens. It involves giving specific powers to regular political representatives so that those of them who have long-term concerns can act upon them. Ekeli proposes that one-third of the legislators would be authorised to make specific demands if they believed a given bill would be harmful to future generations. This submajority of legislators could demand that the enactment be delayed until the next election. Alternatively, they could demand a referendum on any such bill. The public would be given one or two years to deliberate the bill. The legislators who make these demands should prove that the law would harm future generations. Potential conflicts about whether the bill might be harmful to future people would be solved by courts. Ekeli believes delaying votes on bills could promote more public awareness and deliberation on issues related to future generations.

3.2 Creating a special agency and/or appointing a guardian

Instead of reserving seats in legislative assemblies to protect future generations' interests, one could consider establishing a special administrative body, which might either be attached to parliament (as it was the case in the Israeli model discussed in the Appendix) or to the executive branch. Even if such agency does not necessarily have a lawmaking competence, if it bases its opinions on relevant expertise, it might perform an educative function by challenging false beliefs the public might hold regarding future issues (Van Parijs 1998: 321).

(i) National agencies

Mank (1996) proposes creating a superagency to protect the environment for future generations in the United States. The superagency would be a central executive agency. Its members would be appointed by the president, though not in a single term. The superagency would coordinate individual executive agencies and oversee future generations-related regulations. The superagency should have discretion to modify the agenda of individual agencies so that it can make long-term issues a priority. The superagency's proposed regulations might be submitted to legislative revisions. Congress would authorise the superagency to act as a guardian for future generations in courts. In addition, the superagency should also promote public debates and awareness around posterity issues.

(ii) National and international guardians

An international ombudsperson (Ward 2013), a guardian or a group of guardians could represent remote future generations (Stone 2013). Stone considers various options as to where to house these guardians. They might be housed in the United Nations (also proposed by Ward (2013)) or in separate international institutions such as the World Bank or the International Atomic Energy Agency. They could also constitute an independent body. Ward suggests these institutions could be established by a UN General Assembly resolution (Ward 2013: 32). Ekeli (2006) rather looks at the judiciary institutions and proposes national and international courts should have competence to appoint a guardian to represent future generations. What powers might these international representatives have? They could provide assistance to countries and be authorised to be heard by national parliaments and governments before bills are adopted that can have implications for future generations (Stone 2013; Ward 2013). They might advise international institutions on international law concerning future generations

(Ward 2013). They could also intervene and counsel parties in multilateral conflicts involving future generations' interests or initiate legal or diplomatic action on future generations' behalf when future generations are threatened. They could receive complaints and resolve disputes (Ward 2013). Ekeli argues these guardians should have *locus standi* for future generations in courts. They should have the right to initiate proceedings on behalf of future generations. Stone also considers guardians could be authorised to waive the rights of future generations if circumstances require it. Who could be appointed as a guardian? Ekeli suggests that courts should consider this matter on a case-by-case basis. The potential guardians might meet the following conditions: they should demonstrate that they care for future generations, they should have the relevant expertise to perform this function and finally they should also have access to the material resources needed to do so (Ekeli 2006: 392).

Special agencies, appointed guardians and ombudsmen lack coercive powers. According to Beckman and Uggla (2016), this particular feature strengthens the legitimacy of ombudsmen because, by contrast with the inclusion of representatives in decision-making bodies, it does not constrain us to run counter or significantly alter widespread understandings of democratic legitimacy. Moreover, perhaps surprisingly, real-world experiments show that the fact that they do not have the powers to oblige and sanction does not jeopardise their effectiveness.

4 Directions for further research

This overview has shown that, if representation of future generations is neither philosophically nor politically unproblematic, it deserves our attention as a means of securing future generations' interests in contemporary democracies. In particular, we would like to emphasise what Ekeli suggests, that is, that representing future generations in the decision-making process can be a means to trigger changes in presently living citizens' beliefs and in motivations.

Further research may need to focus on policy proposals that take into account the possible effects of various devices to represent future generations on the evolution of citizens' beliefs, motivations, biases and values with respect to future issues. It could be fruitful in articulating proposals to represent future generations at the political level with educational proposals, not only to ensure the efficacy of such representation, but also to ensure its stability (as real-world experiences such as the Israeli and the Hungarian ones, discussed in the Appendix, show, it is difficult to maintain the representation of future people if citizens and officials are not convinced that it is necessary).

So far discussions of the representation of future generations have focused on public institutions, be it at the national or international level. But further discussions should take into account the growing influence of non-governmental actors on environmental and economic problems. It is thus now time to consider whether and how future people should be represented in the decision-making body of organisations such as NGOs, firms or educational institutions.

Appendix: Representation of future generations in public policy and debates

This Appendix reviews the existing legal and political instruments that can represent some of the future generations' interests, outlines existing models of political representation of future generations at the national level[17] and summarises the debate around the implementation of institutions aimed at the representation of future generations at the international level.

A1 Existing legal and political instruments to represent future generations

Although quite a few countries directly represent future generations in democratic decisions, reference is made to future generations in numerous national constitutions, court decisions that have taken future generations into account and parliamentary or special commissions aimed at environmental protection.

(i) Constitutions

The rigidity of constitutions and their precedence over other national legislation make them an appropriate tool to secure future generations' interests (Ekeli 2007; Gosseries 2008b). Many national constitutions refer to future generations,[18] among which the constitutions of Bhutan (Bhutanese Const. art. V, cl. 1), Czech Republic (Czech Charter of Fundamental Rights and Freedoms, preamble), Estonia (Estonian Const. preamble), Poland (Polish Const. preamble), Switzerland (Swiss Const. preamble) and Ukraine (Ukrainian Const. preamble). The constitutions of Norway and Japan even grant future generations rights. Other constitutions explicitly ascribe state institutions the obligation to protect future generations. This can be seen in the constitutions of Armenia (Armenian Const. preamble), Bolivia (Bolivian Const. art. IX, cl. 6), Burundi (Burundian Const. art. XXXV), Cuba (Cuban Const. art. XXVII), Germany (German Const. art. XXa), Sweden (Swedish Const. Ch. 1, art. II). National constitutions often connect the protection of future generations' interests to the protection of the environment. This is the case in South Africa (South African Const. Ch. 1 art. XXIV), Andorra (Andorran Const. preamble), Argentina (Argentinian Const. Ch. 2, s. 41), Brazil (Brazilian Const. art. CCXXV), Ecuador (Ecuadorean Const. Title VII, Ch. 2, s. 1, art. CCCXCV, cl. 1),[19] Uruguay (Uruguayan Const. art. XLVII), France (Loi constitutionnelle N° 2005–205 du 1er mars 2005 relative à la Charte de l'environnement). The protection of posterity has also motivated constitutional clauses for financial sustainability (see Tremmel 2006: 190–191 and 197).

(ii) Court decisions

At the national level, an important Philippine Supreme Court Case (*Minors Oposa v. Secretary of the Department of Environmental and Natural Resources* 1993) has opposed children, represented by their parents, and the state Department of Environmental and Natural Resources on timber-cutting licences. The parents acted as representatives of their children, who in turn represented unborn generations. They asked the court to cancel existing timber licence agreements and to cease allowing new licences in the name of their right and the next generations' right to a healthy environment. Oposa, one of the parents and an environmental activist, referred to 'intergenerational equity'. The court decided that the parents had *locus standi*, that is, that they were qualified to represent the not yet born Filipino generations. The Court ruled in favour of the children and of future generations (see also Allen 1993).

Future generations' rights or interests have on occasion been mentioned in international court decisions. For instance, the dissenting opinion of Judge Weeramantry in the Nuclear tests case (*Nuclear Tests (New Zealand* v. *France)* 1974, 341) cited 'the concept of intergenerational rights' and suggested the International Court of Justice could act as a trustee for future generations:

> Having regard to the information before us that the half-life of a radioactive by-product of nuclear tests can extend to over 20,000 years, this is an important aspect that an international tribunal cannot fail to notice. In a matter of which it is duly seised, this Court must regard itself as a trustee of those rights in the sense that a domestic court is a trustee of the interests of an infant unable to speak for itself.

(iii) Parliamentary and special commissions aimed at protection of the environment

Future generations' interests are to some extent tied to environmental issues and the preservation of natural resources. In that sense, institutions for environmental protection can serve as a tool to represent future generations. For example, since 2004, the Brazilian Comissão de Meio Ambiente e Desenvolvimento Sustentável (commission on environment and sustainable development) is a permanent and independent agency and resides in the Brazilian House of Representatives.[20] The commission's mandate covers the following themes: national environmental policies, environmental law, renewable natural resources, flora and fauna, desertification, sustainable development. With respect to these issues, the commission has the power to deliberate and vote on the bills related to these themes, summon ministers, receive citizens' petitions or reclamations, require assessments and reports, promote public debates, conferences and exhibitions.[21]

New Zealand provides another example. As required by the Environment Act of 1986, the Governor-General of New Zealand appoints a parliamentary commissioner for the environment (*Te Kaitiaki Taiao a Te Whare Pāremata* in Māori) as recommended by the House of Representatives. The commissioner is independent and has the power to investigate environmental matters and to make recommendations. However, she can neither vote on bills nor reverse legislation.[22] An example of activities the commissioner carried out is the report on the impact of two nutrients pollutants, nitrogen and phosphorus, on water quality, which received a lot of public attention.[23] She also proposed an amendment to the National Policy Statement for Freshwater Management in order to prevent further decline of water quality, but the government only followed one of her five recommendations.[24]

Other examples of parliamentary and special commissions for environmental protection include the Canadian Commissioner of the Environment and Sustainable Development, the Chilean Commission on Natural Resources, Environment and National Resources, the German Committee for Sustainable Development or the Council for Sustainable Development in Hong Kong. The effectiveness of these instruments is variable. The environmental mandate is often too narrow to protect all future generations' interests. Some lack independency, institutional support or access to resources to fulfil their task (World Future Council and CISDL 2014: 8).

A2 Existing models of political representation of future generations

Some countries have gone much further in defending future generations' rights and interests and have implemented institutions specifically devoted to the political representation of future generations. Recent experiments have been carried out in Finland, Israel and Hungary.

(i) Finland: Committee for the Future

The Finnish Committee for the Future was created in 1993, after a major economic crisis in the early 1990s induced parliament to ask the government to present strategies for the future.[25] The Committee for the Future has enjoyed permanent status since 2000. It comprises 17 members of parliament who represent different political parties. This free-standing entity defines its tasks independently from the current government's agenda. The purpose of the committee's deliberative and research task is to appraise the long-term effects of political decisions and thus inform parliament and government accordingly. The committee has no authority to prepare legislation or to review the budget proposal made by the Finnish government. But it has the power to comment on all parliamentary documents referring to future issues and to make submissions to other parliamentary committees. The committee also produces research reports on future issues. Therefore, its mandate includes, but is not limited to, environmental issues. Its areas of interests comprise the economy, employment, energy, health, population issues, science and technology. Since its creation, the committee has been engaged in a very active dialogue with the government on the following topics: the future of Finland and Europe, the Finnish economy, employment and technology, the Finnish people's well-being, regional development with a special focus on demographic development, employment and productivity, population policy and the age structure, scenarios for Russia. Each time, the government has submitted a report to the committee (Tiihonen 2006). The committee auditions experts and drafts a report in response to the government's one. The propositions made by the committee are then debated by the parliament. So far, they have been rarely fully rejected (Tiihonen 2006). The implementation of policies is also monitored by the committee. The current committee is working on seven special issues: sustainable growth (how to increase economic growth while resolving the problem of sustainable development?), an inspired society (how to develop a social environment that supports growth entrepreneurialism?), acquiring new knowledge (what kind of skills and knowledge young people will need in 20 years?), can the welfare society endure? (how to define the welfare state of the future?), black swans (what future 'black swans' and their impacts? Black swans are rare and unanticipated events that have major impacts when they happen), crowdsourcing (how to raise the committee's profile in the media?) and radical technologies (what will future technologies be?).[26] Although the Committee for the Future is only a parliamentary commission with little legal authority, the Finnish parliament seems to pay close attention to its recommendations.

(ii) Israel: the Knesset Commission for Future Generations (2001–2006)

The Israeli Parliamentary ('Knesset') Commission for Future Generations was an instrument specifically designed to represent and defend the rights of future generations. The commission operated with a five-year mandate. In 2006, no new commissioner was appointed to replace Judge Shlomo Shohan and the commission ceased to function. In 2010, the Knesset voted a bill dissolving the commission, arguing that the commission was too costly and that it had too much power to interfere with its work (cited in Teschner 2013).

The Israeli Commission for Future Generations was a unit within the Knesset and was financed by the Knesset's budget. It had two main purposes: first, it provided opinions on laws concerning the interests of future generations; second, it advised Knesset members on issues relevant to future generations' interests and rights. The Knesset Commissioner for Future Generations was appointed by the Knesset Speaker, from among the candidates selected by a Public Committee. The Public Committee comprised six members, three of them being Knesset members and the three others were faculty members from higher education institutions and experts in fields that were deemed relevant for future generations (cited in Shoham and Lamay 2006: 263).

The Knesset Commissioner for Future Generations had a broad mandate, including any issue 'of particular relevance for future generations', that is, issues that:

> may have significant consequences for future generations, in the realms of the environment, natural resources, science, development, education, health, the economy, demography, planning and construction, quality of life, technology, justice and any matter which has been determined by the Knesset Constitution, Law and Justice Committee to have significant consequences for future generations.
>
> *(cited in Shoham and Lamay 2006: 263)*

The commissioner had the following powers. He was allowed to participate in Knesset debates and to give the Knesset recommendations on the issues he deemed relevant for future generations (according to the definition above). He had authority to evaluate and comment on bills and secondary legislation he considered being particularly relevant for future generations. The commissioner had also the right to be given enough time to prepare his evaluation and comments. This gave him de facto the power to delay the legislative process. By using this authority, it was indeed within the commissioner's power to block out votes on the state's budget, which would have forced the Knesset to organise new elections. The commissioner had thus an important bargaining power he could use to fulfil his duties. And, indeed, he used this power to force the government to enact a law concerning the integration of children with special needs in the educational system (Shoham and Lamay 2006: 248). Moreover, the commissioner could request almost any information,[27] document or report from a list of institutions including ministries, local authorities and state-owned corporations, including information these authorities had no desire to make publicly available. The former commissioner took this opportunity to request data on water pollution from the Water Commissioner of the Ministry of Infrastructure. When the governmental plant of Electrochemical Industry was discovered to contain hazardous materials which rendered the employees sick, the commissioner requested the medical files of the plant's employees as well as safety regulations (Shoham and Lamay 2006). The commission initiated conferences and workshops (e.g. one on clean air), and it published an opinion supporting a bill on clean air, which was attached to the bill (Shoham 2010, cited in Teschner 2013).

(iii) Hungary: Ombudsman for Future Generations

The institutions discussed so far play (or played) mainly a consultative role, though they enjoy some power thanks to the willingness of decision makers to listen to them, to their material means to investigate future generations-related issues or, as in the Israeli case, to delay decision-making. The Hungarian Ombudsman for Future Generations had gone a step further in the sense that he really participated in political decision-making. The institution of the Ombudsman escapes to some extent the problem that representatives for future people cannot be elected by those they represent, since an ombudsman or parliamentary commissioner is nominated.

In November 2007, the Hungarian NGO Védegylet (Protect the Future)'s lobbyism for a bill establishing the institution of a commissioner for future generations was finally successful.[28] An amendment to the 1993 Hungarian Act on the Parliamentary Commissioner for Civil Rights (the 'Ombudsman Act') established the office of the Ombudsman for Future Generations. The first and unique Ombudsman, Sándor Fülöp, was elected in May 2008 and held the office until August 2012. The Hungarian experiment inspired the World Future Council, an NGO which, among other proposals, campaigns for ombudsmen for future generations at all institutional levels. The new Fundamental Law (Constitution) of Hungary, which entered in force on 1 January 2012, suppressed the Offices of the four Hungarian Ombudsmen, including the Ombudsman for Future Generations,[29] and replaced them with the Office of the Commissioner (Ombudsman) for Fundamental Rights. The Ombudsman for Future Generations is now a Deputy of the general Commissioner for Fundamental Rights. His office is held by Dr Marcel Szabó. The deputy is elected by the parliament, on a proposal by the general ombudsman (himself elected by the parliament on a proposal by the president of the republic).

What are the functions and authorities of the office of the Commissioner for Fundamental Rights with respect to future generations? According to the New Fundamental Law, it is the obligation of the Hungarian state and citizens to protect, maintain and preserve natural resources and cultural heritage for future generations (Fundamental Law of Hungary 2011, art. P (1)). The Ombudsman for Fundamental Rights himself is assigned the task of providing an opinion on draft laws affecting the interests of future generations as defined by the Fundamental Law. He may also propose amendments of these laws (Hungarian Act on the Commissioner for Fundamental Rights 2011, Ch. 1, s. 2 (2)). His deputy responsible for the protection of future generations' interests can also propose the adoption or amendment of laws concerning future generations (Hungarian Act on the Commissioner for Fundamental Rights 2011, Ch. 1, s. 3(1.g)). In addition, he is assigned the task of monitoring the enforcement of the interests of future generations (Hungarian Act on the Commissioner for Fundamental Rights 2011, Ch. 1, s. 3). This means he ought to inform the general Ombudsman for Fundamental Rights as well as the concerned institutions and the public on violations or potential violations of future generations' interests as defined by the Constitution. He has authority to propose that the general Ombudsman institutes proceedings against these violations, or that he turns to the Constitutional Court. He can also participate in investigations led by the general Ombudsman. Finally, he is assigned the task of promoting representation of future generations at the EU and global levels.

In 2013, the deputy investigated or participated in the investigation of more than 400 complaints, commented on more than 50 legislative proposals and was involved in two court cases (Gosseries 2012). The complaints included several relating to environmental protection (Székely and Kovács 2014: 36). The deputy's proposal to institute proceedings *ex officio* for the general Commissioner (Ombudsman) for Fundamental Rights was accepted (Székely and Kovács 2014: 100).

One may point out that the deputy's mandate is too restricted in scope. Besides environmental protection and the preservation of cultural assets and natural resources, other areas of concerns are relevant for intergenerational justice, especially the sustainability of the economy and of the welfare state. In addition, since the constitutional reform of 2012, the independent Ombudsman for Future Generation Office has been replaced by a deputy depending on the general Ombudsman for Fundamental Rights Office, depriving in principle the main representative of future generations in Hungary of the powers to decide which cases should be dealt with and to speak by himself – he must speak through the main Ombudsman's voice (Read 2012: 30, n. 13).

A3 Towards international representation of future generations: proposals and debates

(i) Future generations in international agreements

At the international level, the reference to future generations in international agreements could be a basis for the establishment of political representation for future generations.[30,31] The preamble to the United Nation's Charter settled in 1945 mentions the interests of future generations: the 'peoples of the United Nations' shall be 'determined to save succeeding generations from the scourge of war'. In 1946, the International Convention for the Regulation of Whaling stated present nations have an interest in 'safeguarding for future generations the great natural resources represented by the whale stocks'. In 1972, the UNESCO Convention concerning the Protection of the World Cultural and Natural Heritage referred to 'the duty of ensuring the identification, protection, conservation, presentation and transmission to future generations of the cultural and natural heritage' (art. 4). The publication of the report *Our Common Future* by the Brundtland Commission (WCED 1987) outlined the core principle of sustainable development (development should be such that present and future generations will be able to meet their needs), which constitutes Principle 3 of the Rio Declaration (United Nations Conference on Environment and Development 1992). After 1992, many international conventions started to mention the interests of future generations: the United Nation Framework Convention on Climate Change (1992), whose Article 3 states that 'the Parties should protect the climate system for the benefit of present and future generations of humankind', the Convention on Biological Diversity (1992), the Rio Declaration on Environment and Development (1992), the Vienna Declaration and Programme of Action (1993). In 1997, UNESCO proclaimed the Declaration on the Responsibilities of the Present Generations towards Future Generations, stating that:

> It is important to make every effort to ensure, with due regard to human rights and fundamental freedoms, that future as well as present generations enjoy full freedom of choice as to their political, economic and social systems and are able to preserve their cultural and religious diversity.
>
> *(UNESCO 1997: art. 2)*

The International Law Association agreed on the New Delhi Declaration of Principles of International Law Relating to Sustainable Development in 2002, stating that states policies concerning the use of natural resources must take into account the needs of future people and avoid any wasteful use of these resources. The interests and rights of future generations are also mentioned by many regional agreements, such as the North American Agreement on Environmental Cooperation (1994) or the Aarhus Convention (Convention on Access to Information, Public Participation in Decision-making and Access to Justice in Environmental Matters 1998).

Moreover, the precautionary principle can be understood as a principle required to avoid harming future people. The precautionary principle states that, whenever it is possible that a given action will be harmful in the future, as long as there is no scientific consensus on the existence and the importance of that future risk, the burden of the proof should be on the shoulders of those who want to take such action. The Rio Declaration states that 'where there are threats of serious and irreversible damage, lack of scientific certainty shall not be used as a reason for postponing cost-effective measures to prevent environmental degradation' (United Nations Conference on Environment and Development 1992: art. 15). This principle appears in the Bamako Convention for the conservation of living natural resources (1991), United Nations Convention on Biological Diversity (1992), United Nations Convention on the Law of the Seas Straddling Stock Agreement (1995). The precautionary principle is invoked by Article 191 of the Treaty on the Functioning of the European Union and has informed many European policies with respect to environmental protection, but also to genetically modified organisms for instance.

(ii) Attempts and proposals to establish representation of future generations at the international level

The idea that future generations' interests ought to be protected has made its way into international agreements. Yet the proposal that future people should have their interests represented by specific institutions remains quite controversial. In 1992, delegates from Malta unsuccessfully submitted to the preparatory committee for the Rio Earth Summit (United Nations Conference on Environment and Development 1992) the following proposal: the world community should establish a guardian to represent future generations in various international institutions. This guardian 'would not . . . decide', but would 'plead for future generations, [and counter] the firmly established attitude of our civilization [to discount] the future' (cited in Stone 2013). In 1994 the UNESCO's Future Generations Programme organized a conference called 'A Guardian for Future Generations: Status Under International Law'. The World Future Council also campaigns for an 'ombudsman for future generations' (similar to the Hungarian model) who would be appointed at the global level. Other campaigners for the representation of future generations at the global level include the Foundation for Democracy and Sustainable Development and the Alliance for Future Generations. During the preparatory negotiations for the Rio +20 Summit in 2012, the establishment of a High-Level Representative for Future Generations at the UN was considered. This proposal appeared in the 'zero draft' outcome document of the 2012 Rio+20, *The Future We Want*. Despite strong support from the EU, many countries opposed this draft. The outcome of the negotiations was a much weaker text, where reference to the high-level representative had disappeared, even if the then UN Secretary-General Ban Ki-moon was expected to announce the appointment of a special representative for future generations (see Ward (2011) for a description of the negotiations). The attempts made by defenders of the proposal finally failed. Why did the negotiations fail? Opponents advanced the following arguments: international representation of future generations would (i) threaten national sovereignty, (ii) encourage the proliferation of bureaucracy and (iii) excessively favour the future over the present (Weeramantry et al. 2012).

For now, the following proposals are currently under consideration. A first proposal is to replace the now inactive United Nations Trusteeship Council, whose purpose was to protect the interests of the people of Trust Territories placed under the Trusteeship system, by a Trusteeship Council whose purpose would be to protect the interests of future generations (Sand 2004, cited in World Future Council and CISDL 2014, 19). But the legacy of the UN Trusteeship Council is questionable (it made Nauru a trust territory in 1948, Australia becoming the de facto administrator of Nauru, which allows Australian and British industries to keep control of the phosphate resources in the island, leading to serious environmental damages (McDaniel and Gowdy 1999: 136)). A second proposal suggests establishing an ombudsman or an inspector in international organisations and projects that could impact future people's interests. For example, since 1999 the International Finance Corporation (IFC) which belongs to the World Bank Group has a compliance adviser/ombudsman. The compliance adviser/ombudsman provides assessments of the IFC's compliance with its environmental and social goals, advising the managers of the IFC on matters relative to these goals, as well as a mechanism for handling complaints from persons who are affected by the IFC's policies. A third proposal is to establish the office of a special rapporteur (or working group) on the rights of future generations. The Commission on Human Rights could provide material support for it. Similarly, to the national commissions for the environment and/or future generations existing in New Zealand and Finland, the functions of the special rapporteur would be mainly advisory and investigatory.

Notes

1 The author wishes to thank Marcus Düwell, Axel Gosseries, Pierre-Etienne Vandamme and two anonymous reviewers for helpful comments on earlier drafts, as well as Naomi van Steenbergen for her invaluable editorial work. Versions of this chapter have been presented in September 2017 at the workshop 'Representing the Unrepresented' organised in Fribourg (Switzerland) and at the 'Société, Environnement, Santé' seminar at the university of Paris-Est (France). I am grateful to the participants for their insightful feedback. All errors are my own.
2 See Beckman (2013) on this distinction.
3 For overviews of distributive theories of intergenerational justice, see Gosseries (2008a); Meyer 2016.
4 For a compilation of institutional proposals aimed at securing intergenerational justice, see Gosseries and González-Ricoy (2016).
5 Beckman suggests another reading of the all-affected interests principle, where 'affect' is to be understood in a legal way. According to this reading, 'affecting' a person is '[defining] the entitlements, duties and benefits that apply to [this person] as a matter of law'. In a nutshell, Beckman argues that our decisions do not affect future people in the legal sense, since each generation has always authority to modify the laws it inherits from

the past, at least as long as it follows the correct procedure according to the constitutional arrangements established by preceding generations (Beckman 2013).

6 Let us note this is more an instrumental argument in favour of deliberation, rather than a normative requirement of democracy. I thank Marcus Düwell for having pointed this out to me.

7 This is for this reason, as Goodin (1996) argues, that deliberative democratic practices would be better suited to the defence of nature's interests.

8 See Kavka and Warren (1983) and Gosseries (2008b) for such an elaboration.

9 For a discussion of this assumption, see Mansbridge (2009).

10 This line of answer is closely related to Karnein's model of surrogate representation (2016: 88–92), which is also inspired by Mansbridge's work. Surrogate representation requires the representative to demonstrate, either by her personal characteristics or by the positions she defends, that she is suited to represent a particular group.

11 Representation of future generations could also just provide already future-friendly people with the opportunity to reveal their future-friendly preferences through the decision-making process, without necessarily reshaping their preferences. I thank Mikaël Cozic for having stressed this important point.

12 Another possible objection involves a particular application of the non-identity problem (Parfit 1984: part IV). Suppose the representatives of future people are asked to vote between two policies, resources depletion and ecological conservation. This choice will change many details of the present generation's life, including the time of conception of their children. Hence the choice of each of these two policies will bring different individuals into existence. Hence, depending on the policy they will vote for, future people's representatives will in fact represent different kinds of future people. This leads to the bizarre conclusion that, whatever they vote for, they always speak for their representees' interests. Now, addressing this problem requires addressing the non-identity problem itself, which is beyond the scope of this chapter. For an introduction and a discussion of various possible responses to this challenge, see Meyer (2016: section 3).

13 Three other proposals to represent future people through randomly selected citizens should be mentioned. The first is suited to the British context and involves a non-elected assembly (Tonn and Hogan 2006). Tonn and Hogan argue that the House of Lords could serve as a guardian for future generations. The Lords would appoint a committee on the future of the United Kingdom to hold auditions and provide advices to the Lords. The House of Lords could decide not to approve bills that might harm future generations. Even if the House of the Commons has authority to bypass the House of the Lords' veto after a Second Reading, such delay might increase the public opinion's awareness on this issue. Second, Bourg and Whiteside (2010: 94–95) have proposed a senate for the long term, which would have the power to propose laws and to veto those which would threaten the preservation of environmental goods. One-third of this senate's members would be randomly selected citizens, the other two-thirds being randomly selected people from a list provided by environmental NGOs. Third, MacKenzie (2016b) also imagines a randomly selected second chamber to ensure representation of future interests. The selection procedure would use stratified random sampling to secure adequate representation of salient groups. Half of the chamber would be replaced every year. Members would be remunerated. The chamber wouldn't have legislative power, but only the power to review bills and require amendments from the first chamber.

14 The 2008 French jury's opinion is cited in Vergne (2010). At the time of the completion of this chapter, the website of the jury was not accessible.

15 http://jefferson-center.org/wp-content/uploads/2012/10/Global-Climate-Change.pdf (last accessed 4 December 2014), cited in (Vergne 2010).

16 For other possible critiques, see MacKenzie (2016b: 291–293).

17 The World Future Council provides a complete map of the existing legal mechanisms recognising future generations' interests. See: www.futurejustice.org/resources/global-view-of-mechanisms-recognising-future-generations (last accessed 10 November 2014)

18 For surveys and discussions of references to future generations in constitutions, see World Future Council and CISDL (2014); Ekeli (2007); Tremmel (2006).
19 The Ecuadorean Constitution also protects the rights of nature, independently of human interests. Those rights also involve obligations to protect the environment, but on different normative grounds (and therefore it could imply different environmental policies).
20 See: www2.camara.leg.br/atividade-legislativa/comissoes/comissoes-permanentes/cmads/conheca-a-comissao/index.html (last accessed 9 April 2018)
21 Arts 24 and 32 of Regimento Interno da Câmara dos Deputados. Available at: http://bd.camara.gov.br/bd/bitstream/handle/bdcamara/16119/regimento_interno_9ed.pdf?sequence=9 (last accessed 9 April 2018)
22 See: www.pce.parliament.nz/about-us/functions-and-powers and www.legislation.govt.nz/act/public/1986/0127/latest/DLM98975.html (last accessed 9 April 2018)
23 The report is available at: www.pce.parliament.nz/assets/Uploads/PCE-Water-quality-land-use-web-amended.pdf (last accessed 9 April 2018)
24 Available at: www.pce.parliament.nz/assets/Annual-Report-for-the-year-ended-30-June0-2014.pdf (last accessed 9 April 2018)
25 Available at: http://web.eduskunta.fi/dman/Document.phx?documentId=qs29514121521311&cmd=download (last accessed 9 April 2018)
26 Available at: http://web.eduskunta.fi/dman/Document.phx?documentId=ur13212161619593&cmd=download (last accessed 9 April 2018)
27 Unless it put the security of the state or public safety at risk.
28 For a detailed description of the campaign for the establishment of an Ombudsman for Future Generations, see Jávor (2006).
29 Act 111 of 2011 on the Hungarian Commissioner for Fundamental Rights.
30 This paragraph is partly based on the account proposed by Jávor (2006: 284–285).
31 See Ward (2011: 33–34) for a complete list of the references to future generations in international instruments.

Bibliography

Allen, Ted. 1993. 'Philippine children's case: recognizing legal standing for future generations'. *Georgetown International Environmental Law Review* 6: 713.
Andorran Constitution. Preamble.
Argentinian Constitution. Ch. 2, s 41.
Armenian Constitution. Preamble.
Beckman, Ludvig. 2013. 'Democracy and future generations: should the unborn have a voice?' In Jean-Christophe Merle (ed.), *Spheres of Global Justice*. Dordrecht: Springer, 775–788.
Beckman, Ludvig and Fredrik Uggla. 2016. 'An Ombudsman for Future Generations'. In Iñigo González-Ricoy and Axel Gosseries (eds), *Institutions for Future Generations*. Oxford: Oxford University Press, 117–134.
Bergström, Lars. 2005. 'Democracy and future generations'. In *Democracy Unbound: Basic Explorations*. Stockholm: Stockholm University, I: 190–192
Bhutanese Constitution. Art. V, cl. 1.
Birnbacher, Dieter. 2009. 'What motivates us to care for the (distant) future?'. In Axel Gosseries and Lukas Meyer (eds), *Intergenerational Justice*. Oxford: Oxford University Press.
Bolivian Constitution. Art. IX, cl. 6.
Bourg, Dominique and Kerry H. Whiteside. 2010. *Vers une démocratie écologique: le citoyen, le savant et le politique*. Paris: Seuil.
Brazilian Constitution. Art. CCXXV.
Burundian Constitution. Art. XXXV.
Caney, Simon. 2005. 'Cosmopolitan justice, responsibility, and global climate change'. *Leiden Journal of International Law* 18: 747–775.

Caney, Simon. 2016. 'Political institutions for the future'. In Iñigo González-Ricoy and Axel Gosseries (eds), *Institutions for Future Generations*. Oxford: Oxford University Press, 135–155.

Convention on Access to Information, Public Participation in Decision-Making and Access to Justice in Environmental Matters. 1998. Available at: www.unece.org/fileadmin/ DAM/env/pp/documents/cep43e.pdf (last accessed 9 April 2018)

Crowley, Kate. 2013. 'Pricing carbon: the politics of climate policy in Australia'. *Wiley Interdisciplinary Reviews: Climate Change* 4(6): 603–613.

Cuban Constitution. XXVII.

Czech Charter of Fundamental Rights and Freedoms. Preamble.

Dobson, Andrew. 1996. 'Representative democracy and the environment'. In W. M. Lafferty and J. Meadowcroft (eds), *Democracy and the Environment*. Cheltenham and Northampton, MA: Edward Elgar, 124–139.

Dovi, Suzanne. 2014. 'Political representation'. In Edward N. Zalta (ed.), *The Stanford Encyclopedia of Philosophy* (spring 2014). Available at: http://plato.stanford.edu/archives/ spr2014/entries/political-representation (last accessed 9 April 2018)

Ecuadorean Constitution. Title VII, Ch. 2, s 1., Art. CCCXCV, cl. 1.

Ekeli, Kristian Skagen. 2005. 'Giving a voice to posterity – deliberative democracy and representation of future people'. *Journal of Agricultural and Environmental Ethics* 18(5): 429–450.

Ekeli, Kristian Skagen. 2006. 'The principle of liberty and legal representation of posterity'. *Res Publica* 12(4): 385–409.

Ekeli, Kristian Skagen. 2007. 'Green constitutionalism: the constitutional protection of future generations'. *Ratio Juris* 20(3): 378–401.

Ekeli, Kristian Skagen. 2009. 'Constitutional experiments: representing future generations through submajority rules'. *Journal of Political Philosophy* 17(4): 440–461.

Estonian Constitution. Preamble.

Feinberg, Joel. 1980. 'The rights of animals and unborn generations'. In *Rights, Justice and the Bounds of Liberty*. Princeton, NJ: Princeton University Press, 159–184.

Fundamental Law of Hungary. 2011. Available at: www.ajbh.hu/documents/14315/121663/ basic_law.pdf/6083c0af-bf9c-48b7-9988-9e05660d31d6 (last accessed 9 April 2018)

Gardiner, Stephen M. 2013. *A Perfect Moral Storm: The Ethical Tragedy of Climate Change*. Oxford: Oxford University Press.

German Constitution. Art. XXa.

González-Ricoy, Iñigo and Axel Gosseries. 2016. *Institutions for Future Generations*. Oxford: Oxford University Press.

Goodin, Robert E. 1996. 'Enfranchising the Earth, and its alternatives'. *Political Studies* 44(5): 835–849.

Goodin, Robert E. 2007. 'Enfranchising all affected interests, and its alternatives'. *Philosophy and Public Affairs* 35(1): 40–68.

Gosseries, Axel. 2008a. 'Theories of intergenerational justice: a synopsis'. *Surveys & Perspectives Integrating Environment & Society* 1: 39–49.

Gosseries, Axel. 2008b. 'Constitutions and future generations'. *Good Society* 17(2): 32–37.

Gosseries, Axel. 2012. 'Generations'. In C. McKinnon (ed.), *Issues in Political Theory*. Oxford: Oxford University Press, 301–322.

Hinrichs, Karl. 2007. 'Faut-il accorder le droit de vote aux enfants?'. *Revue philosophique de Louvain* 105(1): 42–76.

Hungarian Act on the Commissioner for Fundamental Rights. 2011. Available at: www. ajbh.hu/en/web/ajbh-en/act-cxi-of-2011 (last accessed 9 April 2018)

Japanese Constitution.

Jávor, Benedek. 2006. 'Institutional protection of succeeding generations – Ombudsman for Future Generations in Hungary'. In Jörg Tremmel (ed.), *Handbook of Intergenerational Justice*. Cheltenham and Northampton, MA: Edward Elgar, 282–298.

Jensen, Karsten Klint. 2015. 'Future generations in democracy: representation or consideration?' *Jurisprudence* 6(3): 535–548.

Karnein, Anja. 2016. 'Can we represent future generations?'. In Iñigo González-Ricoy and Axel Gosseries (eds), *Institutions for Future Generations*. Oxford: Oxford University Press, 83–97.

Kavka, G. and V. Warren. 1983. 'Political representation for future generations'. In R. Elliott and A. Gare (eds), *Environmental Philosophy*. Milton Keynes: Open University Press.

Kotlikoff, Laurence J. 1993. *Generational Accounting: Knowing Who Pays, and When, for What We Spend*. New York: Free Press.

Loi constitutionnelle No. 2005–205 du 1er mars 2005 relative à la Charte de l'environnement. 2014.

McDaniel, Carl N. and John M. Gowdy. 1999. *Paradise for Sale: A Parable of Nature*. Stanford, CA: University of California Press.

MacKenzie, Michael K. 2016a. 'A general-purpose, randomly selected chamber'. In Iñigo González-Ricoy and Axel Gosseries (eds), *Institutions for Future Generations*. Oxford: Oxford University Press, 282–298.

MacKenzie, Michael K. 2016b. 'Sources of short-termism'. In Iñigo González-Ricoy and Axel Gosseries (eds), *Institutions for Future Generations*. Oxford: Oxford University Press, 4–45.

Maltese Sustainable Development Act. 2012. Available at: www.futurejustice.org/wp-content/uploads/2013/05/SD-Act-Malta.pdf (last accessed 9 April 2018)

Mank, Bradford C. 1996. 'Protecting the environment for future generations: a proposal for a "republican" superagency'. *New York University Environmental Law Journal* 5: 444.

Mansbridge, Jane. 2009. 'A "selection model" of political representation'. *Journal of Political Philosophy* 17(4): 369–398.

Meyer, Lukas. 2016. 'Intergenerational justice'. In Edward N. Zalta (ed.), *The Stanford Encyclopedia of Philosophy* (summer). Available at: https://plato.stanford.edu/archives/sum2016/entries/justice-intergenerational (last accessed 9 April 2018)

Minors Oposa v. Secretary of the Department of Environmental and Natural Resources. 1993. Supreme Court of the Philippines.

Niemeyer, Simon and Julia Jennstål. 2016 'The deliberative democratic inclusion of future generations'. In Iñigo González-Ricoy and Axel Gosseries (eds), *Institutions for Future Generations*. Oxford: Oxford University Press, 249–265.

Norwegian Constitution.

Nuclear Tests (*New Zealand v. France*). 1974. International Court of Justice.

Parfit, Derek. 1984. *Reasons and Persons*. Oxford: Clarendon Press.

Polish Constitution. Preamble.

Ponthière, Gregory. 2013. 'On the relevancy of the ecological footprint for the study of intergenerational justice'. In Jean-Christophe Merle (ed.), *Spheres of Global Justice*. Dordrecht: Springer, 735–745.

Preparatory Committee for the United Nations Conference on Environment and Development. 1992. *Principles on General Rights and Obligations. Proposals and Comments Submitted by the Delegation of Malta*. Available at: http://ftp.funet.fi/pub/doc/world/UnitedNations/EnvironConf/PreConfDocs/wg3l8add02 (last accessed 9 April 2018)

Rawls, John. 1999. *A Theory of Justice*. Oxford: Oxford University Press.

Rawls, John. 2001. *Justice as Fairness: A Restatement* (ed. Erin Kelly). Cambridge, MA: Harvard University Press.

Read, Rupert. 2012. 'Guardians of the future. a constitutional case for representing and protecting future people'. Dorset: Green House Think Thank. Available at: www.greenhousethinktank.org/files/greenhouse/home/guardians_inside_final.pdf (last accessed 9 April 2018)

Sand, Peter H. 2004. 'Sovereignty bounded: public trusteeship for common pool resources?'. *Global Environmental Politics* 4(1): 47–71.

Shoham, Shlomo. 2010. *Future Intelligence and Sustainability: The Story of the Israeli Parliament's Commission for Future Generations*. Gütersloh: Bertelsmann Foundation.

Shoham, Shlomo and Nira Lamay. 2006. 'Commission for Future Generations in the Knesset: lessons learnt'. In Jörg Tremmel (ed.), *Handbook of Intergenerational Justice*. Cheltenham and Northampton, MA: Edward Elgar, 244–281.

South African Constitution. Ch. 1., Art. XXIV.

Stone, Christopher. 2013. 'Safeguarding future generations'. In Emmanuel Agius and Salvino Busuttil (eds), *Future Generations and International Law*. Abingdon: Routledge.

Swedish Constitution. Ch. 1., Art. II.

Székely, László and Zsolt Kovács. 2014. *Report on the Activities of the Commissioner for Fundamental Rights and His Deputies – 2013*. Budapest: Office of the Commissioner for Fundamental Rights.

Teschner, Naama. 2013. *Official Bodies That Deal with the Needs of Future Generations and Sustainable Development – Comparative Review*. Jerusalem: Knesset Research and Information Center. Available at: www.knesset.gov.il/mmm/data/pdf/me03194.pdf (last accessed 9 April 2018)

Thompson, Dennis. 2010. 'Representing future generations: political presentism and democratic trusteeship'. *Democracy, Equality, and Justice, Critical Review of International Social and Political Philosophy* 13(1): 17–37.

Tiihonen, Paula. 2006. 'Committee for the future – a new institution to discuss the future in Finland?'. In Benedek Jávor and Judith Racz (eds), *Do We Owe Them a Future?*. Budapest: Vedegylet, 72.

Tonn, Bruce and Michael Hogan. 2006. 'The House of Lords: guardians of future generations'. *Futures* 38(1): 115–119.

Tremmel, Jörg. 2006. 'Establishing intergenerational justice in national constitutions'. In Jörg Tremmel (ed.), *Handbook of Intergenerational Justice*. Cheltenham and Northampton, MA: Edward Elgar.

Ukrainian Constitution. Preamble.

UNESCO. 1997. Declaration on the Responsibilities of the Present Generations Towards Future Generations. Available at: http://portal.unesco.org/en/ev.php-URL_ID=13178&URL_DO=DO_TOPIC&URL_SECTION=201.html (last accessed 9 April 2018)

United Nations Conference on Environment and Development. 1992. Rio Declaration on Environment and Development. Available at: www.un.org/documents/ga/conf151/aconf15126-1annex1.htm (last accessed 9 April 2018)

Uruguayan Constitution. Art. XLVII.

Van Parijs, Philippe. 1998. 'The disfranchisement of the elderly, and other attempts to secure intergenerational justice'. *Philosophy & and Public Affairs* 27(4): 292–333.

Vergne, Antoine. 2010. '"L'avis de monsieur Tout-Le-Monde?" Jurys citoyens et urgence écologique'. *Revue critique d'écologie politique* 34(10).

Wallimann-Helmer, Ivo. 2015. 'Can youth quotas help avoid future disasters?'. In Jörg Tremmel, Antony Mason, Igor Dimitrijoski and Petter Godli (eds), *Youth Quotas and Other Forms of Youth Participation in Ageing Societies*. London: Springer.

Ward, Halina. 2011. 'Beyond the short term: legal and institutional space for future generations in global governance'. *Yearbook of International Environmental Law* 22(1): 3–36.

World Commission on Environment and Development (WCED). 1987. *Our Common Future* [Brundtland Report]. Melbourne: WCED. Available at: www.un-documents.net/our-common-future.pdf (last accessed 9 April 2018)

Weeramantry, C. G., Ashok Khosla and Scilla Elworthy. 2012. 'Guardians for the future: safeguarding the world from environmental crisis'. *Guardian*, 20 April. Available at: www. theguardian.com/environment/blog/2012/apr/20/guardians-for-the-future-environment (last accessed 9 April 2018)

Wolfe, Matthew. 2008. 'The shadows of future generations'. *Duke Law Journal* 57(6): 1897–1932.

World Future Council and Centre for International Sustainable Development Law (CISDL). 2014. *National Policies and International Instruments to Protect the Rights of Future Generations.* Available at: www.worldfuturecouncil.org/fileadmin/user_upload/PDF/Representation Future_Generations.pdf (last accessed 18 May 2017)

7

INTERGENERATIONAL JUSTICE IN THE CONTEXT OF DEVELOPING COUNTRIES

Adrian-Paul Iliescu, Ileana Dascălu, Thierry Ngosso and Naomi van Steenbergen

1 Introduction

As we have seen, environmental degradation, global warming and overuse of natural resources have long-term adverse effects whose prevention or mitigation require imposing costs in the very near future. While many of these problems are global in scope, though, they do not affect all countries with equal severity. Developing countries, especially those engaged in subsistence agriculture, are generally more vulnerable to climate change and environmental degradation, and less able to cope with the economic and societal costs brought about by the destruction of productive croplands, extreme weather events, and natural disasters. In many cases, they face particular problems and dilemmas – such as institutional failure and economic and social traps – that do not apply in equal measure to the industrialised world. The situation of less developed countries and the corresponding economic, political and moral challenges therefore requires a dedicated discussion. The main question that will be addressed in this chapter, correspondingly, is: how do the particular situations and difficulties of developing countries bear upon their responsibility for future generations?

This question has both practical and normative aspects. On the practical side, it is important to ask to what extent policies designed with an eye on developed countries can be fruitfully employed by developing countries. What kinds of future-oriented policies are practicable for developing countries, and how do these differ from those that apply to developed countries? On the normative side, it is clear that we cannot require developing countries to apply themselves to the care for future generations with the same intensity as we can expect of developed countries. Nevertheless, there are important questions about the boundaries of what we can expect of them, both in the light of historical circumstances and given their current situation. The question, then, is: under which conditions and constraints, and in which ways, can people in developing countries be expected to be responsible towards future generations? Roughly, ways to deal with the situation of developing countries fall in between two extremes. The one extreme is the belief that developing countries always can and should replicate the policies of developed countries. The other extreme is the conviction that due to immediate pressures, poor countries simply should not be expected to care for future generations at all. We reject both extremes, and shall in this chapter present some considerations that should allow the reader to reflect on these challenges with greater subtlety and insight.

2 The situation of developing countries

Importantly, there is no single criterion according to which we can neatly split the world into 'developed' and 'developing' countries. Indeed, what lies between relatively clear cases of highly developed countries such as Norway and underdeveloped countries such as the Central African Republic is a continuum. Moreover, what is often referred to as 'development' consists of several aspects – not only income, but also institutional stability, education, life expectancy, etc. – and some countries may appear highly developed when judged by one measure while severely lacking according to another. When we speak of developing countries in this book, then, we do not mean to speak of a certain well-defined group of particular countries. Rather, we shall identify certain circumstances, problems and vulnerabilities that place a strain on the capacity of nations to meet intergenerational duties. Developing countries, in this book, are merely loosely defined as those that are particularly affected by these issues.

In this chapter, we shall proceed as follows. First, we shall introduce some important circumstances, problems and vulnerabilities at the national level that are relevant in the context of sustainability and intergenerational justice. We shall, in turn, discuss economic circumstances, institutional failure, and entrapment (though as will quickly become evident, these factors are tightly intertwined). For clarity, we separate identifying these factually relevant circumstances from a consideration of their moral and political implications. That is, the issues identified should initially be understood merely as factors that ought to be taken into account, not as arguments against duties for developing countries. Only after having identified relevant circumstances shall we consider the implications of such issues for the duties of developing countries with respect to future generations.

2.1 Economic circumstances

The first factor, which rather suggests itself, is economic circumstances. The most basic issue is that countries with very low gross national incomes have obvious problems in their ability to meet duties of intergenerational justice, given that addressing the needs of future generations comes at a direct cost for the current generation. Very poor countries will have trouble sparing anything for future generations without jeopardising the basic needs of the current generation.

Countries with low GDPs will, moreover, often have substantial foreign debt. In addition to curtailing expenditure on services that would benefit the current generation (healthcare, nutrition, education), the accumulation of debt transfers a financial burden to future generations, who will not only have responsibility for the debt, but also for an ever-increasing amount of interest. In a negative scenario, this places a cap on future consumption and development, because of the additional duty to restore depleted resources (economic or environmental) to a state required to sustain growth (Clark 2008). This means that their prospects for welfare are jeopardised from the outset. Therefore, a debt crisis generates a vicious circle for developing countries, which find themselves unable to fulfil their moral duties simultaneously towards the present generation and towards future generations.

Often, the lack of financial resources with which many developing countries find themselves confronted acts as an amplifier of other deficiencies, and perhaps the most striking effect is that of financial debt compounding ecological debt. When developing countries need to rely on loans to finance current consumption and investment – which primarily benefit the present people – ecological debt is often simultaneously accumulated, either as an effect of rapid industrialisation without environmental protection measures or as a result of the trading of natural resources to finance the debt contracted. The impact on the welfare of future generations may be significant, as they are likely to inherit reduced biodiversity, damaged terrestrial and aquatic ecosystems, low-quality land for agriculture and reduced forested areas. In other words, if the loans obtained by the present generation are not used to accomplish considerable improvements in living conditions that extend into the future, future generations of developing countries may well find themselves deprived of the very conditions that would have allowed them to sustain the financial debt contracted by their predecessors. Both financial and ecological debt may be forms of uncompensated disadvantages generating poverty for future generations.

However, from the viewpoint of sustainability and future generations, just as important as the state of the economy at a given time is the question of what fuels it. Many of the countries generally considered to be characterised by a lack of development have economies with an incipient industrial base and still depend heavily on (subsistence) agriculture. In comparison to industrialised countries, weakly developed countries are consequently far more vulnerable to environmental changes, which are likely to have a direct impact on agricultural productivity. Frequent and prolonged draughts, changing temperature and rainfall patterns as well as catastrophic natural events disproportionately threaten the economies of societies that depend on agriculture. Unfortunately, for many countries this is not merely a bleak future prospect. Climate-related events such as these have already triggered pandemics and famines in the poorest countries of the world. The populations of these countries, already deprived of basic nutrition and healthcare, are among those hardest hit by changes in the climate.

Besides the issue of agriculture, special attention is due to the role of natural resources. Some very weakly developed countries have great abundances of natural resources. Curiously, precisely some of the countries richest in natural resources are those who are the poorest and least competitive in economic terms, and politically the most unstable and authoritarian. This paradoxical situation is known in the literature as the 'resource curse' (Auty 1993; Sachs and Warner 2001; Ross 2013). This term denotes a situation in which an abundance of natural resources, inadequately managed and vulnerable to fluctuations of international markets, generates low economic growth rates and economic instability. To make things worse, natural resources are often used by those in power to gather excessive wealth and to stay in power, at the expense of the great majority of the population (Wantchekon 2002; Wenar 2008; Ross 2013). Furthermore, not only does the resource curse translate into civil conflicts over resources; it is also likely to increase dependence on foreign aid, leading, in some cases, to a debt crisis.

While a global transition to sustainable resources, and particularly away from fossil fuels, might at first sound like a doom scenario for countries whose economies are supported by little more than oil or mining, in light of the resource curse it could actually turn out to be a blessing. Given that near-exclusive dependence on natural resources and thus on a highly volatile market makes an economy unstable, being forced to transition to a more diversified set of sources of income could actually turn out to be economically beneficial. Furthermore, a loss of income from natural resources is likely to lead to the need for governments to start raising taxes. While this may not seem initially beneficial for citizens, taxes can encourage more transparency and democracy: since the state will depend on its citizens for revenue, it will be forced to demonstrate accountability about the way money is spent. Moreover, authoritarian leaders will lose the funds on which they relied to maintain power and repress dissidents, which, in a positive scenario, may further democracy. All will depend, however, on how the transition takes place – whether it will carry with it changes in power structures, or whether those currently abusive of their resource-dependent power will once more be the ones benefiting.

2.2 Institutional failure

As the issue of the resource curse already indicates, a very important practical factor in the context of weakly developed countries is institutional failure. There is a broad consensus in the development literature that institutional dysfunction, which often leads to massive economic inefficiency, generates particular obstacles for developing countries. Conversely, the effect of the quality of institutional performance on growth and prosperity has been emphasised as one of the prime drivers of development, trumping other factors such as geography and market integration in international trade (Rodrik et al. 2004). Some of the general criteria used to define 'good institutions' are genuine property rights, enforceable contracts, a broadly equal distribution of power (Olson 2000), community participation in policymaking and insurance options for the poor, both coupled with anti-fraud mechanisms (Banerjee and Duflo 2011), and inclusive, as opposed to extractive, political institutions (Acemoğlu and Robinson 2012).

It should be noted that the task of demonstrating causal connections between such deficiencies on the one hand and economic growth and productivity on the other is usually carried out by relying on a mix of quantitative data and perception-based indicators, which help outline a general picture of the differences between developed and developing countries. However, most often the focus is on political institutions, which in developing countries generally fail to act as impartial enforcers of contracts aligned with the public interest, thus blocking the economic changes necessary to reduce the political power of corrupt elites.

Institutional weakness in developing countries affects the distribution of resources, which are often being channelled into obscure avenues, resulting in difficulties for many citizens to secure their basic needs. Where political institutions are taken over by a corrupt minority and fail to take responsibility for the public interest, intense conflicts over the distribution of resources may result, and the preferences of various powerful groups stand to be served to the detriment of social justice. And while some authors express confidence in the incremental institutional progress across a generation by changes in the margin that would eventually prompt a virtuous circle of development (Banerjee and Duflo 2011), others insist that institutions are quite difficult to reform and that, consequently, there is a strong tendency for bad institutions to maintain themselves:

> There are two sources of persistence in the behaviour of the system: first, political institutions are durable, and typically, a sufficiently large change in the distribution of political power is necessary to cause a change in political institutions, such as a transition from dictatorship to democracy. Second, when a particular group is rich relative to others, this will increase its de facto political power and enable it to push for economic and political institutions favourable to its interests. This will tend to reproduce the initial relative wealth disparity in the future.
>
> *(Acemoğlu and Robinson 2006: 677)*

Again, there is a potential difference between the role and strength of this tendency in developed versus developing countries. Countries without consolidated democracies are far more likely to face this issue, and their institutional weakness means that targeted intervention is far less likely to yield good results. For example, while corruption affects both developed and developing countries, in the case of the latter the problem is often part of a system of vulnerabilities which would require wholesale reforms. Since, as is often highlighted, institutions are to large extent formed by those in power, so that the concentration of political power determines the structure of political and economic institutions, it would not suffice to address various deficiencies in isolation, as their interrelations – stronger and deeper in developing countries than in developed ones – require measures that can address the cumulative negative effects they have on each other (Uslaner 2008). Therefore, efforts directed at institutional improvement are more costly (and initially likely to be less efficient) for countries that are underdeveloped in political terms.

Without drawing any normative conclusions at this point, these considerations make clear that institutional failure is a very important factor to take into account when considering the prospects for future generations of weakly developed countries, since there is a serious chance that efforts to diminish the negative environmental legacy for those generations are undermined by deficient institutions.

2.3 Entrapment

A less immediately apparent, but nonetheless very important factor influencing the situation of the poorest countries is that this situation tends to be characterised by a mechanism known as 'entrapment'. In general, traps are defined as self-reinforcing mechanisms leading to bad (inefficient) equilibria, or as vicious circles that maintain negative states of affairs. Entrapment, then, is the result of a tendency of certain bad things to perpetuate themselves: poverty generates more poverty, conflicts generate other conflicts, bad governance stimulates bad governance (partly because incompetent or dishonest politicians promote other incompetent or dishonest politicians), illness causes other illnesses (directly or via treatment) and so on. The most widely discussed traps, poverty traps, are mechanisms that transfer and prolong poverty. However, developing countries may face not only poverty traps, but also geographical traps (characteristic of 'hot, dry, land-locked countries' (Azariadis and Stachurski 2005: 33)), social traps (Rothstein 2005), backwardness traps, institutional traps, bad governance traps, conflict traps, unemployment traps, inactivity traps, bad health traps and even rigidity traps.[1] Azariadis and Stachurski elaborate:

> inefficient equilibria have a bad habit of reinforcing themselves. Corrupt institutions can generate incentives which reward more corruption. Workers with imperfectly observed skills in an unskilled population may be treated as low skilled by firms, and hence have little incentive to invest large sums in education. Low demand discourages investment in increasing returns technology, which reduces productivity and reinforces low demand. That these inefficient outcomes are self-reinforcing is important − were they not, then presumably agents would soon make their way to a better equilibrium.
>
> *(2005: 4)*

The point of such observations is the following: it is not the case that there is no conceivable way out of a difficult economic and social situation, but for someone who is entrapped in such a situation it will, precisely for that reason, be very difficult to use those ways to get out. For instance: high-level education is a potential way out of poverty, but someone who is poor will, precisely for that reason, be unlikely to have access to high-level education. Loans can be means to escape from poverty and helplessness, but someone who is poor will, precisely for that reason, have no collateral and thus be unable to get a loan (when banks ask for collateral (Dercon 2003: 3–4)). Illnesses can be treated, but treatment can be expensive and someone who is ill is not in a position to earn money to pay for treatment.

Much the same mechanism is operative on the level of nations. The richer a country is and consequently the richer the country that is inherited by future generations, the less need there is to provide for them in specific ways. Wealth and development make it more likely (although, of course, not absolutely certain) that future generations will be able to deal with any problems they may encounter. In contrast, the poorer a country is and consequently the poorer the country the next generation inherits, the more likely it is that this generation will have a reduced capacity for solving the problems it faces. At the same time, affluent and developed nations can afford to take care of future generations: the richer a country, the greater its ability to take all sorts of measures (saving, investment, technological modernisation, avoiding resource exhaustion, etc.) to facilitate the prosperity and safety of future generations. In contrast, a poor nation often cannot afford to save and to take measures to protect future generations, and thus has difficulties to care for them effectively. This is a well-known but still disturbing situation: precisely those nations that have less reason to worry about future generations on account of being prosperous can afford to take measures to protect their future citizens; whereas nations whose future generations will likely be in the worst position cannot afford to protect them.

Moreover, in the case of developing countries, entrapment is often exacerbated by the fact that the problematic situation does not consist of a series of separate hard-to-escape problems, but rather of a set of difficulties that are interrelated and mutually reinforcing. These burdens may include poverty, lack of resources, institutional dysfunction, endemic corruption, low social capital, inequality (Uslaner 2008: 42–50), acute conflicts, counterproductive traditions, bad governance, powerful prey groups, high levels of criminality and global institutional factors (Pogge 2008: 147). Poverty, then, leads to illness and illness leads to poverty, poverty attracts corruption and corruption increases poverty, corruption brings backwardness, etc. So, while all countries face a diversity of problems, in the case of developing countries the scope and gravity of the individual problems paired with the mutually reinforcing relation in which they stand makes for a very particular and extremely difficult predicament.

2.4 Vulnerable international position, vulnerable groups

Finally, countries with weak economies and weak institutions are often vulnerable in contexts in which they deal with more developed countries or internationally operating companies. This again can expose them to environmentally damaging practices. For example, companies looking for sites to dump toxic waste tend to seek out underdeveloped countries. This is what happened in the *Probo Koala* case, when toxic chemicals were dumped in poor neighbourhoods of Abidjan, Ivory Coast in 2006 by the Dutch company Trafigura Beheer BV (Denoiseux

2010). Exporting hazardous goods to poor countries has been part of the Western multinational agenda for a long time (Shue 1981).

Similar mechanisms may mean that vulnerable groups within developing countries are disproportionately burdened, not only by environmental degradation, but indeed by measures to combat it. A recent example can be found in Kenya where in order to combat abusive and uncontrolled logging in the Mau forest, government authorities decided to forcibly deport all inhabitants of the forest, including the Ogiek communities who had been living there for centuries (Calas 2009). Thus, environmental protection can create what Mark Dowie (2009) has termed 'conservation refugees': poor and vulnerable people, often indigenous, forcibly displaced by their own governments, without any financial compensation, in order to create areas of conservation, biodiversity reserves or national parks. Their number is now estimated to exceed 14 million in Africa alone. While such projects to protect nature may have the appearance of being environmentally virtuous, it is clear that their consequences are harmful and unjust to poor indigenous populations.

Finally, less developed countries often have weaker standing on the global political stage, and may have difficulty making their voices heard (again, there is a very significant difference here between the poorest, least developed countries, and those whose economies have steep growth curves). Whenever this is the case, chances are that the results of any negotiations will be unfavourable to them. This comprises another barrier to their ability to adequately provide for their future generations.

3 Normative considerations

Having outlined a number of relevant circumstances and vulnerabilities of developing countries, we are now in a position to consider some normative implications. Concerted attempts to mitigate climate change and to stop negative developments such as resource exhaustion or environmental degradation have given rise to the identification of a number of desirable changes. Implementing these changes is burdensome, and a great deal of theoretical and political attention has been devoted to the question how such burdens should be divided between strongly developed and less developed countries. There are several reasons to think that less developed countries should be allocated proportionately fewer burdensome changes than more developed ones.

3.1 The urgency of existing problems

One rather obvious reason why developing countries cannot be expected to apply themselves to care for future generations with the same intensity as can be expected from strongly developed countries has to do with the urgency of existing problems and needs. Because developing countries face such severe problems, many people living in these countries typically have basic needs that go unsatisfied. If we assume (following authors such as Shue 1980, Pogge 2008, Löfquist 2011 or indeed the Universal Declaration of Human Rights, arts 25 and 28), that every person has a fundamental right to have his or her basic needs fulfilled, this entails that the fundamental rights of many citizens of developing countries are not met.[2]

The urgency of care for the present generation means that in the case of developing countries, the question of future generations has two important characteristics that are absent in the case of developed countries. First, since funds dedicated to the future could be used to satisfy basic needs and to protect basic rights, care for future generations comes at an extremely high opportunity cost. In this respect, developing countries differ from developed countries, for which the opportunity costs of investing in future generations take the form not of absolute needs, but of 'self-cancelling relative wants' (Daly 2002: 4). When authors who plead for prevention of harm to future generations claim that 'the costs of prevention are moderate, although far from insignificant' (Shue 2014: 269), they obviously have the case of developed countries in mind, not that of desperately poor countries.[3]

The second, corresponding characteristic is that the existence of needs that should be met immediately and of neglected rights that warrant immediate redress, results in a very high discount rate of investments in the future. That is, the perceived relative value of future goods (in this case, properly taken-care-of future generations) is low in light of the urgency of present needs. The following example is illustrative:

> Haitians were able to cut down the last tree because the individuals taking the specific actions had high personal discount rates. On any given day the value of a tree cut down was worth significantly more than one standing one year later, just as the starving man dismissed the future value of $10,000 in the face of a sandwich in hand immediately. The tree today meant fuel for cooking and money to buy food for hungry mouths. The forests of Haiti and the sardines of Namibia and the blue fin tuna in the Atlantic were depleted by people acting rationally, even if with very different motivations.
>
> *(Schweitzer 2010)*

The high opportunity costs of prioritising future needs and rights and the reality of a high discount rate make it rational for developing countries to allocate resources to the present rather than to the future. As Shue points out:

> It may ultimately be in the interest of the poor states to see ozone depletion and global warming stopped, but in the medium term the citizens of the poor states have far more urgent and serious problems – such as lack of food, lack of clean drinking water, and lack of jobs to provide minimal support for themselves and their families.
>
> *(2014: 193)*

Moreover, the aim of satisfying basic needs and fulfilling basic rights is not only perfectly rational or economically sound – there are moral reasons in its favour, too. Many authors argue that the fact that many of the present needs of very poor people in developing countries are survival needs gives rise to direct moral obligations and preclusions. Some hold that basic needs may never be neglected for the sake of prevention, however great the threat (Shue 1993). On this basis, theorists such as Shue argue that, for instance, considerable amounts of greenhouse gas emissions are excusable, because they are 'subsistence emissions', the elimination of which would jeopardise survival in the most deprived societies. Moreover, when survival is at stake, devoting resources to protect future generations at the expense of the present (desperately) poor seems unacceptable:

> Right now, on the order of eighteen million people are dying each year of readily remediable chronic poverty for want of relatively small sums of money and related institutional changes. One could not sanely claim that unlimited sums should be devoted to blocking the possibility of future severe climate change if that entailed that one would, in consequence, refuse to spend what it would take to eliminate severe poverty.
>
> *(Shue 2014: 275)*

The right of people in developing countries to dedicate resources to satisfying their own basic needs at the cost of future burdens on their descendants has been compared to the right of self-defence:

> In these cases, we may with good reason speak of having so strong or so rationally compelling a reason to emit that, in spite of the harm these emissions will cause to (future) others, we are excused for our maleficence. Much like self-defense may excuse the commission of an injury and even a murder, so their necessity for our subsistence may excuse our indispensable current emissions and the resulting future infliction of harm they cause. Subsistence emissions are emissions we cannot reasonably be expected not to make, because they are rationally compelling emissions, and we are excused for making them.
>
> *(Traxler 2002: 106)*

From this perspective, requiring very poor countries to save for the future or invest in technologies meant to avoid imposing costs on future generations is morally problematic in situations where the basic needs and rights of present generations are not met. Correspondingly, developing countries in this sense seem to have a restricted duty to spend their resources on protecting future generations, and that in some cases it seems indeed morally impermissible for them to do so.

However, it is very important to recognise the limits to this type of argument. First of all, future generations of poor countries not only stand to be severely harmed by the consequences of environmental degradation and climate change, they are in fact likely to be worse off than their current generations even in the absence of catastrophic environmental changes. The fact of entrapment and the mutually reinforcing nature of many of the problems confronting developing countries mean that the low levels of welfare, economic development, productivity, and technological innovation typical of developing countries are not only unlikely to improve, but indeed stand to worsen over time. Future generations of underdeveloped countries, then, are likely both to face more severe problems and to be less equipped to deal with them. So even though poor countries' current generations do not have much to spare, there is even more reason to be concerned for their future generations. As Shue points out:

> failing to deal with climate change constitutes not only failing to protect future generations but inflicting adversity on them by making their circumstances more difficult and dangerous than they would have been without as much climate change, and much more difficult and dangerous than circumstances are now for us.[4]
>
> *(2014: 269)*

According to this type of argument, the fact that future generations are likely to face worse circumstances than exist today means that any duties towards them cannot be annulled by current poor circumstances. Even current poor circumstances, after all, are likely still better than those of future generations that are not provided for. The fact that future generations are likely to be worse off than current ones constitutes a reason to prioritise their rights over the rights of current generations, even those that are already suffering.

In this vein, it could furthermore be argued that even high opportunity costs cannot be invoked as an argument against developing countries spending resources on future generations. While opportunity costs are indeed high, the magnitude of expected problems for future generations in the absence of protective measures far outweighs them.

In this respect, though, it is important to distinguish between deeply underdeveloped countries and relatively underdeveloped countries that are on a very steep development curve. The latter countries may, for instance, currently be relatively poor, but likely to see great economic and technological advances in the coming decade or so, which will impact favourably on their future generations. Still, it remains a valid question whether the future generations of these countries will truly be better off if all resources are poured into development, rather than some being simultaneously spent on, say, measures to protect the environment.

Second, it is crucial to heed the fact that the argument concerning poor and problematic circumstances in the present only constitutes an argument against certain developing countries imposing such costs on their present generations *themselves*. There is no reason to think that the *rights* of those future generations to be protected from harm are at all restricted, and it may well be that it falls upon other parties to provide such protection or to assist developing countries in offering it. As we shall see below, there are plenty of reasons to think that such duties must fall on (certain) richer or more strongly developed countries. Furthermore, we shall see that the dilemma sketched here – to help either current generations or future ones – will not always apply. Indeed, as we shall see below, in many cases what benefits present generations and what benefits future ones will coincide.

3.2 Moral limits to sacrifice

A similar angle from which prioritising present needs over the needs of future generations might appear justified is grounded in the idea that there are moral limits to sacrifice.

Unchained consumerism, generational selfishness and irresponsible polluting behaviour have created global natural disaster that threatens future generations. Many benefits that present people enjoy will sooner or later require sacrifice from future generations. Conversely, it is obvious that some arrangements which would improve the situation of future generations will be detrimental to currently living people. Trying to stop the existing harmful activities and to repair the damage already created almost inevitably implies the disruption of what has come to be perceived as 'normal' economic activity (stimulating growth), 'reasonable' aims (economic development or higher economic competitiveness) or 'modern' life-styles, and consequently some sacrifice from all of us who now reap the benefits of this peculiar 'normality'. Of course, even if they feel normal, many of these entrenched habits could be justifiably classified as luxuries. However, some benefits that we might have to give up might be understood as rights: the right to development, the right to welfare, the freedom to choose one's lifestyle or one's aims, etc. (though it should be noted that all of these are controversial). If extreme measures are deemed necessary to ensure minimal provisions for future generations, the more basic rights of current generations may come under threat. In this case, appropriate provisions for future generations are likely to lead to conflicts of rights. Avoiding both unacceptable conflicts and the neglect of important rights requires balancing the relevant indispensable rights. Thus, one of the relevant problems is the task of securing both the legitimate rights of future generations and those of the present ones. As Henry Shue remarks:

> The most that can be demanded of us is a level of sacrifice that does not compromise our secure enjoyment of the same rights that, we are acknowledging, belong as well to persons in the future. To deprive ourselves of basic rights in order to guarantee those same basic rights to people in the future would be in effect to treat our generation as inferior – as somehow entitled to less than equal minimum rights.
>
> *(2014: 174)*

In other words, it is acceptable for the protection of rights for future generations to come at a cost for current generations, but no measure should cause current generations to fall below the level we attempt to secure for future generations. Of course, in many circumstances this still leaves room for drastic changes. Yet given the scarcity of immediately available financial resources that characterises most developing countries, it may well be the case that in those countries, policies aimed at protecting the rights and interests of future generations require reductions or cancellations of public policies that secure some fundamental interests or basic rights of present people. Some authors insist that this would be an injustice, and that no matter how generous our intentions towards future people might be, we must first of all make sure that our efforts in this respect do not harm present generations in essential ways.

In his contribution to the *Oxford Handbook of Climate Change and Society*, Jon Barnett defends this perspective by introducing the idea of human security, which comprises at least three fundamental elements: basic needs fulfilment, human rights protection and respect for one's core values. Public policies, he argues, should guarantee human security for any person, no matter whether she belongs to a future generation or to a present one. Even if our policies are deliberately designed to protect future generations from the negative effects of climate change, resource exhaustion or environment degradation, the fundamental security of present people should not be affected either:

> Policies that increase human insecurity by undermining people's access to enjoyment of basic needs, human rights and core values should be considered maladaptive, and all potential policies for both climate change mitigation and adaptation should be screened for these effects.
>
> *(Barnett 2011: 273)*

From this point of view, the protection of basic rights of future generations is limited by the fundamental rights of persons currently alive. However, in the case of developing countries, the same reservations as those elaborated above apply. In other words: the rights of future generations are not affected by this argument, and the argument has no force against the stipulation that other parties, such as developed countries, ought to spend the resources necessary to protect these generations, as long as such spending is balanced against the fundamental rights of those who presently depend on the resources in question.

3.3 The relationship between the duties of developing countries and those of developed countries

It is often taken for granted that each state ought to take care of its own citizens, whether current or future ones. This would entail that there is no relationship between the duties of developing countries and those of developed countries. The assumption, however, is highly problematic.

As many theorists have argued in detail, compared to now highly developed countries, developing countries played a far smaller role in causing the global problems that affect the future generations of the world (Shue 1999; Neumayer 2000; see also Pogge 2008). This means that requiring developing countries to share the burden of mitigating the effects of resource exhaustion or environmental degradation entails making them pay for problems that they had only a marginal role in causing. From this perspective, it seems at least plausible that developing countries ought to take up a smaller part of the burden of mitigating harmful effects of environmental change, regardless of who will benefit from such mitigation. This may be interpreted in terms of historical responsibilities for those countries, now relatively developed, that used environmentally unfriendly paths to promote their immediate development interests. This idea is often referred to as the 'polluter pays principle'. A similar conclusion would result from the 'beneficiary pays principle', which does not allocate the mitigation burdens according to historical responsibility, but on the basis of the question who has benefited from the industries that have caused environmental degradation (see Caney 2005; Shue 2010; Singer 2010). Practically, the main difference is that most of the current citizens of developed countries cannot be said to have been responsible for their state's substantial emissions in, say, the 1950s, but they certainly do benefit from them. The assumption that each state is responsible for its own, then, mostly favours developed countries, and the grounds for it are questionable. There are also authors who argue that the expected environmental crises and their impacts are so significant that we should not merely consider the question who is responsible or who benefits, but also simply allocate duties according to which countries are able to contribute to a solution (see Caney 2005; Shue 2010).

The problem of responsibility and differentiation is in fact a dual one. One question is how the fact that certain parties bear more responsibility for current problems should influence the distribution of burdens in counteracting the effects of previous harmful actions. Yet the use of exhaustible resources, pollution and the like are not problems of the past, but ongoing practices; and indeed – as is pointed out in Chapter 8 on economics – to a certain extent this seems justifiable. This raises a second question: if developed countries owe their development in part to their past engagement in harmful practices, don't developing countries have a right to engage in those practices at least relatively more than the countries that have already reaped substantial benefits from them? If this is indeed the case, this would have a great impact on the moral status of the current global emissions patterns. At the very least, it would mean that the current distribution of ongoing emissions (which per capita are still many times higher in the developed countries than in the developing ones) is deeply morally problematic.[5] Moreover, present practices of people in wealthy nations disproportionately threaten the current and future generations of poor countries, and this fact ought to bear upon their duties towards those whom they expose to harm (see, e.g., Zhang et al. 2017).

Regardless of one's answer to the question whether there is such a thing as a right to development, then, it is quite clear that given both historical developments and the current situation, the assumption that each state simply is responsible for its own citizens cannot stand. Instead, the developed countries have a duty to aid the underdeveloped ones, at least when it comes to mitigating the harmful effects of the (past and present) practices of the former.

4 Where the interests of present and future generations coincide

The preceding discussion may have raised the impression that the interests of present and future generations are always at odds, and that they may at best be balanced against each other. However, this is certainly not always the case. First of all, it must be kept in mind that substantial environmental crises are already ongoing, and these stand to worsen drastically within the next centuries. The future, unfortunately in this respect, is not far off at all. On the positive side, there are situations in which provisions that are beneficial to the present poor have a positive impact on future generations. Diminishing air pollution in China, say, is an urgent task beneficial to both present and future Chinese citizens. There are strong indications that the best way to reduce population growth is to encourage education for women. This obviously directly benefits the women who will be educated and the next generations of the family, but it also is likely to have a beneficial effect on the economic health of the country as a whole, including its future generations (see Dilli 2017). Here, the interests of the present and future generations can be made to coincide. Indeed, in the context of developing countries some of the most promising avenues for change involve measures that benefit both the current and future generations. And while current generations may selfishly favour economic development over care for future generations, such development may ultimately favour future generations, too. As Gardiner remarks, 'not all of the rewards accrue to the present generation. Some are passed on in the form of technological advances and increases in the capital stock' (2001: 403).

At the same time, policies aimed at protecting the environment and the rights of future generations can contribute to the well-being of the current generation, both when they involve investments and the creation of jobs, and when current generations already suffer from the problems such measures are targeted at mitigating. An example of the first is the Green Belt Movement founded by the Kenyan environmental activist Wangari Maathaï, a movement that is strongly involved in reforestation in Kenya while at the same time employing local women. It was thanks to this initiative that Wangari Maathaï won the Nobel Peace Prize. The fact that current generations are already burdened by the environmental problems that threaten future generations is obvious in the case of some emerging economies, where industrial development endangers the health of present generations at a large scale. The adoption of industrial strategies aimed at a green future would dramatically improve not only the prospects of future generations, but also the quality of life of present people.

An important caveat, though, is that even if measures to protect the environment are beneficial for the present generation, they may still be associated with costs so high that overall they appear, from the perspective of the very poor, as an unaffordable luxury. As Jan Narveson remarks:

Environmental standards are expensive, and it is perfectly possible that a given standard in a given country is too expensive. Applying it in that country will, again, make many people there unemployable, given the costs of meeting those standards. And the chances of dying earlier if you are unemployed may well be higher than if you are employed in an area with lower environmental standards. That is perfectly possible, and the enthusiast for environmentalism, if he has his way, is likely to occasion the deaths as well as the continued impoverishment of many people in the country that is the victim of politically powerful people who succumb to his arguments. In short, the wealthy can afford squeaky-clean environments, perhaps, but for most others, they are not worth having. A pollution that will cause your death when you get to be 80 is not worth paying to reduce at the cost of the money that will only enable you to live to 60 anyway.

(2004: 342)

Of course, as many of the arguments above, Narveson's argument only has any force against the idea that developing countries should spend their own resources on their future generations. As we have argued, though, it is morally quite implausible that this burden should fall on developing countries alone.

In a somewhat similar vein, several authors have stressed that even if economic development threatens to exhaust natural resources, pollute and produce dangerous climate change, it also has positive consequences for future generations, who stand to benefit from technological progress, enhanced industrial capacity, greater productivity, etc. This undeniable fact has led some authors to conclude that the exhaustion of natural resources should not be considered very dramatic. Paul Collier, for instance, has advocated the view that we could deal fairly with both natural resources and future generations even if we use natural resources intensively, because we are not curators of natural treasures, but custodians of their value. This means that we can freely use existing resources as long as we pass on to future generations all sorts of other benefits: advanced technologies, higher industrial capacity, higher economic productivity, higher levels of welfare, etc. (Collier 2010). But as Gardiner notes, a view according to which development should be seen as not being fundamentally problematic because it is bound to bring compensation does not appear satisfactory:

> future generations might be compensated for the damage they inherit through having better resources with which to deal with them. Such arguments are no doubt warranted in some cases: for example, some developing countries are probably right to think that they do best to improve their economic infrastructure rather than abate emissions at the moment, especially since the planet is already committed to some warming. However, in general, the point is limited by such factors as (a) that much of the benefit of emissions is not passed on but simply consumed; (b) that technology and capital are far from perfect substitutes for environmental quality; and (c) that the precise physical effects of global warming are likely to be unpredictable, severe, and possibly catastrophic (so that effective deployment of the inherited benefits to mitigate them may be extremely difficult).

(2001: 403)

Many authors, most notably Shue and Gardiner, insist that we should not surrender to the disjunction 'development or intergenerational justice', because intermediate solutions and trade-offs can reconcile the two opposite sets of moral preferences or pressures. An adequate way of establishing an intergenerational community of rights does not have to imply sacrificing one party in order to provide for another. The optimism implied in the idea that in most cases we do not have to choose between doing the right thing for present people and doing the right thing for future people is encouraging, but not completely reassuring just by itself. It remains to be seen if and when trade-offs are feasible and reconciliation is possible, and this will require rigorous and detailed studies. This is one important area on which it would be productive to focus research efforts in the coming years.

5 The necessity of an integrated approach

Given the particular circumstances of developing countries, it is not enough to simply pump money into environmental conservation programmes or sustainable industries. The tasks of preventing anthropogenic natural disaster and of prioritising the needs of future generations require institutional arrangements, without which no policy aimed at protecting future people can be successful. Unfortunately, though, many developing countries are institutionally weak, and thus deficient in this respect. Indeed, many authors insist that it is the very fact of institutional underdevelopment and inefficiency that is responsible for most of the poverty of such countries (Rodrik 2007; Acemoğlu and Robinson 2012). Institutional failure and entrapment severely hinder the adequate protection of future generations. Here is a telling example:

> Norway, about the richest country in the world, parks some of its oil revenue in a 'future-generations fund', and several countries of the bottom billion have sought to imitate it. This may be a good idea for Norway, which has capital coming out of its ears, but it is a pretty doubtful one for the bottom-billion societies, since they are extremely short of capital . . . Future-generations funds are even politically risky in low-income countries: as they accumulate they are a mounting temptation for populism. Consequently, future-generations funds are unlikely to make it through to some future generation and more likely to be a transfer from the prudent governments that establish them to the imprudent governments that dismantle them. Sadly, that is what the record to date bears out.
>
> *(Collier 2007: 142)*

Of course, such findings ought not to be taken to imply that the duty to care for future generations is reduced under these circumstances. But they do mean that we have to think very carefully about the best ways to do this – ways that are capable of dealing with the particular vulnerabilities developing countries face. This means that in the case of developing countries, we cannot simply pour money into programmes for environmental improvement while disregarding political, economic and institutional weaknesses. Rather, securing a safe environment for the future generations of developing countries requires an integrated approach.

6 Conclusion

As we have seen, in the context of intergenerational justice and long-term responsibility, the situation of developing countries is, for several reasons, relevantly different from that of highly developed countries. Moreover, it has emerged that the issue is a complex one. We have introduced a number of reasons to think that it is particularly important to protect the future generations of developing countries. At the same time, the first part of the chapter has shown that there are complex vulnerabilities that in some extreme cases seem to justify that developing countries reserve their resources for meeting short-term responsibilities. Moreover, there are strong reasons to think that developed countries bear significant responsibility for the situation threatening present and future generations of developing countries, and that they have corresponding duties to mitigate the ill effects of their practices and bear a significant part of the burden for tackling environmental problems. In any case, what it is absolutely clear and quite unanimously accepted is that developed countries and developing countries cannot solve these problems in isolation from one another. Resource exhaustion, environmental degradation and related issues are global problems, which require a cooperative solution.

Notes

1 Remarkably, not only shortages and deficiencies, but also otherwise positive events such as sudden enrichment can generate traps. Such traps are known as 'huge resources traps'. Perhaps the most famous of these was the 'Dutch disease', a situation in the 1970s where a newly discovered wealth of natural gas and corresponding soaring exports ultimately ended up having a detrimental effect on the Dutch economy.
2 Rights to the fulfilment of basic needs is sometimes interpreted as a kind of positive right. The very idea of positive rights is, however, not universally accepted. There are authors who argue that genuine rights are always negative (e.g. the right not to be harmed) and who, correspondingly, do not accept the idea of a right to have one's needs fulfilled. Against such a standpoint it could be argued that the right to have one's basic needs fulfilled is in fact identical to a right not to be harmed, since the very definition of a basic need is that its absence entails harm. See Chapter 2 for more on this issue.
3 The idea that opportunity costs for developed countries are modest is not uncontroversial either, however. Adequate measures to prevent climate change, for instance, would lead to disruption of economic activity, entrenched lifestyles, competitiveness, etc.
4 On the ethical dimensions of exposing people to danger, see Chapter 3.
5 See World Bank (2017). Just to give an indication: the figures from 2014 show that the USA, Canada and Australia were each responsible for about 16 metric tonnes per capita and the average for EU countries was 6.4, while a country such as India remained below 2 and the least developed countries averaged 0.3 metric tonnes per capita. As can be expected, China was one of the outliers, its emissions having risen from 1.2 in 1960 to 7.5 in 2014, though it certainly is not the 'emissions world leader' it is made out to be by those relying on absolute numbers.

Bibliography

Acemoğlu, Daron and James Robinson. 2006. 'Paths of economic and political development'. In Barry R. Weingast and Donald A. Wittman (eds), *The Oxford Handbook of Political Economy*. Oxford: Oxford University Press, 673–692.

Acemoğlu, Daron and James Robinson. 2012. *Why Nations Fail*. New York: Crown Publishers.

Auty, Richard. 1993. *Sustaining Development in Mineral Economies: The Resource Curse Thesis*. London: Routledge.

Azariadis, Costas and John Stachurski. 2005. 'Poverty traps'. In Philippe Aghion and Steven N. Durlauf (eds), *Handbook of Economic Growth, Volume 1A*. Amsterdam: Elsevier, 295–384.

Banerjee, Abhijit and Esther Duflo. 2011. *Poor Economics. A Radical Rethinking of the Way to Fight Global Poverty*. New York: Public Affairs.

Barnett, J. 2011. 'Human security'. In John S. Dryzek, Richard B. Norgaard and Davis Schlosberg (eds), *The Oxford Handbook of Climate Change and Society*. Oxford: Oxford University Press, 267–277.

Calas, Bernard. 2009. 'La crise kenyane de 2008: les leçons du Kuresoi'. *Transcontinentales* 7: 7–30.

Caney, Simon. 2005. 'Cosmopolitan justice, responsibility and global climate change'. Originally printed in *Leiden Journal of International Law*. Reprinted 2010 in Stephen M. Gardiner, Simon Caney, Dale Jamieson and Henry Shue (eds), *Climate Ethics: Essential Readings*. New York: Oxford University Press, 122–145.

Caney, Simon. 2010. 'Climate change, human rights and moral thresholds'. Originally printed in Stephen Humphreys (ed.), *Human Rights and Climate Change*. Cambridge: Cambridge University Press. Reprinted 2010 in Stephen M. Gardiner, Simon Caney, Dale Jamieson and Henry Shue (eds), *Climate Ethics: Essential Readings*. New York: Oxford University Press, 163–180.

Collier, Paul. 2007. *The Bottom Billion*. Oxford: Oxford University Press.

Collier, Paul. 2010. *The Plundered Planet: Why We Must – and How We Can – Manage Nature for Global Prosperity*. Oxford: Oxford University Press.

Daly, Herman E. 2002. 'Sustainable development: definitions, principles, policies'. Invited address, Washington, D.C., MD: World Bank.

Denoiseux, Delphine. 2010. 'L'exportation de déchets dangereux vers l'Afrique: le cas du Probo Koala'. *Courrier hebdomadaire du CRISP* 26(2071).

Dercon, Stefan. 2003. 'Poverty traps and development: the equity–efficiency trade-off revisited'. Paper prepared for the Conference on Growth, Inequality and Poverty organized by the Agence française de développement and the European Development Research Network.

Dilli, Selin. 2017. 'The deep causes of economic development: family systems and female agency'. In Jan Luiten van Zanden, Auke Rijpma and Jan Kok (eds), *Agency, Gender and Economic Development in the World Economy 1850–2000: Testing the Sen Hypothesis*. Abingdon: Routledge.

Donnelly, Jack. 1985. 'In search of the unicorn: the jurisprudence and politics of the right to development'. *California Western International Law Journal* 15: 473–510.

Dowie, Marc. 2009. *Conservation Refugees: The Hundred-Year Conflict between Global Conservation and Native Peoples*. Boston, MA: MIT Press.

Gardiner, Stephen M. 2001. 'The real tragedy of the commons'. *Philosophy and Public Affairs* 30(4): 387–416.

Harris, Paul (ed.). 2011. *China's Responsibility for Climate Change: Ethics, Fairness, and Environmental Policy*. University of Bristol: Policy Press.

Löfquist, Lars. 2011. 'Climate change, justice and the right to development'. *Journal of Global Ethics* 7(3): 251–260.

Luterbacher, Ulf and Detlef Sprinz (eds). 2001. *International Relations and Global Climate Change*. Cambridge, MA: MIT Press.

Narveson, Jan. 2004. 'Welfare and wealth, poverty and justice in today's world'. *Journal of Ethics* 8(4): 305–348.

Neumayer, Eric. 2000. 'In defense of historical accountability for greenhouse gas emissions'. *Ecological Economics* 33(2): 185–192.

Olson, Mancur. 2000. *Power and Prosperity: Outgrowing Communist and Capitalist Dictatorships*. New York: Basic Books.

Pogge, Thomas. 2008. *World Poverty and Human Rights: Cosmopolitan Responsibilities and Reforms*, 2nd edn. Cambridge: Polity Press.

Posner, Eric and David Weisbach. 2010. *Climate Change Justice*. Princeton, NJ: Princeton University Press.

Rodrik, Dani. 2007. *One Economics, Many Recipes*. Princeton, NJ and Oxford: Princeton University Press.

Rodrik, Dani, Arvind Subramanian and Francesco Trebbi. 2004. 'Institutions rule: the primacy of institutions over geography and integration in economic development'. *Journal of Economic Growth* 9(2): 131–165.

Ross, Michael L. 2013. *The Oil Curse: How Petroleum Wealth Shapes the Development of Nations*. Princeton, NJ and Oxford: Princeton University Press.

Rothstein, Bo. 2005. *Social Traps and the Problem of Trust*. Cambridge: Cambridge University Press.

Sachs, Jeffrey and Andrew Warner. 2001. 'The curse of natural resources'. *European Economic Review* 45: 827–838.

Schweitzer, Jeff. 2010. 'Seed corn, discount rate and our endangered future'. *Huffington Post*, 27 July. Available at: www.huffingtonpost.com/jeff-schweitzer/seed-corn-discount-rate-a_b_660559.html (last accessed 9 April 2018)

Shue, Henry. 1980. *Basic Rights*. Princeton, NJ: Princeton University Press.

Shue, Henry. 1981. 'Exporting hazard'. *Ethics* 91(4): 579–606.

Shue, Henry. 1992. 'The unavoidability of justice'. Originally printed in Andrew Hurrell and Benedict Kingsbury (eds), *The International Politics of the Environment*. Oxford: Oxford University Press, 1992. Reprinted 2014 in Henry Shue, *Climate Justice: Vulnerability and Protection*. Oxford: Oxford University Press, 27–44.

Shue, Henry. 1993. 'Subsistence emissions and luxury emissions'. Originally printed in *Law & Policy* 15(1). Reprinted 2010 in Stephen Gardiner, Simon Caney, Dale Jamieson and Henry Shue (eds), *Climate Ethics: Essential Readings*. New York: Oxford University Press, 200–214.

Shue, Henry. 1999. 'Global environment and international inequality'. *International Affairs* 75(3): 531–545.

Shue, Henry. 2010. 'Global environment and international equality'. In Stephen Gardiner, Simon Caney, Dale Jamieson and Henry Shue (eds), *Climate Ethics: Essential Readings*. New York: Oxford University Press, 102–111.

Shue, Henry. 2013. 'Climate hope: implementing the exit strategy'. Originally printed in *Chicago Journal of International Law* 13(2). Reprinted 2014 in Henry Shue, *Climate Justice: Vulnerability and Protection*. Oxford: Oxford University Press, 319–339.

Shue, Henry. 2014. *Climate Justice: Vulnerability and Protection*. Oxford: Oxford University Press.

Singer, Peter. 2010. 'One atmosphere'. In Stephen Gardiner, Simon Caney, Dale Jamieson and Henry Shue (eds), *Climate Ethics: Essential Readings*. New York: Oxford University Press, 181–199.

Traxler, Martino. 2002. 'Fair chore division for climate change'. *Social Theory and Practice* 28(1): 101–134.

Uslaner, Eric. 2008. *Corruption, Inequality and the Rule of Law.* Cambridge: Cambridge University Press.

Wantchekon, Leonard. 2002. 'Why do resource dependent countries have authoritarian governments?'. *Journal of African Finance and Economic Development* 5(2): 57–77.

Wenar, Leif. 2008. 'Property rights and the resource curse'. *Philosophy and Public Affairs* 38(1): 2–32.

Wolf, Clark. 2008. 'Justice and intergenerational debt'. *Intergenerational Justice Review* 8(1): 13–17.

World Bank. 2017. 'CO_2 emissions (metric tons per capita)'. Collected by the Carbon Dioxide Information Analysis Center, Environmental Sciences Division, Oak Ridge National Laboratory, USA. Available at: data.worldbank.org/indicator/EN.ATM.CO2E.PC

Zhang, Qianget al. 2017. 'Transboundary health impacts of transported global air pollution and international trade'. *Nature* 543: 705–709.

8

CLIMATE ECONOMICS AND FUTURE GENERATIONS

Klaus Steigleder

1 Introduction

While in the Paris Agreement of 2015 it was stipulated by the participants of the United Nations Framework Convention on Climate Change that global warming should be kept 'well below' an increase of 2 °C above preindustrial levels, prominent climate economists argue for years that global warming should instead be limited to no lower than 3 °C. This is not meant as a prediction that it is probably too late to limit global warming to below 2 °C and that it would be prudent to be prepared for a much greater extent of global warming. Instead, it is meant as a prescription. The economists are convinced that the costs of striving for a more ambitious limitation of global warming are too high as compared to the costs that will be connected with an increase of average global temperature to 3 °C or even more.

This chapter has mainly two aims: first, I would like to show that these claims of mainstream climate economics are deeply wrong and cannot call for being based on the authority of economics. Instead, they are based on problematic moral presuppositions. Second, I would like to make comprehensible why highly intelligent and mostly well-meaning economists are convinced of these claims. Their arguments are based on an impressive theoretical framework and on important considerations and insights which at certain points are connected with questionable assumptions and doubtful decisions. Because of the great influence economics and economists exert on policymaking, it is of great importance to understand both the strengths and the weaknesses of current mainstream climate economics and to see exactly where and why it is going wrong.

For this it is necessary to understand some of the basics of neoclassical natural resource and environmental economics. I will therefore start by explaining them. This will require some patience from readers, but I hope they will find that the benefits outbalance the costs. I will criticise the moral presuppositions of mainstream climate economics from the standpoint of rights-based moral theories which assume that each person possesses equal rights to the conditions necessary for being able to lead her life (such as life, physical and psychological integrity). These are assumptions on which not only the constitutions of modern states are mainly based but which also form the basis of current international law. Thus, they ought to guide all (climate) politics. Besides these more pragmatic considerations the basic assumptions of rights-based moral theories could be justified more directly, but doing so would go beyond the remit of this chapter.

Thus, I will start with an introduction to some basics of neoclassical natural resource and environmental economics which focuses on certain kinds of market failures, i.e. constellations in which systematically too much or too little of a good is produced on a market. In our context so-called 'negative externalities' are an especially relevant kind of market failure. Negative externalities exist when not all costs of production and consumption are covered by the traders on the market (the sellers and the buyers) but some of the costs fall on uninvolved third parties. A typical result is that the amount of the production of certain goods (and of the damage connected with it) is too high. After a first overview of environmentally relevant market failures, I will explain the concept of a negative externality in more detail and then highlight the presumptions neoclassical natural resource and environmental economics makes when employing the concept. This will then allow us to understand the search for the optimal amount of global warming which guides mainstream climate economics.

2 Some basics of neoclassical natural resource and environmental economics

Mainstream climate economics is a part of neoclassical natural resource and environmental economics. Neoclassical economics, whose roots go back to the second half of the nineteenth century, which builds upon classical economics and which still provides a viable framework for research, is the dominant approach to economics and is what you mainly get in the standard textbooks on (micro-)economics. It focuses on the individual actor, who is conceived of as self-interested and rational, attempting to maximise the satisfaction of his or her preferences under conditions of scarcity and therefore being constantly forced to make trade-offs. Neoclassical economics is interested in the effects of individual actors' decisions on markets and on society as a whole. Like the classical theorists the proponents of neoclassical economics see the potential of markets to generate social benefits, wealth and welfare (well-being) out of the self-interested actions of the market participants. But unlike their predecessors, neoclassical theorists have increasingly realised that this is often not the case. Due to a variety of reasons, markets frequently do not work effectively when left alone. Instead, several kinds of market failures repeatedly occur, many of which derive from inexistent or ill-defined property rights.

Three kinds of market failures are especially relevant for environmental economics (and climate economics): the overuse of common property resources, the underproduction of collectively beneficial goods and, finally, externalities.

Fishing areas are a standard example of the overuse of common property resources. As each fisherman is concerned about the maximisation of his individual profit and new fishermen will enter the market as long as their expected individual returns are above their expected (private) average costs overfishing will eventuate. Individual restraint cannot solve the problem, for others will catch the fish a forward-looking fisherman would forgo. Thus, each fisherman has the incentive to fish individually profitable, but collectively unsustainable quantities.

Measures to clean up the environment often amount to the provision of public goods. While private goods are, as the economists call it, rival and exclusive in use (the smartphone I buy can no longer be bought by you and my use of it on the whole excludes your use of it) public goods are nonrival and nonexclusive. At least up to a point they are not used up by the use of others (that I have it does not prevent you from having it too) and their use does not prevent others from using them too. An example of such a public good pertinent to our context is clean air. Now, the difficulty surrounding public goods is that markets tend to undersupply them. Because of the characteristics of public goods, individual actors who would provide them cannot see to it that those who benefit from them pay for them and bear part of their costs. As a result, individual actors have no incentive to produce public goods in sufficient quantities, say to restore clean air in a region.

The problems of the overuse of common property and of the undersupply of public goods can often be overcome by government intervention, be it by assigning property rights, by limiting or regulating use or by providing the public goods. But things are difficult if international or even global measures are needed.

It should be evident that analyses that focus on the motivations of the involved actors and that use the existing incentives and incentive structures to explain why certain environmental damage is created in the first place and why the necessary actions to repair it are not taken, are highly relevant and important. Economics has many pertinent explanations to offer as to why it is especially difficult to stop anthropogenic climate change and fossil fuel-based global warming (e.g. powerful vested interests, coordination problems and other impediments for taking the necessary measures on a global level, incentives to wait, defer and try to free ride). Besides, climate economics has the means to assess the expectable effectiveness of proposed policies that aim at overcoming such difficulties, and it is also able to devise policy proposals of its own.

Interesting and important such inquiries may be though, they will not form the object of the following investigation. The focus will instead be on another fundamental aim of neoclassical environmental economics, namely to determine the 'optimal amount of pollution', which in climate economics translates into the search for the 'optimal amount of global warming'. As this concept and aim is closely connected with the third (and most prominent) of the three kinds of market failure mentioned above, namely externalities and here with the so-called 'negative externalities', I will now focus on this concept in some detail.

3 Negative externalities

Externalities are costs or benefits which market participants impose on or provide to third parties. As the so-called 'positive externalities' are closely related to the provision of public goods, let us focus here solely on the negative externalities, which impose costs on others. These are costs which arise with the production or consumption of goods or services but are not paid for by the producers or the consumers and are therefore not reflected in the market prices. A standard example of negative externalities caused by production is a plant that disposes of the chemicals used in its production by dumping them into a nearby river. This will negatively affect those who are accustomed to using the river downstream, say fishermen, swimmers and the owners of hotels sited at the river, and will impose various costs on them. The fishermen will no longer be able to catch or sell river fish, the swimmers must switch to further away places and the hotel owners will lose customers.

In so far as such costs on third parties are not reflected in the market prices, the market prices incorporate only the private costs of the producers or the consumers and not the social costs of the production or consumption. The social costs are the sum of the private costs and of the costs imposed on the affected third parties. Consequently, the prices paid on the markets are too low (they do not reflect the true costs) and the quantities produced or consumed are therefore too high. Thus, when externalities are involved, the quantities produced or consumed on the market are inefficient, meaning that the production or consumption leads to less overall welfare (well-being) for all the involved people than possible.

But perhaps the way the example of negative externality is put is a bit pessimistic. The plant dumps such an amount of chemicals into the river that fishing is no longer possible or sensible either because the fish are so much reduced or can no longer be eaten and besides it is implied that the river is so much altered (colour? smell?) that the hotels seem to lose even their customers not interested in swimming. So, let us introduce more nuances into our example and confine us to the impacts on fishing. We will assume that the impact of the chemicals on the river fish varies with the amount of chemicals fed into the river, with a small quantity having almost no effect and with the negative impact gradually increasing with the rise of the quantity of the chemicals poured in. We will further make the assumptions that each unit of what is produced in the plant is directly connected with a certain and constant amount of chemical waste to be dumped into the river and that the plant can reduce the amount of the chemical waste only by reducing the quantity of what it produces.

Because the costs imposed on the fishermen are external to the firm, it has no incentive to take them into account. In order to maximise its profits, it will only consider its private costs, which are lower than the social costs, and it will therefore produce too much and will dump too many chemicals. This is, as we have seen, in a certain sense ineffective. The socially effective level of production is that level at which the marginal benefits of the production, i.e. the benefits of producing one more unit, equal the marginal social costs of the production, i.e. the social costs of producing one more unit, and not only the marginal private costs, i.e. the private costs of producing one more unit (the field of study dealing with such calculations is marginal analysis).

The neglect of the external or social costs can be avoided or rectified by trying to make sure that the social costs connected with the production or consumption of a good are internalised. Ways to achieve this are for example prescriptions, fines or taxes. Laws could prohibit polluting more than a certain amount of a substance and punish transgressions with large fines. Or a tax could be raised on certain amounts of pollutive substances which would thereby put a price on certain kinds of pollution. Thus, there seem to be good reasons for market failures in the form of negative externalities to be corrected from the outside by government intervention and that the corresponding markets should not be left alone. But whether such interventions are really necessary or what their extent should be is a matter of lively disagreement between the neoclassical economists and their different schools. While some call for massive and widespread interventions, others are sceptical of the abilities of governments to get things right or to better the outcomes on the markets and are convinced that the interventions will often make things worse.

Economists commonly analyse anthropogenic climate change as a negative externality. By significantly contributing to global warming, the burning of fossil fuels imposes costs on current and future third parties; costs not reflected in the prices we pay for the various forms of our carbon consumption, e.g. the use of electricity, cars, planes, heating our homes or by buying all the diverse goods produced with considerable emissions of carbon dioxide. But as was stressed in the so-called *Stern Review* the externality associated with the burning of fossil fuels:

> has a number of features that together distinguish it from other externalities:
>
> - It is global in its causes and consequences;
> - The impacts of climate change are long-term and persistent;
> - Uncertainties and risks in the economic impacts are pervasive.
> - There is a serious risk of major, irreversible change with non-marginal economic effects.
>
> *(2007: 25)*

In another paper Stern wrote that these externalities 'represent the biggest market failure the world has seen' (Stern 2008: 1).

But before dealing in more detail with the economic treatment of climate change, it will pay off to make several assumptions of the analysis of externalities more explicit or to elaborate on them. As I will ultimately attempt to criticise mainstream environmental and climate economics from the perspective of a rights-based ethics, I will bring up this perspective at a later stage of my analysis as a point of comparison. Subsequent to this section I will explicitly introduce the perspective of a rights-based ethics.

4 A closer look at the assumptions behind the analysis of negative externalities

In order to get a better understanding of what is involved in the analysis of negative externalities, we should, first, make sure that we have a good grasp of the evaluations involved. On the basis of what criteria is the economist able to judge a level of production or consumption as too high and to regard externalities as a market failure to be avoided or corrected? An ethicist or other high-minded person might be inclined to assume that, all other things being equal, it is unfair to impose costs on others against their will. But fairness is normally not a part of the economist's toolbox. The economist is instead concerned with the welfare (well-being) of society (or of the people living in an economic region or in the world) overall.

Markets and the market system have the ability to create social wealth and to raise the level of the welfare (well-being) of the people living in a society. This is conceived as an unintended effect of what the actors or players on the market do or pursue. The individual actors or players pursue their own interests and contribute to the market and enter market transactions because they expect that this will be beneficial to themselves, but by producing for and competing and trading on the market they create a surplus which goes beyond the immediate benefits they intend to reap. The (well-founded) fascination with this phenomenon is palpable in the classical economic treatises like Adam Smith's *Wealth of Nations* (1776) and is still conveyed today by every textbook on the principles of economics.

In the case of externalities, society on the whole is less well off than it could be. The individual pursuit of maximal preference satisfaction leads for all affected people or for society overall to suboptimal results. A higher total surplus, more benefits or welfare, could be derived from market production or consumption and therefore the balance of the overall benefits and costs could be improved. Thus, the point of reference of the evaluations that the economic treatment of negative externalities involves seems to be social welfare, while the evaluative criterion proper seems to be efficiency.

But the understanding of efficiency presumed in this context probably deviates from an everyday understanding of the term. In this latter understanding efficiency signifies, I suppose, an instrumental relation between means and ends and focuses on the question of how well the employment of the means brings about a presupposed end. If with the same input or effort more is achieved or if the same is achieved with less input or effort, the employment of the means is more efficient. Accordingly, such employment can be optimal and suboptimal in terms of efficiency. Besides, there is a direct link between such an efficient pursuit of one's ends and the rationality of an agent who tries to maximise the satisfaction of his preferences. For employing the means at her disposal efficiently (in the sense explained) will allow her to achieve more of what she wants, either more of one specific end or more of her overall ends (because means at her disposal remain for the pursuit of other ends).

At first appearance, the presumed understanding of efficiency in the criticism of externalities might seem quite similar to the understanding of efficiency just explained: markets have the potential to further social welfare and they can do this to different degrees. They work efficiently or optimally if their potential to bring about social welfare is maximally actualised and they work inefficiently or sub-optimally if the actual workings of the markets bring about less social welfare than possible. But the relation between social welfare and the workings of the market is not an instrumental one in the sense explained, for (the workings of) the market cannot simply be treated as a means to the end of social welfare which the market players have. We have seen that it is instead assumed that the market players by and large pursue their own interests and not the maximisation of social welfare. While it might be the case that the (open) maximisation of one's self-interest is counter-productive and that people are on the whole better off when they are prepared to restrict the pursuit of their self-interest (see Gauthier 1986), there is certainly no simple connection between the maximisation of social welfare and rationality. The maximisation of social welfare may be conducive to the interests of many people, but it is far from clear that it will make all people better off, let alone contribute to the maximisation of their self-interest. For individual players, it might best serve their interests to neglect the social costs and to impose externalities on others, e.g. to continue with fossil fuel-based production or consumption.

Thus, by addressing the market failure of externalities as inefficiencies the economists disguise, most probably also to themselves, that they treat the max-imisation of social welfare as an end that ought to be pursued and that they therefore hold it to be right or required to restrict the self-interested actions of individual market players when these conflict with this end. Now, to hold one required to restrict the pursuit of one's interests for the importance of the interests of others is a decisive characteristic of moral evaluations and norms. Hence the analysis is based on moral judgements and prescriptions. But to discern this is only to discern a certain kind of judgement and does as such imply nothing about its quality. It remains to be seen whether the moral claims behind the analysis of the economists are good or convincing. In any case, they are to be distinguished from the economic analysis proper.

A second point to note is that the proposed internalisation of social costs does not amount to the complete avoidance of costs to third parties but only to a certain reduction of these costs. To return to our example of the plant dumping chemicals into a nearby river, the economic analysis will normally not lead to the recom-mendation that the plant not pollute the river at all, but that its decision of how much to pollute reflect the social costs. To put it more generally, social welfare is on the whole not maximised by forgoing all environmental pollution, but by restricting it to that amount that aligns its benefits with the (real) costs. All in all, you cannot have production or consumption and a functioning market economy without any negative impacts on the environment and on third parties. But many of these impacts and a certain amount of them are worth the cost, because the benefits derived from them outweigh the costs, because social welfare is increased or the affected people are benefited overall. It would therefore be irrational, suboptimal or wrong to avoid certain pollution and damage to the environment if certain benefits could not be had without them. An important consequence of this is that environmental pollution and damage cannot only be too high but also too low. From this perspective, the question what the optimum amount of environmental pollution (and resource use) is becomes understandable, sensible and important. It is one of the guiding questions, if not the guiding question, of neoclassical natural resource and environmental economics.

But while it is important to ask what the optimal amount of pollution is much depends on how one attempts to answer this question. In the following I would like to highlight mainly two things. First, I would like to point out that the way neoclassical natural resource and environmental economics evaluates the benefits and costs of pollution does not adequately reflect the rights of the involved parties. Second, I would like to emphasise that the general importance of determining the optimal pollution notwithstanding one must be more prepared than the neoclassical economists seem to be that concerning certain kinds of pollution the optimal amount of pollution might be (close to) zero.

To begin with, the outlined economic approach sees the value of the environment and of functioning ecosystems confined to (or at least deals with it only in so far as) the benefits conveyed to the economy and to market participants to the extent that they are willing to pay for them. Thus, a clean river alive with fish will have a direct market value, say, for fishermen or for people working in the tourist business. Consumers will be prepared to incur costs in order to visit nice places, to hike in forests or to swim in seas. There is also the indirect market value of so-called 'ecosystem services' when functioning ecosystems provide, for example, protection against floods, storms or droughts. Besides such use values economists also acknowledge non-use values when people are prepared to pay for the protection of the environment or of ecosystems because they want them to exist or to be preserved for one's own potential later use or for the use of later generations. Economists have developed various methods to measure the willingness to pay for such existence, option and bequest values of the individual persons or their willingness to accept losses of them when compensated. As the values and valuations are expressed in monetary terms the benefits and costs can ultimately easily be offset against each other.

Such an approach is often criticised because it does not do justice to the intrinsic value of the environment, ecosystems or plant and animal species. But even if it is appropriate to assume such intrinsic value, one should be aware that intrinsic value can come in degrees and accordingly some entity can possess more or less intrinsic value than another. Thus, even if it is plausible to conceive of the environment, of ecosystems or species as imbued with intrinsic value, this does not as such imply that this value cannot be overridden by the higher intrinsic value of persons and that the morally crucial aspect is ultimately not the relevance of an intact environment and intact ecosystems for the ability of each and any person to lead a self-fulfilling life. From the perspective of a rights-based ethics the decisive question is not whether the economic valuations of the environment sufficiently reflect its intrinsic value, but whether the monetary valuations of the use and non-use values of the different aspects of the environment and the corresponding cost–benefit analysis do sufficiently reflect the rights of all affected people.

Thus, a moral evaluation based on the rights of people is not readily in opposition to the economic approach to allow for environmental pollution or damage and to search for an optimal amount of environmental pollution. Any attempt of persons to lead a self-fulfilling life will probably have an impact on the environment. Besides it is certainly correct that a functioning market economy cannot be had without environmental damage. At the same time the relevance of the wealth-creating features of a functioning market economy for the provision and the protection of the rights of persons can hardly be overrated. My claim is not that a market economy will automatically provide for the rights of the affected persons, but that if certain framework conditions, including welfare state measures, are in place, a market economy is at least for the time being instrumental to the provision and the protection of rights. In terms of its potential to create sufficient wealth for all it is probably correct to hold that a market economy represents the best economic system that we know so far. Thus, environmental damage can from the perspective of a rights-based ethics be not only morally permissible but also morally required.

This is of course no licence for any kind or amount of environmental pollution or damage. It is also not to be expected that the ways or degrees of environmental pollution justified by the economic analysis will in any case be in accordance with the evaluations made from the perspective of the rights of all affected persons. Moreover, despite the moral relevance of a functioning market economy the existing market based economic system or market economies seem to be unsustainable because of their impact on the environment, the involved destruction of ecosystems, elimination of species and overuse of natural resources. It is much disputed whether this betrays a sort of 'system error', i.e. an ultimately ineliminable problem, of market economies or whether it constitutes a serious but eventually rectifiable problem (for such an appraisal, see, e.g., Helm 2015). But even if it turned out that the market economy is inherently unsustainable, we would have to recognise that so far, we neither have a viable alternative to hand and nor do we know how to bring about the necessary transformations. Thus at least for the time being the necessary corrections have to be achieved within the existing system as far as possible. This is especially important in the context of climate change, because here we seem to be confronted with only a small window of opportunity to set things right.

Finally, it is important to note that from the fact that the search for the optimal amount of environmental pollution or damage is sensible we cannot infer without further argument that this will also be the case for special kinds or areas of environmental pollution at least as long as we preserve the meaning of 'optimal amount' as signifying an amount which is neither too low nor too high. For it is at least conceivable that with regard to some kinds of environmental pollution any pollution of this kind will be too high. Of course, nothing prevents us from using 'optimal amount of pollution' in a technical sense which also allows for 'zero pollution'. But then my initial point is just to be restated as follows: despite the fact that generally speaking the amount of environmental pollution may be too low one must always be prepared that concerning particular kinds or areas of environmental pollution any pollution may be too high. Thus, the assumption that in particular applications or problem areas of environmental pollution or damage the optimal amount of pollution is not zero pollution is always in need of an argument. As a consequence, it is not possible to infer without further argument from the fact that generally speaking the search for an optimal, non-zero amount of environmental pollution is justified that the search for an optimal, non-zero amount of global warming is also justified. I am not claiming here that this search cannot be justified. I am only claiming that such a justification cannot be waived.

With this remark, I would like to close the second point of my analysis of the economic treatment of negative externalities focusing on the extent of the proposed reduction of social costs and turn to a third and final point. We have already seen that the economic treatment of negative externalities is guided by the aim of the maximisation of social welfare and that this aim is morally charged. If this is so the evaluations constitutive of this will also constitute moral evaluations and are therefore also open to ethical criticism.

The two most important features of the maximisation of social welfare taken as a moral aim are on the one hand that social welfare is understood as a function of individual welfare and on the other hand that social welfare is understood as an aggregate of individual welfare. This implicates that the effects, benefits and costs on all involved people are taken into account. However, only the aggregative results are decisive and thus a distribution of the benefits and costs of the involved people that leads to the maximum of the achievable social welfare. As a consequence, any individual costs are justified in so far as they are part of a distribution of costs and benefits which will lead to the maximisation of overall social welfare. This can involve a treatment of persons which is normatively not very plausible or at least at odds with the view that people possess equal moral rights. Thus, before looking at how mainstream climate economics attempts to determine the optimal amount of global warming, let us have at least a short look at rights-based moral theories (for a more detailed treatment of rights, see Chapter 2).

5 A short look at rights-based moral theories

Irrespective of the many differences between rights-based moral theories, they all share at their core the tenet that persons possess a fundamental moral importance which grounds an entitlement that certain of their fundamental interests be mutually respected. These are the rights the persons possess. The rights are again the basis and rationale of the duties all persons have, namely to respect the rights of persons. A rights-based ethical theory therefore judges actions, institutional settings or policies by the consequences on the rights of all affected persons. I will presuppose here that all persons possess equal rights to the necessary preconditions for being able to lead a self-fulfilling life, like life, physical integrity, property, and that these rights form a certain hierarchy depending on their importance for being able to lead one's life. Therefore, situationally the life of one person can take precedence over the property of another person (if the property in question is not needed for survival). But all persons ultimately constitute strict normative limits to each other and must not be sacrificed for the well-being of others. Thus rights-based theories are often not aggregative as is maximisation of social welfare. I will also presuppose that the rights of people are not only negative rights, i.e. rights to the forbearance of certain actions, but also positive rights, i.e. rights to assistance, if important rights are threatened, a person cannot help herself and another person (or other persons collectively) can help without endangering her (their) own rights of the same or a higher level as the threatened right. But some rights-based theories acknowledge only negative rights. Finally, the rights of persons include a right to the effective protection of their rights. This makes certain institutions, like state and international institutions and a functioning economic system, necessary.

This is not the place to justify these claims (but see, e.g., Gewirth 1978, Shue 1996, Steigleder 1999). Here I would like to confine myself to the remark that the outlined theory is much in agreement with the nationally or internationally acknowledged basic or human rights.

6 In search of the optimal amount of global warming

From a practical or policy perspective, two questions concerning anthropogenic climate change are arguably the most fundamental ones. One is the question what increase in average global surface temperature as compared to pre-industrial levels will be still tolerable. The increase in carbon dioxide due to the burning of fossil fuels, deforestation and soil use is the main cause of global warming. It is a more recent discovery that the emitted carbon dioxide that is not absorbed by the oceans, by plants or soils, has a long persistence time in the atmosphere lasting hundreds or even thousands of years. Thus, the carbon dioxide accumulates in the atmosphere and the increase in average global temperature is mainly a function of the cumulative amount of carbon dioxide. Therefore, the second most funda-mental question concerning climate change is what cumulative amount of carbon or carbon dioxide in the atmosphere corresponds to what increase in average global temperature. The two questions could be condensed into the question of what cumulative amount of carbon in the atmosphere is tolerable.

The standard answers to the two questions are that the increase in average global temperature should be limited to 2 °C and that this corresponds to a cumulative amount of 1 teraton of carbon (1 tt = 1 trillion tons) in the atmosphere. But this is far from certain. Others claim that 700 gigatons of carbon (1 gt = 1 billion tons) will already lead to the increase of 2 °C (note that 1 ton of carbon equals 3.67 tons of carbon dioxide). This makes a huge difference. As the cumulative amount of carbon in the atmosphere so far is estimated to lie somewhere between 590 and

600 gt, under business as usual 700 gt might be hit in about ten years while 1 tt might be approached somewhere between 2040 and 2050.

The significance of the fact that carbon dioxide accumulates in the atmosphere and that human-induced global warming is a function mainly of the cumulative amount of carbon dioxide is on the one hand that dangerous climate change can ultimately not be avoided by a mere reduction but only by an almost complete avoidance of further emissions of carbon dioxide on a global basis and on the other hand that the moment at which this can still be achieved can be missed. But what amount of increase in average global temperatures constitutes dangerous climate change? The rationale behind the claim that global warming should be limited to 2 °C is that under these conditions a 50 per cent chance exists that the effects of the corresponding climate change will be on the whole still 'tolerable' and 'manageable'. Note that even this estimate involves a 50 per cent or by most standards very high risk that the effects will on the whole not be tolerable or manageable. It is therefore argued that the aim of limiting global warming by 2 °C should be reduced to a target of 1.5 °C.

It is striking that in mainstream climate economics the 2 °C aim is often or even mostly considered as being too low. Instead (up to) 3 °C or even more are proposed as better targets. The respective targets derive from the attempt to determine the optimal amount of global warming. As we already know from our examination of the economic treatment of negative externalities, the optimal amount of global warming is considered as that amount which aligns the (marginal) social benefits and costs of the production and consumption which lead to global warming on the one hand and of the measures effecting (changing) the existing production and consumption patterns in order to limit global warming on the other hand. In comparison to the treatment of the relatively simple externalities considered so far, the cost–benefit analysis employed in this context involves some complexities many of which are not confined to climate change but are especially pertinent to it.

Of these complexities, the perhaps most important one is to take account of the huge time frame climate change involves. While the effects of global warming have already been experienced globally for many years and while for instance by way of increased heat waves and other extreme weather events climate change has already taken a considerable death toll, the costs of uninhibited global warming will to a much greater extent and increasingly felt in the future and will over hundreds of years progressively affect future generations to come. Thus, not only the benefits and costs of different measures will accrue at different times, but also the differences in the timing of measures will be connected with different benefits and costs.

It is important to be clear on what the respective costs and benefits are in this context. On the one hand, the benefits and costs of different levels of climate change and global warming are considered. Here the benefits are mainly the benefits producers and consumers derive from the use and burning of fossil fuels. But the warming caused by the carbon emissions might also be connected with certain benefits, at least up to a certain level. For instance, the cold and harsh climates in the polar regions of the north might be mitigated, the warming of the Arctic Sea will make the passage of ships and the mining of natural resources possible or easier, and the increased presence of carbon dioxide in the air might be conducive to the growth of some crops and thus increase yields. The costs are the many negative effects to be expected in connection with global warming, e.g. increased droughts, floods, torrential rains, storms, heat waves, rising sea levels, crop losses, starvation, inhabitability of land, climate induced forced migration, the spread of tropical diseases to formerly milder climatic zones, species loss on an increasing scale, death. A more recent discovery is that the accumulation of carbon dioxide emissions has led to a progressive acidification of the oceans, which may give rise to potentially huge ecological and economic damage. On the other hand, the costs of different measures of reducing and stopping carbon emissions in different time frames and with different depths of intervention and paces in terms of losses in production and consumption are compared with the benefits of the damage avoided which come along with different levels of global warming.

Things are complicated by the fact that two different strategies seem to be available for combating or preventing the negative effects of climate change. The first strategy is called 'mitigation' and aims at the prevention or limitation of global warming mostly by the reduction of the emissions of carbon dioxide and other greenhouse gases. The second strategy is called 'adaptation' and aims at combating and reducing the negative effects connected with global warming, e.g. better irrigation or sea water desalination in order to prevent or confront droughts, improved or more widespread air conditioning in order to resist heat waves and the building of dykes or migration as a protection against rising sea levels. This complicates the cost–benefit analyses because for at least up to a certain level of global warming one must decide whether one should take into account the expected costs of certain unchecked damage which results from climate change or the expected costs of the different measures aimed at preventing the damage from coming into effect. Economists recommend taking the latter route. It is also seen to have the advantage of heightening our awareness of which damage can be potentially hedged and which cannot.

While the attempted cost–benefit analyses can in many ways be instructive they are nonetheless in many respects deeply problematic. In the following I will try to emphasise some of the most important problems.

7 Valuing the life of (future) people in monetary terms

As already mentioned, many (thousands of) people have already died due to current anthropogenic climate change. With the increase in global warming much more people will die owing to climate-related causes. The economic cost–benefit analysis, which aims at determining the optimal level of global warming, treats these fatalities as costs and tries to measure them in monetary terms. For this it will normally plug into the equations a standard price in terms of which the value of a statistical life is measured. We cannot go into the details here of the methods or considerations on the basis of which the value of a statistical life is determined. One method is to derive such a value from the willingness of workers to accept certain (relatively small) work-related risks of death for a certain increase of payment. Another and to my mind more sensible method is to compare the implied costs of preventing a fatality which come along with different safety measures and to try to standardise the cost or value of preventing a fatality in order to be able to compare the effectiveness of different measures.

Here, I would like to argue for two claims. First, it is often sensible and unavoidable to base decisions whether to save the lives of people on the monetary costs involved, and cost–benefit analyses can be important instruments in assisting such decisions. Second, the considerations justifying such decisions do not license the evaluations of the life or death of future people in monetary terms as they are undertaken in the context of the climate change-related cost–benefit analyses. To assume that one may proceed from the first kind of evaluation to the second kind, or to overlook that really different kinds of evaluations are involved, is a widespread mistake in cost–benefit analyses. At its root is the neglect of distinguishing between approaching existing risks or risk constellations and the imposition or creation of new risks.

When approaching existing risks or risk constellations policymakers deal with risks from the outside or from an external perspective. In this perspective, the question of the genesis of the risks is of at most secondary importance. The risk constellations may be the result of many actions by which certain agents have recklessly created risks (think e.g. of financial markets) or the risks may have built up unnoticed behind the backs of the involved parties, for instance due to cumulative effects (think e.g. again of financial markets). The risks may result from the human condition, our natural environment or from the forces of nature. In the face of different existing risk constellations an important policy question is which constellations or problem situation should be given priority. Should for instance rail safety or road safety be improved, this disease or that disease be combated by means of screenings, this or that chemical content in drinking water be reduced? In the context of such questions and in the face of scarce resources an important consideration is how many lives can be saved by which measures and at what cost or which investments in possible improvements or prevention will probably save more lives. It might turn out that the projected costs of preventing a fatality resulting from certain rail safety improvements are much higher than those resulting from certain road safety improvements. All things being equal, this might be both an economically and a morally good reason to prioritise the road safety measures over the rail safety measures (for an argument that things are often not equal, see Wolff 2006; 2007).

It is important to note that the distributive focus of rights-based ethical theories notwithstanding, such theories have many areas of application where they prescribe the pursuit of a maximising strategy. This is the case when those responsible for enacting or devising a certain policy must take an external perspective on a situation or problem situation, because the responsible persons do not have special obligations to anyone affected and no one affected has special rights to be given priority. In such situations or constellations, the appropriate treatment of all affected is to try to help, save (etc.) as many people as possible. For this is the only way to do justice both to the fact that each of the affected persons possesses the same utmost moral importance and that none possesses any special claim to special considerations.

If only the second (no special claim) condition were relevant, one could argue that it is unessential who is (and thus how many people are) saved, because none of those who are not helped can complain, for none has a right to be treated with priority. But if more can be helped, it betrays a neglect of or disrespect to the moral status of all the affected when one does not try to do so. Therefore, all else being equal, that strategy has to be chosen which will probably save as much people as possible, and it follows (at least in part) from this strategy whom one must try to save. Take as an example an accident involving many severely injured people. In order to save as many people as possible the emergency physicians and paramedics arriving on the scene may choose the strategy of 'triage'. In this the injured are first divided into the three groups of those who will probably survive without help, those who will probably die even with help and those who will probably survive with help, and then one concentrates only on those in the third group.

A distinction must be made then between the choice involved in giving priority to one existing risk or risk constellation over another, and the evaluation of the creation of risks affecting others. Here the focus is on the agent or agents who generate the possibility that others will be harmed. Because as agents they are able to control what they do, it depends on them whether an additional risk of a certain quality comes into the world or not. Whether it is permissible to impose a certain risk on others depends on the answers to the following questions (for a more detailed account of the foundations of a rights-based risk ethics, see Steigleder 2016). First, what is the possible impact of the imposed risks on the rights of those affected by the risk imposition? (What is the potential harm? Which rights are endangered?) Second, how will an agent be affected in her rights if she is not allowed to perform the actions connected with this risk imposition? Third, how do the respective impacts on the rights of the affected people and on the rights of the agents compare? The important point to note is that the agent and the recipients of her actions possess the same rights to the preconditions necessary for being able to lead a self-fulfilling life. If the possible impact of the imposed risks on the rights of the affected people is relatively low, while the impact of the prohibition of the actions connected with the risks on the ability of the agent to lead a self-fulfilling life is high, then the prohibition will be disproportionate and unjustified. The agent has a right to perform the actions which are connected with the risks in question. But if the possible impact of the imposed risks on the rights of the affected people is high, while the impact of the prohibition of the actions connected with the risks on the ability of the agent to lead a self-fulfilling live is relatively low, then the prohibition is not disproportionate and therefore in principle justified. Persons have a right not to be exposed to such risks without justifying reasons.

There may be border cases where it is not clear whose rights should take precedence, but this does not speak against the many cases in which the criterion allows one to decide which risk impositions are morally permissible and which are (in principle) morally wrong and therefore morally prohibited. This is always to be assumed when actions involve or contribute to the imposition of clear risks of death, severe physical injury or extensive disruptions of the preconditions of being able to lead a self-fulfilling life. As already suggested, there can be justifying reasons for the imposition of risks which are in principle prohibited. Here, I will only mention two such reasons or criteria. One criterion is consensus. The explicit and free and informed consent of an affected person that a certain prohibited risk is imposed on her can often justify the imposition of the risk. Another criterion is what one might call the normative inevitability of prohibited risks. Sometimes greater risks for all affected persons can only be avoided by imposing relatively smaller risks on them. This criterion can justify for instance risks which are connected with certain technologies, technological systems or modes of social organisation.

Now, the emission of carbon dioxide and the corresponding global warming imposes not only risks of grave harms on existing people but also risks of much greater harm (quantitatively as well as qualitatively) on future people. If we concentrate for the moment on the possible harms to future people, these can neither be justified by the consensus criterion nor by the normative inevitability criterion, because it seems not to be the case that even greater risks of harm can be averted from the people living in the future only through global warming or in connection with it. Thus, as it is in principle (strongly) forbidden to create or increase the risks of global warming, it is also in principle (strongly) forbidden to contribute to global warming by further emissions of carbon dioxide.

But things are, of course, more complicated. First, global warming is a cumulative effect of the many carbon dioxide emissions. While (almost) any emission of carbon dioxide contributes to the accumulation of carbon in the atmosphere, taken individually they will mostly be marginal and no single actor can stop global warming or avert the potential dangers connected to it. This can only be achieved by comprehensive and far-reaching policies. One question is what the aim of such policies must be. In light of the risks involved, the answer to this question is that the aim must be to stop global emissions of carbon dioxide as quickly and as comprehensively as possible. In contrast to this, mainstream climate economics assumes considerably more global warming should be allowed and that therefore for the time being some measures, but no drastic measures should be taken.

Second, even if there is a need to proceed as fast as possible, one must acknowledge that the developed and emerging economies are based on fossil fuels and that the transition to a non-fossil fuel-based economy will take time. To ignore this would risk serious disruptions of the economy and thereby endanger the livelihood and thus the rights of many people. Third, as Henry Shue (2014: 333–337) has pointed out, for many poor people fossil fuels, especially coal, are the only fuels they can afford. Neither are they able to forgo them without help, nor will they be able to stand increases in their price which might result from policies aimed at overcoming the use of fossil fuels. Shue has shown that it is of the utmost importance that one is always aware of such potentially far-reaching side effects of well-meant policies and is prepared to flank them by the necessary countermeasures.

If global warming and emitting carbon dioxide are to be understood as risk creation, they constitute large-scale infringements of the most basic rights of people living in the future (as well as of people living today). These can only be justified in so far as they cannot be avoided without having the same consequences on the rights of the agents themselves or their contemporaries. But as long as the destruction of functioning market economies by imprudent or overambitious measures which aim at a fossil fuel-free economy at a moment's notice is avoided, this will not be the case. For the many hardships and dangers connected with the transition to a fossil fuel-free economy can be alleviated by welfare state measures and other assistance. Thus, there is the double duty both of restricting global warming and the emissions of carbon dioxide as fast as possible and of organising the assistance necessary to avoid threats to the livelihood of those negatively affected by the implementation of this.

The important point to note is that for instance unemployment or a loss in the standard of living well above subsistence level, regrettable as they may be, do not compare with the loss of life, of the basis of one's existence, or with debilitating injuries or diseases. But this gets lost when, as it is the case in the climate economic cost–benefit analyses, the different costs and benefits are all measured in monetary terms. For then the projected decline in global economic output can potentially outweigh the calculated costs of the projected number of lives lost. Furthermore, there is no justification for putting into these calculations the numbers derived from the attempted standardisation of the values of preventing a fatality (as is legitimately done in the context of tackling existing risk constellations).

8 The discounting of future damage and people

As already mentioned, the climate economic cost–benefit analysis must deal with different benefits and costs accruing at different times. In finance, in order to be able to compare different investment opportunities or financial instruments, the present value of future payments or payoffs is calculated. The reason behind this is that one normally prefers having a dollar today than waiting for a year, because the value of a dollar today is greater than the value of the dollar one will get in a year. For one could invest today's dollar so that it will have earned interest in a year, and $X (1 + r)$, where r stands for the interest rate, is more than $X (if r is positive). Thus, the present value of $X next year in the context of an investment that constantly earns an interest of r per year is $X / (1 + r)$. If interest compounds the present value of an amount of money $X in a certain number of years t (next year t equals 1, in two years t equals 2, in ten years t equals 10 and so on) is $X / (1 - r)^t$. So, if r is 5 per cent or 0.05 (in these days of low interest rates this may sound a bit outdated or futuristic, just as you like), the present value of a dollar in a year is about $0.95, of a dollar in two years is about $0.90, of a dollar in ten years is about

$0.61 and of a dollar in 50 years is less than $0.09. A further reason why one prefers money today to money in the future is what is called 'time preference'. Normally one does not like to postpone consumption and thus prefers having money available today to having it later (this topic is discussed in more detail in Chapter 9) (one may interpret the interest payments as compensation for postponing the use of money and the differences in the interest rates of different investments as surcharges depending on different risks connected with the investments. The higher the risks the higher the risk premium).

In economic cost–benefit analyses (including climate economic analyses) that deal with costs and benefits accruing at (or over) different times, the present value of all the costs and benefits is calculated so as to be able to compare them. In order to be able to calculate the present value a discount rate r has to be chosen. It can easily be seen that the level of the discount rate chosen will have a huge impact on the results and recommendations of any climate economic cost–benefit analysis. For the more the future costs and benefits are discounted, the more weight is given to the present costs and benefits. Now, a significant part of the future costs consists in the monetary value of climate-related premature deaths of the people living (at different times) in the future and in the monetary value of the many other climate-related negative effects on the future people. Likewise, a significant part of the future benefits accrues from the avoidance – by means of mitigating global warming – of the costs these premature deaths and negative effects would mean. Thus, the level of the discount rate incorporates at least in part a measure of how much more significance is attributed to the costs and benefits accruing to the people living today and ultimately to the people living today themselves in comparison to the costs and benefits accruing to the future people and to these future people themselves. For while in the relatively small time horizon of financial investments the different payoffs in principle accrue to the same people at different times, the costs and benefits connected with the long time horizon of global warming will accrue to people different from those making the decisions or to whom the recommendations are made. So, with what justification can the calculation of the present value of future costs and benefits be transferred from the area of financial or other investments to the long time horizon of climate economic cost–benefit analyses?

There are mainly two different approaches to determining the discount rate to be applied in such analyses: a descriptive and a prescriptive one. The descriptive approach tries to derive the discount rate from the going interest rates on the markets. The rationale behind this is to orient the discount rate on how the actors on the markets in reality discount costs and benefits accruing in the future in order to calculate their present values. However, there is no single going interest rate, but many different ones. So, which of them should guide the discount rate to be employed in the climate economic cost–benefit analyses or by what method and considerations should the different interest rates be weighed to derive a discount rate which still reflects how economic actors actually behave? More importantly, why should one suppose that (rational) actors who use (different) interest rates for comparing costs and benefits which they expect to accrue to themselves at different times from different assets will also use this method for comparing the costs and benefits of different policies to them and to their contemporaries on the one hand and to the (distinct) people living at different times in the future on the other hand?

The prescriptive approach is oriented towards the aim of maximising social welfare from the perspective of today's actors. The discount rate proposed is a composite of especially two elements. A first element is the pure rate of time preference of those living and acting today. As we have seen, a (positive) discount rate based on time preference implies that the present actors may or should hold themselves and the costs and benefits accruing to them as having priority over the people living in the future and the costs and benefits accruing to the future people. A second element is the expectation that due to continuing economic growth, as measured in terms of economic output, the people living in the future will be much better off than we are today and will therefore be better positioned to deal with the problems caused by (certain levels) of global warming. For instance, an annual growth of the world economy by 3 per cent will lead to a more than fourfold increase in the level of prosperity after 50 years and to a more than sixteenfold increase in the level of prosperity after 100 years. In order to be able to compare the different economic circumstances against the backdrop of which the climate-related costs and benefits are perceived, the expected economic growth rate is included in the discount rate usually adjusted (multiplied) by a factor which accounts for the changing (diminishing) impact additional costs or benefits have with increasing income. Thus, in the prescriptive approach the proposed discount rate is basically the sum of the pure rate of time preference and of the weighted rate of the expected annual economic growth.

The already mentioned *Stern Review* caused uproar among climate economists because it used the prescriptive approach and argued for moral reasons that the pure rate of time preference must be (almost) zero. Otherwise the fundamental normative equality of all persons, which cannot depend on where or when (today or in the nearer or further-away future) a person lives, is neglected. Stern also incorporated a relatively low expectation of global annual economic growth, so that the *Stern Review* worked with a discount rate of 1.4 per cent (instead of the much higher discount rates often used in climate economic cost–benefit analyses). A consequence of the comparatively low discount rate used by Stern is that the future costs of unmitigated climate change are expected to be quite high. At the same time Stern came to the conclusion that the costs of the necessary measures of mitigation to avoid the future damage are relatively low.

Therefore, the *Stern Review* recommends immediate and extensive measures of mitigation confronting global warming. It does this by working within the conventional neoclassical framework of climate economics. Apparently, many of the other members of the guild considered this being more challenging and deserving of more censure than the work of any other dissenting climate economist criticising the framework itself. Let us just look at three criticisms levelled against Stern's morally motivated choice of an almost zero-time preference.

One criticism is that the approach is paternalistic (see Nordhaus 2007: 691–693; Weitzman 2007: 707). It presents, it is said, the approach of the social planner who tries to impose the moral (and other) aspects of his world view on the people living today. To this e.g. William D. Nordhaus objects in mainly two ways. First, one should better orient oneself on how people and countries actually behave and on what they base their investment decisions (namely, on the real return of capital). Thus, Nordhaus favours the descriptive over the prescriptive approach. But Nordhaus sees the role of economics not confined to the prediction of what economic decisions will be made confronting increasing climate change. Instead, climate economics should give guidance as to how people and countries can employ efficient climate policies.[1] We have already seen that the 'efficiency' of such efficient measures is not necessarily in the self-interest of the affected people, but is guided by a morally normative aim (the maximisation of social welfare), an aim that is not argued for. For Nordhaus, as a typical (and leading) neoclassical economist, climate policy seems to come down to the timing and scope of investment and savings decisions, the resulting economic growth and capital accumulation. Climate change poses a certain threat on future economic growth and the corresponding economic wealth. Therefore, measures to counter global warming will have to be taken. But one should not expect the corresponding investment decisions to be based on new or far-fetched criteria. Within this diagnosis prediction and prescription seem to overlap. Neither will people base their climate-related investment decisions on new criteria nor are they (morally) required to do so.

The sense of calm Nordhaus radiates in his analysis irrespective of his palpable annoyance about the *Stern Review* seems to derive from the fact that the impacts of different climate policies seem to come down for him to more or less future wealth of people who will in all probability be much better off than we are. But if global warming will increasingly be a matter of life and death, then a discount rate can contribute to obscure this (possible) fact and to obscure the moral relevance of it. This makes Nordhaus's second objection interesting. It says that Stern's choice of an almost zero rate of time preference is, without arguments, based on utilitarianism. As utilitarianism is much disputed and rivalled by many other normative theories ranging from Rawls to the 'morals of major religions' (Nordhaus 2007: 693), Stern should not feel justified to prescribe utilitarianism to non-believers.

But, as far as I can see, Stern's choice of the rate of an almost zero-time preference is not based on utilitarianism, but on the equal moral status of each and any person (wherever and whenever she lives) (see Stern 2007: 35). This could well be considered a common denominator of many (most?) theories of normative ethics, in any case of utilitarianism in all its variants and of Rawls's theory, but perhaps not of all 'morals of major religions'. But more importantly, it is difficult to see what convincing argument could be raised against this basic presumption. And in case I have misinterpreted the somewhat vague formulations in Stern, it should be clear that the zero rate of time preference is in intergenerational matters well founded, given the presumption of the equal moral status of all people.

Dieter Helm interprets Stern as prescribing strict impartiality 'through time', and objects that this is not the way the world functions nor how we behave (Helm 2013: 62–67). He refers to David Hume (1711–1776) (see also Helm 2011: 244–247) who has pointed out that we consider people in our vicinity as being more important to us than distant strangers. This is of course an important observation, but it is not clear how relevant it is in the context of fixing a discount rate concerning the benefits and costs to future people. First, times have changed since Hume. The impact of our actions can be much more far-reaching both in space and time than Hume could ever imagine. Second, in the context of carbon emissions we are not concerned with possible positive duties, i.e. duties of assistance, but with negative duties to avoid inflicting harms on other. It is certainly not the case that our duties not to inflict harm on others are confined to our near vicinity. This leads to a third point, namely the distinction between what ought to be done and what is normally done. While Helm is certainly right that incentives are important and that the question of what ought to be done cannot be answered by a neglect of our motivational possibilities, it is nevertheless important to keep the questions distinct. Normally, we have first to answer the question of what ought to be done and then the question of how the existing incentive structures can be brought in line with this. While the urgency and extent of action demanded by Stern deviates from what climate economists usually recommend, it does not seem to be in any way far-fetched or unfulfillable, even if many very difficult policy questions on how the necessary measures could be taken on a global level remain open. Relating to this, Helm makes the important point that we will possibly have stronger incentives to take action when we focus more on the dangers of climate change on us and our children than on future people (Helm 2013: 65). Fourth, from the equal moral status of all people, which Stern presupposes, the strict impartiality Helm imputes to Stern does not necessarily follow, as I will try to explain in connection with the following point.

A further criticism of a zero rate of time preference is based on the fear that the potentially infinite time horizon of future generations could lead to a potentially infinite amount of future costs or benefits, so that the people living today are required to neglect their comparably tiny welfare in order to serve the welfare of future generations (see Nordhaus 2013: 192f.). But from the perspective of a rights-based theory, which presupposes the equal moral status of all people, this is not the case. All people, wherever and whenever they live, possess the same rights, but these rights are to be approached from the internal perspective of the agents. As no person does possess more rights to the necessary preconditions to lead a self-fulfilling life than any other person, no agent can ever be required to give up her basic rights. In this regard, the asymmetry between negative and positive rights is important. We are obliged not to inflict (serious) harms on others, but our obligations to help others are limited (for an account of some of the intricacies related to harming future people, see Steigleder 2016).

It was not my aim to defend the *Stern Review* here, but to show that the problematic implications of measuring the death and serious infringements of people in monetary terms as it is done in climate economic cost–benefit analyses are dramatically increased by discounting these measurements regarding future people.

9 Discounting by probabilities

There is an additional way of discounting the future costs and benefits involved in climate economic cost–benefit analyses and this is by introducing probability weights. If for instance the occurrence of a future damage of say $1 million has only a probability of 10 per cent, the expected value of the future damage is calculated by multiplying the projected costs and the probability number (0.1 x $1,000,000 = $100,000). This approach is burdened with mainly two further problems. First, there are on the whole no reliable ways to derive the probability numbers. The numbers constitute subjective estimates which create the appearance of precision. Second, it seems quite clear that global warming will not develop in linear ways. Positive and negative feedback mechanisms are involved and there are so-called 'tipping points' (or 'points of no return') which lead to processes which can no longer be stopped. We do not know where the different tipping points lie and when developments like sea level rise and climate change will switch from linear to exponential. We only know that this can occur all of a sudden and that, looking at paleoclimatic precedence, 2 °C could already bring us into the danger zone. In short, potential catastrophes are lurking and ultimately, we must treat them as uncertainties.[2] The rosy picture of ever-increasing economic growth is far from certain, and global warming and other environmental hazards may well have the consequence that the people living in the future will have a much lower living standard than we have. The normative consequence of all this can only be to try to stop global warming as quickly, extensively and effectively as possible – without endangering the basic rights of the people who will be affected by our measures.

10 Concluding remarks

In this chapter I tried to show that despite the many positive uses economic cost–benefit analyses may have, current mainstream climate economic cost–benefit analyses are deeply flawed and even dangerous. For they convey the picture that the current anthropogenic global warming is a less urgent problem than it actually is, and they do not adequately deal with the dangers to the life and the physical and psychological integrity of the affected people. As one should expect from the prescription of aims like the optimum amount of global warming, mainstream climate economics involves many morally normative judgements. I have tried to make some of them more visible and I have pointed to their problems. In my opinion climate economics should content itself with finding and evaluating means for given aims, like the aim of stopping global warming as quickly and extensively as possible. Here its help is urgently needed.

Notes

1 See Nordhaus (2007: 692): 'The calculations of changes in world welfare from efficient climate-change policies examine potential improvements within the context of the existing distribution of income and investments across space and time'.
2 This is taken seriously by some economists: see Weitzman (2009); Weitzman and Wagner (2015).

Bibliography

Ackerman, Frank. 2009. *Can we Afford the Future? Economics in a Warming World*. London and New York: Zed Books.
Ackerman, Frank and Elisabeth Stanton. 2014. *Climate Economics. The State of the Art.* Abingdon: Routledge.
Gauthier, David. 1986. *Morals by Agreement*. Oxford: Clarendon Press.
Gewirth, Alan. 1978. *Reason and Morality*. Chicago, IL: The University of Chicago Press.
Harris, Jonathan M. and Brian Roach. 2017. *Environmental and Natural Resource Economics. A Contemporary Approach*, 4th edn. Abingdon: Routledge.
Helm, Dieter. 2011. 'Sustainable consumption, climate change and future generations'. *Royal Institute of Philosophy Supplement* 69: 235–252.
Helm, Dieter. 2013. *The Carbon Crunch: How We're Getting Climate Change Wrong – and How to Fix It*. New Haven, CT and London: Yale University Press.
Helm, Dieter. 2015. *Natural Capital: Valuing the Planet*. New Haven, CT and London: Yale University Press.
Nordhaus, William D. 2007. 'A review of the Stern Review on the economics of climate change'. *Journal of Economic Literature* 45: 686–702.
Nordhaus, William D. 2013. *The Climate Casino: Risk, Uncertainty, and Economics for a Warming World*. New Haven, CT and London: Yale University Press.
Shue, Henry. 1996. *Basic Rights: Subsistence, Affluence, and U.S. Foreign Policy*, 2nd edn. Princeton, NJ: Princeton University Press.
Shue, Henry. 2014. *Climate Justice: Vulnerability and Protection*. Oxford: Oxford University Press.
Steigleder, Klaus. 1999. *Grundlegung der normativen Ethik: Der Ansatz von Alan Gewirth*. Freiburg and Munich: Verlag Karl Alber.
Steigleder, Klaus. 2016. 'Climate risks, climate economics, and the foundations of a rights-based risk ethics'. *Journal of Human Rights* 15(2): 251–271.
Stern, Nicholas. 2007. *The Economics of Climate Change: The Stern Review*. Cambridge: Cambridge University Press.
Stern, Nicholas. 2008. 'The economics of climate change'. *American Economic Review* 98(2): 1–37.
Weitzman, Martin L. 2007. 'A review of the Stern Review on the economics of climate change'. *Journal of Economic Literature* 45: 703–724.
Weitzman, Martin L. 2009. 'On modeling and interpreting the economics of catastrophic climate change'. *Review of Economics and Statistics* 91(1): 1–19.
Weitzman, Martin L. and Gernot Wagner. 2015. *Climate Shock: The Economic Consequences of a Hotter Planet*. Princeton, NJ: Princeton University Press.
Wolff, Jonathan. 2006. 'Risk, fear, blame, shame and the regulation of public safety'. *Economics and Philosophy* 22: 409–427.
Wolff, Jonathan. 2007. 'What is the value of preventing a fatality?'. In Tim Lewens (ed.), *Risk: Philosophical Perspectives*. Abingdon: Routledge.

9

MOTIVATIONAL ASPECTS OF A POLITICS OF SUSTAINABILITY

Dieter Birnbacher

1 The 'motivation problem'

Questions of motivation are crucial for any future ethics understood as a discipline that deals with ethical questions essentially involving states and actions in the distant future. They are crucial especially for a future ethics that aspires to have an impact on how things are in reality and how real people act. Moral proposals are one thing; the motivation to follow them is another. Normative statements, whether in ethics, aesthetics or technology, cannot, by themselves, compel conformity. All they can do is prescribe or recommend a certain course of action. In order to make someone act accordingly, morality has to rely on further factors: dispositions of the addressee such as self-interest, rationality, sensibility, and moral and other attitudes. Even if the prescription, or piece of advice, is categorical and tells others what they must do, their addressees are free in choosing whether to follow or ignore it.

The problem of how to bridge the gap between norm and conformity has sometimes been called the 'motivation problem' (Care 1982; Baumgartner 2005). 'Motivation problem' is not a commonly used term within ethics. Nevertheless, it can serve as a convenient label for an inquiry into the conditions that have to be fulfilled in order to make a norm, prescription, recommendation or any other action-guiding statement effective in the sense of making the addressee behave in conformity with it.

As far as the addressee of a norm is concerned, a norm, however urgently expressed, does not by itself involve a motivation to follow it. This is different for the person sincerely expressing the norm. It is plausible that if a person accepts a norm, she is at least in some degree motivated to act on it. Although even for such a person the norm is not action-compelling, it is at least action-guiding. The person has a reason to act in the way the norm prescribes, however strongly this reason may compete with other reasons pointing in the opposite direction.

In the context of future ethics, the 'motivation problem' has a specific edge. Compared to other areas of ethics, there seems to be a more striking discrepancy in this field between the motivation to accept ethical principles and the motivation to act in accordance with them. The motivation to accept principles of future ethics is much less problematic than the motivation to adopt such principles as personal maxims or by translating them into concrete action. We live in a moral culture deeply impregnated with the universalistic moral tradition of the Enlightenment. Most people who accept a fundamental moral norm like *neminem laede* ('injure no one' – Schopenhauer's 'principle of justice') will in general understand this norm in such a way that not only current but also future beings susceptible to being harmed are included in its domain. There does not seem to be a big difference between what motivates holding the unextended and the extended norm. Once a norm of non-harming is accepted, it seems plausible to include potential future people along with present ones as far as they are affected by present action or inaction. It is no surprise, therefore, that the moral imperative to take the interests of future generations into account is firmly established in most parts of the industrialised world. According to what people reply to relevant survey questions, only few people in the more well-to-do parts of the world deny that the present generation has responsibilities towards future generations. Future-oriented norms such as preventing future climate-driven catastrophes, keeping intact the natural conditions on which human life depends, or protecting biodiversity from irreversible losses, are widely recognised, a recognition prominently reflected in the well-known 'first commandment' of Hans Jonas's ethics of responsibility (Jonas 1979: 186) not to jeopardise the future existence of humanity.

Nevertheless, there is an undeniable gap in moral motivation. Moral emotions such as love of humanity, a sense of justice and international solidarity are readily affirmed in the abstract, but rarely lived in the concrete. Their motivational force is throughout inferior to competing particularistic emotions such as egoism, family bonds, group solidarity and patriotism. However much the evolutionary origins of morality in the immediate concerns of the family, the clan and the tribe are deliberately disavowed in the principles of universalistic moralities such as Kantianism and utilitarianism, these origins stubbornly reappear in the limits of motivation documented by social psychology and political science. It even has to be doubted whether the whole of humanity, spread out over the past, present and future, can at all be a proper object of moral emotions. This can be seen especially in the field of the ethics of climate change, where the 'lag' between professed aims and principles and concrete (collective and individual) behaviour is obvious.

This chapter will explore the motivational resources available for a consistent climate politics. I will, first, give an overview of the psychological factors that stand in the way of an adequate care for the global future and pose serious obstacles to a practical acceptance of policies designed to slow down climate change. The following sections propose avenues that might circumvent these obstacles by relying on indirect motivations (section 3) and self-binding through institutional arrangements (section 4). The chapter concludes with some tentative remarks on what further work has still to be done to overcome motivational deficiencies in regard to future threats.

2 Concern about the future – theory versus practice

Let me begin with some remarks on the factors that determine our attitudes to future events. There is a large body of psychological research on various aspects of attitudes to the future, but it is only rarely that they are brought together systematically.

Psychologically, the discrepancy between words and deeds in long-term political action is far from surprising. Issues with a pronounced long-term dimension bring a number of factors into play that are known to have a negative influence on the motivation to comply with these norms in behaviour. Among them are: (1) pure time preference; (2) non-reciprocity: (3) uncertainty; and (4) threats to the maintenance of habitualised lifestyles.

First, let's consider pure time preference. Future dangers rarely catch our spontaneous attention without constant efforts to keep them on the agenda. Pure time preference seems part of the explanation of the relative ease with which, for example, the Montreal Protocol was established in 1987. This protocol banned gases destroying the ozone layer that led to a dramatic increase in skin cancer around the globe. Apart from the fact that only small adaptations on the part of producers were necessary to reduce emissions, the fact that the results promised to be visible in the immediate future greatly helped in coming to an agreement. In the case of greenhouse gases this is much more uncertain, not only because much more comprehensive changes are at stake, but also because the victims of global warming have not yet made their appearance and the impact of present styles of production will only be felt in the generations to come. All this explains why future ethics does not, in general, provoke the 'visceral response' (Weber 2006: 103) prompting appropriate action.

A second factor is that obligations in respect to the far-off future are necessarily non-reciprocal. From future people, you can expect neither positive nor negative sanctions for actions done in the present. They will benefit from what they inherit from preceding generations, or will have to cope with damages and losses caused by them. In all probability, the inheritance of later generations will consist of an enormous amount of theoretical and practical knowledge for which they will not be able to thank the people who accumulated it except in symbolic terms. Less positively, future people will have to live with an enormous loss of exhaustible resources such as arable land, water resources, primeval vegetation and biodiversity. In both cases there will be no chance to reciprocate or to threaten reciprocation. At the point of time climate change can be expected to have its most deleterious consequences for many of the poor countries of the South, the people responsible for them will have disappeared in the abysses of the past. While children and grandchildren have an opportunity to demand their due and to protest against harms imposed on them by their parents and grandparents (for example in the context of pension payments and other forms of social security) great-grandchildren necessarily remain silent. If they have a voice, then only by advocacy, through people speaking for them in anticipation of their future legitimate claims (the issue of representation will be discussed extensively in Chapter 6).

A third aspect of the motivational gap is the inherent uncertainty of the future and the difficulties in judging how present action will impact on future living conditions. Even if some estimates are more certain than others – the estimates of future demographic developments, for instance, have much less variance than the estimates of how climate change will reduce biodiversity – uncertainty is ubiquitous. Uncertainty comes in many kinds, and affects more than one important psychological dimension (see Jamieson 2012: 191ff.). There is, first, limited certainty about which of the different scenarios on which future ethics is based will actually materialise. For example, even if the physical side of the future development of the climate can be predicted within relatively narrow boundaries, the impact of changes in the climate on the economy and quality of life is far more diffuse. The motivation to lower emissions of greenhouse gases seems to depend to a large extent on the consequences envisaged for oneself and for one's immediate descendants. Therefore, uncertainties about the local and regional impacts of climate change will be crucial for motivation, including the probability of a massive climate-driven exodus of Africans into the well-to-do fortress Europe. Another dimension is the uncertainty concerning the results of technical progress. It cannot be ruled out that technical progress will yield new methods of neutralising the effects of carbon dioxide that are less risky than technologies of 'geo-engineering', such as carbon capture and storage (CCS), the depositing of carbon dioxide in caverns and other places where it will not enter the atmosphere (see Wilcox 2012). And, third, it is uncertain whether present measures to lower emissions will have an impact on any ethically relevant future parameters at all. It might well be that the impact of an increasing number of civil wars will be much more disastrous. Everywhere we are summoned to make provisions for future generations there is a critical lack of feedback on success or failure. We have to act without 'control beliefs'. 'Control beliefs' about success and failure are, however, crucially important for the motivation to act in accordance with certain principles. Without them, motivation is unstable and vulnerable.

An additional aspect is the uncertainty about the extent to which later generations will maintain strategies initiated today for the sake of the long-term future. No individual and no collective can be certain that later people will share our norms and values to an extent necessary to prolong their efforts into the indefinite future. Much depends on the extent to which the present generation succeeds in demonstrating to their successors that it is possible to care for the long-term future without substantial losses in present goods and without thwarting prospects for people in the more immediate future. Psychologically, uncertainty substantially reduces motivation. When it is uncertain whether the morally necessary changes on behaviour pay off, one has to assume that preparedness to effectuate or support these changes will be low (see Evans and Jacobs 1981: 116f. for the case of environmental deterioration).

A fourth obstacle is perhaps even more prohibitive: the necessity to make habits and lifestyles conform to the requirements of future-oriented ethical demands. It is, in general, difficult to change ways of life to which one has grown accustomed, and politicians have understandable scruples to take positions that move too far off the common run, especially in democracies. The recent change in the social norm about smoking cannot really count as a counterexample. Carbon dioxide emissions do not endanger one's own health or the immediate environment. The risks remain abstract, so that a tension persists between high-minded principles and the reluctance to question behaviour incompatible with them. An example is the coexistence of high ambitions in climate protection and the maintenance and even furtherance of habits stably integrated in people's way of life, such as individual motorised mobility. Germany is the best example of this kind of contradiction. A nation that claims to be a model in environmental and climate protection (and actually is in many respects) at the same time floods the world with luxury playthings for adults: gas-guzzling and high-emission 'premium' cars. The Stuttgart-based sociologist Zwick found in a survey that 50 per cent of respondents think that the climate problem has a 'high or very high' catastrophe potential and that it implies 'a great or very great' social peril, but that his attitude does not correlate with a corresponding preparedness to find the source of the peril in one's own behaviour (Zwick 2001: 302). Similar denial attitudes have been observed in the US (Stoll-Kleemann et al. 2001: 11; Leiserowitz 2006: 56). Even those Americans who do not belong to the large group of climate change deniers are not willing to drive less (or to change to public transport) and oppose higher fuel taxes (O'Connor et al. 1999: 464ff.). As is shown by the difficulties of reducing (or indeed stopping the expansion of) car traffic by means of taxation, strongly habitualised and lifestyle-determining behaviours seem to be resistant to political control efforts. It seems doubtful that political measures that would really limit car traffic would at all be realisable, unless in special circumstances such as the oil price crisis of the 1980s. As far as commitments in the long term require changes in the stable behaviour patterns of society at large, the prospects of realising them seem gloomy.

Phenomena of 'avoidant maladaptation' are not exclusive to the industrialised world. As the anthropologists Grothmann and Patt have shown in an African study, information on risks transmitted merely by cognitive means has little chance of changing irrational behaviours in developing countries too. More effective are role playing and confrontations with concrete alternative behaviours – techniques that involve the emotions significantly more than pure information does (Grothmann and Patt 2005: 208).

A further factor that acts as an obstacle to active commitment to long-term aims is that problems of the future are harder to get across to people than problems of the present. TV reports on catastrophes in today's poorest countries often motivate substantial preparedness to donate. Future catastrophes have much less appeal. Often, negative utopias in the media are too overdramatised to be perceived as trustworthy.

A further factor is social distance. Since the people primarily affected by present long-term decisions live in the (far) future, they are anonymous. When it is threatened that they will be harmed or disadvantaged, agents in the present will view them as 'statistical' instead of 'identified' victims. Feelings of solidarity, on the other hand, are aroused much more strongly by victims 'under our eyes', such as the victims of mining accidents, earthquakes and epidemics, even in cases in which a sober calculation would suggest that it is more rational to use the resources spent for future-directed preventive purposes (see Calabresi and Bobbitt 1978). In the case of climate change, this factor assumes a prominent position since the future people primarily harmed by it will live in regions with non-European cultures, while people in the industrialised world with the highest emission of greenhouse gases (Americans 20 tons, Germans 10 tons, the sustainable amount being 2 to 3 tons per head and year) tend to think that they will not be negatively affected or will even profit (see Giddens 2009: 113). Even on the assumption that the loyalties of Europeans will in the future move away from the nation to supranational entities such as the European Union, the people primarily affected will still be 'too far-off'. They will be beyond the horizon of people's spontaneous sympathies.

It is interesting, in this context, to compare this situation with the list of factors identified by the development ethicist Peter Unger for the preparedness to offer international aid: (1) physical proximity; (2) social proximity; (3) informational immediacy; (4) picturability; (5) emergency character (1996: 73). Judging from this list, the people primarily affected by climate change do not satisfy the majority of the factors substantially enough to encourage solidarity. Possibly, the climate problem is simply too massive for the human motivation system, which, for evolutionary reasons, is better adapted to more immediate objectives (see Leist 2015: 126).

In sum, there is a considerable gap between cognition and motivation, between what people believe (or say they believe) and how they act. And there are a number of factors that, taken together, can help to explain why there is such a motivational gap between ethical norms concerning the long-term future and action in conformity with these norms. Pure time preference, uncertainty, social distance and conservatism of lifestyles, among others, jointly prevent that dangers recognised as such result in behaviour changes. Temporally more proximate events, events involving oneself or people in one's affective horizon and events that can be managed without thoroughgoing changes in lifestyle tend to have a much greater impact on present action. From an ethical and political point of view, the question is how these motivational obstacles to consistent future-oriented action might be overcome or at least circumvented.

3 Indirect motivations

There is every reason to doubt whether the motivations flowing from the mere recognition of abstract future ethical norms are sufficiently powerful to counteract the motivations flowing from more immediate moral and non-moral values. But this should not reduce us to absolute pessimism. In the next section, we will explore the possibility that more indirect motivations than the recognition of abstract norms and principles or sympathy with far-off people might function as motivational substitutes.

Indirect motivations are defined as motivations that are not directed at future people themselves but at other and more immediate aims the attainment of which can be expected to have a favourable influence on future people. The great advantage of indirect motivations is their more reliable emotional basis. This is because they mostly belong to the category of 'quasi moral motives' that support genuinely moral motives such as responsibility, dutifulness and moral integrity, without being themselves of a distinctly moral character (see Birnbacher 2009: 283). Classical examples of 'quasi-moral motives' are love, pity, care and solidarity. They tend to be equivalent to moral motives as far as their consequences are concerned but are more strongly bound up with affective relations and needs. They are more a matter of the heart than of cold intellect.

The most well-known model of an indirect motivation in future ethics is the so called 'chain of love' (Passmore 1980: 88f.). According to this model, each generation cares exclusively for the generation of its children and grandchildren, with the result that the sequence of limited responsibilities has the same or even better effects on the whole series of generations than postulates of a more future-oriented responsibility. On the assumptions that parents' behaviour plays the role of a model for the behaviour of children, provisions for the generations n+x are no less good than the provisions for generation n in the agents' temporal proximity. The resulting provisions for generation n+x might even be better than they would be if provisions are directly made for generation n+x.

As generally in morality, the results of moral effort are more reliably attained if motivations are of an indirect rather than a direct kind because genuinely moral motivations are often abstract and more remote from the concreteness of human emotional life. Caring instincts, spontaneous compassion and the loyalty resulting from long-standing personal relations are, in general, more reliable motivators than conscientiousness or feelings of duty.

Another source of indirect motivation is the preservation and cultivation of intrinsic values. The valuation of cultural values such as certain forms of art, music, literature, philosophy and science, but also of social virtues and political institutions, is closely tied, psychologically, to the motivation to preserve these values, or to entrust appropriate institutions with their preservation. Whoever loves the music of Bach, for example, does, as rule, also have an interest in knowing that this kind of music will be handed down to later generations even by generations who are unable to feel or even to understand these valuations: 'To love is, amongst other things, to care about the future of what we love' (Passmore 1980: 88). It is hardly imaginable that values such as scientific truth, artistic creativity or the principles of democracy can be seriously held by someone who does not at the same hope that they will last forever. The most important intertemporal project that answers to this description and is immediately relevant to catastrophe prevention is the project of human rights. However fragile human rights may be as products of an arduous and by no means accomplished development, it is clear that they essentially claim an everlasting validity. Whoever holds them in high esteem now wishes that they will never get lost.

Another indirect motive that may serve as the basis for a morality of sustainability is the need for overarching aims transcending one's person, one's lifetime and one's immediate environment. Objectives of the global future offer themselves as appropriate targets for this need, especially in the secularised parts of the world. Ernst Partridge has called these motives motives of 'self-transcendence' (1980: 204). They might alternatively be called 'motives of historical meaningfulness'. Acting for the future of mankind may be particularly rewarding in this respect because the individual satisfies three needs at a time: the need for giving life meaning, the need for self-respect, and the need for feeling embedded in a larger community. A person then views his or her limited existence as a link in a chain of generations held together by an intergenerational feeling of community, with obligations towards of the future and feelings of gratitude towards the past.

To sum up, there are quite a number of indirect motivations that might support acting for the distant future even in case the direct motivations fail to have an impact. The question remains, however, whether these motivations are sufficiently strong and reliable to act as a substitute.

4 Self-binding through institutions – self-binding of institutions

In this section, we will consider another class of motivations that might also be classed 'indirect', which are, however, more fruitfully discussed as a class of its own because they essentially involve social rather than psychological mechanisms.

Self-binding through future-oriented institutions can be understood as a way of shifting the burdens of duty from direct to indirect motivations. Self-binding is a mechanism by which direct motivations are replaced by indirect motivations in cases in which direct motivations do not seem sufficiently reliable to bear the weight of recognised obligations (see Heidbrink and Reidel 2011). Whoever makes a long-term commitment, as, for example, in contracting life assurance or regularly giving money to a charity, makes fidelity less burdensome and raises the threshold for deviations. Repeated payment of instalments, for example, is more burdensome and has a higher risk of being forgotten than a respective once-for-all order to one's bank. Especially in moral matters long-term commitments have clear advantages. They limit room for manoeuvre and prevent backsliding and disloyalty. Whoever knows that he tends to yield to impulsiveness and knows, at the same time, that this tendency will spoil his long-term projects, will have good reasons for opting for self-binding.

As for the modalities of self-binding, it has become customary to distinguish between internal and external self-binding. Internal self-binding means adopting principles and maxims that sanction opportunistic deviations by feelings of guilt and shame. To yield to a temptation may be highly pleasurable for a time. But even a hard-boiled egoist must take into account the expectable sequel of feelings of guilt and shame. External self-binding means to make use of other persons or institutions to limit one's options and to reinforce self-discipline by external sanctions. This kind of self-binding, often called a 'Ulysses contract', following the story of Ulysses who ordered his men to bind him to escape seduction by the sirens, can be viewed as a kind of self-paternalism: an agreement is made with some outside agency to restrict one's own freedom for the sake of one's own rational self-interest.

Given the liability of conscience to corruption, delegating control of one's behaviour to an external agency will, as rule, be more effective than delegation to an internal one. Conscience too easily falls prey to the same temptations against which it should act as a fortress. If the task is to prevent 'short-termism' for opportunistic reasons, external sanctions such as those offered by legal prohibitions will in general be more reliable. They are attractive in particular to those who have the least reason to rely on their spontaneous impulses, such as addicts wishing to be cured from their compulsions. Gambling addicts are among the most fervent advocates of individual gambling bans.

The distinction between internal and external self-binding applies on an individual as well as on a collective level. Internal self-binding on the collective level means that society commits itself to contractual or other obligations that keep it from succumbing to temptations. This function is exercised by quite a number of bodies, especially councils, commissions and expert rounds. They function as agencies that keep politicians away from the temptations of opportunistic populism, and protect them to some degree from the pressures of lobbies, party politics and campaigning. At the same time, politicians continue to be free in forming their own judgements and to rule against the advice of these bodies. One might think of endowing these bodies with legislative or executive powers. But this would be hardly compatible with the principles of democracy according to which all power of governments ultimately derives from the people governed. Councils should not be permitted to usurp the functions of elected representatives.

Realising political aims in the field of long-term environmental and climatic policies requires complex prognostic estimates and strategic calculations. It is impossible to succeed in these without the assistance of scientific expertise. On the other hand, scientific expertise is not sufficient for competent counselling on chances and risks. The very concept of risk has a value component (the possibility of harm, that is, a loss of value), and even warning against future risks necessarily involves value judgements. Political counselling, therefore, is unthinkable without moral and political components, such as advocacy of later generations affected by present decisions – in analogy to the often-practised advocacy of children, born and unborn, in urban planning.

Experience shows that the path from scientific warnings concerning future risks to correspondingly future-conscious politics is long and thorny. There is a long, sometimes fatally long, time lag between warnings and political reactions. In part, this lag has a rational basis. Not every warning is equally well founded (an example is the 'Waldsterben' in the 1980 which proved to be far less dramatic than originally thought), and some catastrophe scenarios are far from realistic. But to a great extent the lag reflects the difficulties of politicians to confront new challenges and their fear to openly declare unpleasant truths, even if many of these truths have long been well known, though possibly carefully suppressed.

On the level of the collective, several external self-binding mechanisms with a clear relevance to future ethics are already in operation. Some of them take the form of international law and international contracts, others of transnational organisations and authorities. A model of an internationally effective agency able not only to give advice to national governments but also to implement their future-directed policies independently of national politics is the European Central Bank. It functions independently of national governments and is bound exclusively by the criteria of the European Union Treaty. However, given the fact that governments are the key agents of most future hazards, such as the destruction of large parts of tropical rain forest, the reduction of biodiversity, and the degradation of soils by intensive agriculture, there is still much to be done. There are quite a number of proposals about how change may be effected. One option that should be taken into consideration is the global court for future issues proposed by Weiss (1989: 121). A court of this kind, even if it lacks the authority to check the 'obliviousness of the future' of national governments by sanctions, would at least be able to protest against policies that endanger the interests of future people and to encourage the search for sustainable alternatives.

In Germany, as in some other countries, the constitution in its present form contains a number of provisions against an excessively opportunistic political decision-making. One such provision is the introduction of a new article into the constitution (art. 20a) in 1994 which explicitly charges the government with provisions for future generations and the maintenance of the natural living conditions on which human life depends. Since then, expansions of this article have been proposed that make care for the future more stringent (see Tremmel et al. 1999). Another example is the so-called 'debt brake' in article 109(3), introduced in 2011, in order to control public debt. The most important constitutional safeguard against 'short-termism', however, is the institution of indirect democracy according to which the members of the legislative have no imperative mandate but are free to follow their own convictions and party discipline. By locating the control of the executive not immediately with the electorate but with elected representatives, the possibility is reinforced to temper potential pressure from citizens in the direction of opportunism and to give priority to long-term objectives.

5 Research agenda

Further research is urgently called for to fill the lacunae left by the present state of the art concerning the motivation problem. A problem this research has to face is that it has to bring together a number of disciplines that still primarily follow different paradigms and rarely speak the same language: applied ethics, environmental science, motivation theory, social psychology, sociology and political science. There are several issues closely connected with the motivation problem that still have to be cleared up. First, the processes that lead from moral conviction to moral action and from political long-term strategies to concrete political action are still poorly understood. In the context of economic sustainability, for example, it is largely unclear what the factors are that have to come together to transform grass-roots practices into established social practices backed up by widely accepted norms and social control mechanisms. One thing that the ongoing discussion in the social sciences, and especially in social practice theory (see Hielscher 2013: 151f.), makes highly probable is that neither preference changes in individuals nor changes in political orientation can be expected to effect the relative fundamental changes necessary to attain the aim of a sustainable world economy and to reduce the risks of climate change. It is widely agreed, on the contrary, that bottom-up (individualistic) and top-down (structural) effects have to go together in order to change consumption patterns in accordance with formally approved sustainability objectives. What is classified as 'normal' is continually redefined, in small steps that often go unrecognised and in which spontaneous (or seemingly spontaneous) changes in individual attitudes and dispositions to act enter into interactions with external incentives (of economic, legal or social sorts). These changes, though barely noticeable, are so many steps towards sustainability. An interesting example, in this respect, is the change in the patterns of consumption of energy in Germany that is supported both by the typically 'green' idea of decentralised energy production in small communities and the strategic aims of giving up nuclear energy production in the mid-term and to reduce the dependence on fossil fuel imports on a national scale. It would be interesting to see how far changes of individual preferences in a 'green' direction on the one hand, and legislative breakthrough such as the German Alternative Energy Law on the other will, in the long run, work together as mutual catalysts of changes in energy production and consumption practices.

Another relevant research topic is how relevant changes in attitudes in the past came about and what the mechanisms were that gave them the stability they have proved to maintain up to the present. The most prominent example is, naturally, the so-called 'ecological crisis' in the 1980s, and the enormous effect it had on individual attitudes and collective practices. Though the motivation to act for an improved quality of the environment one experiences every day can be expected to be much stronger than the motivation to act for the quality of life of an anonymous and distant future, it might be helpful to ask what lessons can be learned from the relatively successful political responses to environmental pollution for a similarly successful climate politics. It might be interesting, too, to reconstruct the factors that made the recent campaigns against smoking as successful as they proved to be. To all appearances, this campaign had a lasting effect, on attitudes as well as on behaviour. Which factors prevent the success of similar campaigns against excessive use of fossil fuels, excessive car traffic and excessive meat consumption?

Finally, ethics as a philosophical discipline should be more courageous in taking up issues of public concern and to confront its abstract models with real-life problems. There have been, in the last years, a number of highly interesting attempts to integrate ethical theory and political science into a realistic ethics of sustainability (see, e.g., Birnbacher and Thorseth 2015; Bos and Düwell 2016). Much more, however, could be done to make the rich resources of academic ethics available to public discussion.

Bibliography

Baumgartner, Christoph. 2005. *Umweltethik – Umwelthandeln. Ein Beitrag zur Lösung des Motivationsproblems*. Paderborn: Mentis.

Birnbacher, Dieter. 2009. 'What motivates us to care for the (distant) future?'. In Axel Gosseries and Lukas Meyer (eds), *Intergenerational Justice*. Oxford: Oxford University Press, 273–300.

Birnbacher, Dieter and May Thorseth (eds). 2015. *The Politics of Sustainability. Philosophical Perspectives*. Abingdon: Routledge.

Bos, Gerhard and Marcus Düwell (eds). 2016. *Human Rights and Sustainability*. Abingdon: Routledge.

Calabresi, Guido and Philip Bobbitt. 1978. *Tragic Choices*. New York: Norton.

Care, Norman. 1982. 'Future generations, public policy, and the motivation problem'. *Environmental Ethics* 4: 195–213.

Evans, Gary and Stephen Jacobs. 1983. 'Air pollution and human behavior'. *Journal of Social Issues* 37: 95–125.

Giddens, Anthony. 2009. *The Politics of Climate Change*. Cambridge: Polity Press.

Grothmann, Torsten and Anthony Patt. 2005. 'Adaptive capacity and human cognition: the process of individual adaptation to climate change'. *Global Environmental Change* 15: 199–213.

Heidbrink, Ludger and Johannes Reidel. 2011. 'Nachhaltiger Konsum durch politische Selbstbindung'. *GAIA* 20: 152–156.

Hielscher, Sabine, Gill Seyfang and Adrian Smith. 2013. 'Grassroots innovations for sustainable energy: exploring niche-development processes among community-energy initiatives'. In Maurie J. Cohen, Halina Szejnwald and Philip J. Vergragt (eds), *Innovations in Sustainable Consumption. New Economic, Socio-technical Transitions and Social Practices*. Cheltenham and Northampton, MA: Edward Elgar, 133–158.

Jamieson, Dale. 2012. 'Ethics, public policy, and global warming'. In Stephen M. Gardiner, Simon Caney, Dale Jamieson and Henry Shue (eds), *Climate Ethics: Essential Readings*. Oxford: Oxford University Press, 71–86.

Jonas, Hans. 1979. *Das Prinzip Verantwortung. Versuch einer Ethik für die technologische Zivilisation*. Frankfurt: Insel.

Leiserowitz, Anthony. 2006. 'Climate change risk perception and policy preferences: the role of affect, imagery, and values'. *Climatic Change* 77: 45–72.

Leist, Anton. 2015. 'Schadenverursachen und Kooperation beim Klimawandel – zwei Weisen, auf das Ende zu sehen'. In Angela Kallhoff (ed.), *Klimagerechtigkeit und Klimaethik*. Berlin and Boston, MA: Springer, 107–134.

O'Connor, Robert et al. 1999. 'Risk perceptions, general environmental beliefs, and willingness to address climate change'. *Risk Analysis* 19: 461–471.

Partridge, Ernest. 1980. 'Why care about the future?'. In Ernest Partridge (ed.), *Responsibilities to Future Generations*. Amherst, MA: Prometheus Books, 203–220.

Passmore, John Arthur. 1980. *Man's Responsibility for Nature. Ecological Problems and Western Traditions*, 2nd edn. London: Duckworth.

Stoll-Kleemann, Susanne et al. 2001. 'The psychology of denial concerning climate mitigation measures: evidence from Swiss focus groups'. *Global Environmental Change* 11: 107–117.

Tremmel, Jörg et al. 1999. 'Die Verankerung von Generationsgerechtigkeit im Grundgesetz – Vorschlag für einen erneuerten Artikel 20a GG'. *Zeitschrift für Rechtspolitik* 32: 431–438.

Unger, Peter. 1996. *Living High and Letting Die: Our Illusion of Innocence*. New York: Oxford University Press.

Weber, Elke. 2006. 'Experience-based and description-based perceptions of long-term risk. why global warming does not scare us (yet)'. *Climatic Change* 77: 103–120.

Weiss, Edith Brown. 1989. *In Fairness to Future Generations. International Law, Common Patrimony, and Intergenerational Equity*. Tokyo and Dobbs Ferry, NY: Transnational.

Wilcox, Jennifer. 2012. *Carbon Capture*. Dordrecht: Springer.

Zwick, Michael. 2001. 'Der globale Klimawandel in der Wahrnehmung der Öffentlichkeit'. *GAIA* 10: 299–303.

10

GOVERNANCE TOWARDS A GREEN FUTURE

May Thorseth and Fabian Schuppert

1 Introduction

Achieving a green future for all is – as the other chapters in this book have shown – no simple task. Some of the key limitations and obstacles to sustainable development and to avoiding the dangerous consequences of environmental change are partly due to the structures and workings of political institutions. In order to govern in accordance with the vision of a green future for all, one needs the right kinds of institutions, norms, principles, actors and power balances. As discussed throughout this book, we take a human rights-based approach to be particularly promising, since enshrining ethics of a green future would provide us with an established political, legal and moral starting points for distributing entitlements, responsibilities, duties and burdens so as to make a green future for all possible. However, as this chapter will show, environmental governance is an extremely complex field and it thus would be naive to assume that the establishment of rights to a green future would in and of itself provide a panacea for existing shortfalls in governance practice.

The aim of this chapter is to bring together some of the key observations made in the other chapters, to utilise the rights-based framework developed earlier and to address particular challenges to devise legitimate and effective governance for a green future. In so doing, we will draw on a couple of cases that demonstrate obstacles to sustainable politics and governance following from the prevailing discourses of (un)sustainability, economic feasibility and national interest short-termism. In response to these issues, we will highlight possible roads to sustainable politics and governance which draw on the idea of rights to a green future and which seem to require institutional changes, motivational changes and a shift in sustainability discourses in order to address – among many other issues – the differences between affluent and poor countries more adequately.

As it stands, existing environmental governance practice has significant deficits, no matter whether regarded at the local, regional, national, transnational or global level. Some of the problems seem to stem from democratic governance, since, for example, the attitudes of political decision makers in democracies can be expected to have a great deal of overlap with those of their constituencies, which means that the limitations of future-oriented moral attitudes and the motivational barriers to future-oriented action of citizens are likely to have a considerable impact on politics. At the same time, though, many transnational institutions for environmental governance lack democratic legitimacy and accountability. Additionally, many environmental policies tend to be implemented according to standardised procedures in accordance with internationally acknowledged rules and regulations, such as Agenda 21, many of which are controversial from the normative viewpoint of intergenerational global justice and sustainability. On top of this, politics in general struggles to adequately prepare for and regulate in light of future risks and uncertainties. In other words, to make our world future-proof is something politics struggles with because of its generally flawed understanding of risk. Last but not least, a particular obstacle to achieving a green future for all concerns how the differences between developed and developing countries tend to be glossed over, and the way in which global power politics shapes the normative landscape of global to local governance regimes.

Our approach in this chapter is to flag up how roads to sustainable politics depend on a successful interplay between the right kind of normative framework, the wide use of different governance tools, careful institutional design and underlying motivational driving forces. We hope to show that in order to succeed we need to look for roads in plural, i.e. roads that are suitable for the different contexts of sustainable politics and that achieve a green future for all.

In the following sections we will first outline a generic overview of issues in relation to environmental governance. We will touch on issues such as the rebound effect, future-proofing policymaking, and motivational obstacles to sustainability, before moving on to three concrete cases which will make the issues discussed tangible and which highlight the need to contextualise our governance responses. In section 7 we connect our discussion on governance to important findings from the other chapters of the book. Finally, in section 8 we offer some concluding remarks on roads to sustainability.

2 Global environmental governance: some preliminary remarks

The focus in this section is to give a brief generic overview of global environmental governance and its multifaceted nature. *First of all*, it is important to be clear about what falls under the umbrella term 'governance'. Governance refers to processes of governing, including the agents that participate in particular practices of governance. Hence governance is not limited to actions and structures of states but also includes markets, trade, law, civil society, networks and individuals. Moreover, tools for governance come in many different shapes and forms, including but not limited to laws, norms, treaties, language, culture and power.

Environmental governance proves to be particularly complex since its object, that is, the environment, is affected by a whole range of processes, practices and policies, including those that are not directly aimed at the environment and occur on many different levels. Moreover, 'the environment' as the object of governance is in itself too opaque and complex to be treated as a unified whole. This is perhaps why we often see that laws, norms and treaties within environmental governance normally single out particular aspects of the environment that they aim to regulate, such as the levels of toxins in soil and water or the taxation of fossil-based combustibles. When over ten years ago Ronald Mitchell (2003) counted the number of international environmental agreements, there were more than 750. This number has been increasing even further since. There is a vast array of bilateral, multilateral, transnational, international and global environmental governance norms, treaties and principles, spanning the whole spectrum from the informal via soft law to hard law. For the remainder of this section we will focus on a few key examples and explain some of the main prospects and challenges of international environmental governance.

One aspect of the current global environmental governance regime that is particularly often subject to criticism is the fact that the current system is very fragmented, with no central and powerful environmental agency in place by which it could shape international policy and exert a certain amount of pressure onto non-complying states to be more sustainable. Critics argue that the world needs a stronger central agency for environmental matters since existing institutions like the United Nations Environment Programme (UNEP) lack the cohesion, power and political support to adequately address global environmental issues, especially if individual states oppose UNEP's policies. This criticism often goes hand in hand with the observation that international environmental law lacks the backing of an international court solely designed to adjudicate environmental disputes. While the International Court of Justice (ICJ) is in theory equipped with the power to process environmental cases, in its actual practice the ICJ has not only never used its existing (on paper) environmental chamber, but it has also treated the few environment-related cases it had in a distinctly non-environmental way, that is, strictly in terms of whether particular international agreements had been violated (for details, see Stephens 2009). Therefore, some commentators have called for the establishment of an international court of the environment, a forum in which newly enshrined environmental rights could be claimed and protected.

Both these proposals, i.e. the suggestion that states should create a world environment agency as well as an international court for the environment, point to problems with a central feature of the current global environmental governance regime, namely, the fact that most environmental governance is based on voluntary collaboration between states, supported by customary norms, non-binding agreements and other soft law instruments. Some critics think it would be better to have binding norms which are centrally enforceable, which is one of the primary reasons why these critics call for the establishment of a central agency and a court of the environment. It is true, that the bulk of existing global environmental governance tools is not intended to strictly enforce environmental goals and establish legal liabilities for parties that fail to comply, but rather to develop and sustain collaborative efforts among individual sovereign states to make our world safer and more sustainable. However, while this approach has obvious downsides (e.g. no legal enforceability of most norms) and a mixed track record (e.g. the slow and thus far insufficient response to global anthropogenic climate change), it should be noted that this approach has also delivered on several occasions (e.g. the phasing out of CFCs through the adoption of the Montreal Protocol) and that stricter regulations might be hard to establish, which means one should be careful not to throw out the child with the bathwater. For instance: past attempts to establish strict liability principles, such as the Council of Europe's (CE) Convention on Civil Liability for Damage Resulting from Activities Dangerous to the Environment, have been ill-fated. All that was needed to put the CE's convention into effect was its ratification by three member states. However, in the end, the convention failed. It is not very surprising, then, that the 1972 Stockholm Declaration of Principles, which was adopted at the end of the 1972 United Nations Conference on the Human Environment, does not propose any liability mechanisms, but only mentions liability as a future principle (see Chapter 5).

For better or worse, it is therefore still sovereign states that wield significant power within the existing international environmental governance regime. It is states that are the parties to existing multilateral environmental agreements and it is often (no matter whether openly or covertly) state interests that shape policies, recommendations and norms developed within existing environmental governance institutions. The effects of state-led global environmental governance vary significantly. While the 1992 Earth Summit is often credited with establishing the precautionary principle in international environmental governance, Agenda 21, which was intended to put the idea of sustainable development into law, has been heavily criticised for being too business-friendly and neoliberal in its outlook.[1] Precaution and sustainable development are both among the ten core principles of the existing global environmental regime. The other eight principles are: cooperation, sovereignty, no harm, sustainable use, equitable use, intergenerational equity, the polluter pays principle and common but differentiated responsibilities (Stephens 2009). Even though most of these principles are not without controversy, they provide the backbone of today's climate and environmental governance. Hence it is not surprising that all these principles have played a major role within the negotiations of the United Nations Framework Convention on Climate Change. Principles like precaution have gradually changed the discursive governance landscape, leading to a partial shift in justificatory logic from something being permissible until shown to be harmful to a more precautionary approach, which calls for scientific evidence to show that certain actions are not harmful and to adopt the strategy 'better safe than sorry' (see section 4).

What is important when talking about global and international environmental governance is to disaggregate its various dimensions. Apart from the obvious, that is, the political and legal dimensions, environmental governance includes an economic dimension, a social dimension, a psychological dimension and a technological dimension.

The political dimension, as pointed out above, is dominated by the governments of sovereign states. It is states that shape agendas and make agreements, while there is basically no democratic control over the myriad of transnational environmental organisations that exist. This points to the worry about a distinct lack of legitimacy in current environmental governance arrangements. Environmental governance is often technocratic, since it is elites and experts who decide what kind of policy is adopted and for which reasons. While the rise of expert-led policymaking is in part due to the complexities of the environmental problems we face today, there is a worry that important decisions about societal risk-taking and future well-being are made by a group of unelected technocrats, bureaucrats and industry representatives. Thus, many governance schemes lack democratic legitimacy and accountability, that is, they are not democratically controlled.[2]

The legal dimension, as also pointed out above, is dominated by soft law instruments, since global environmental hard law is somewhat underdeveloped and difficult to enforce within the existing legal fora. At the same time the implementation, interpretation and enforcement of new and existing legal tools is crucial for advancing the future-proofing of society. However, in some cases different legal and normative orders conflict with one another, such as for instance in the case of EU-imposed border tax adjustments for making sure that the EU's internal carbon tax/emissions trading regime would not disadvantage EU products, which some lawyers deemed to be incompatible with existing WTO legislation.[3]

The economic dimension does not only concern the costs of adopting certain measures, such as whether the countries of the developed global North should compensate Ecuador and its citizens for the income they forgo by choosing to preserve the Yasuni National Park and its biodiversity rather than exploiting the large amounts of oil reserves that were discovered below the park (see section 6). The economic dimension also includes questions such as whether one should invest more in alleviating poverty or saving the environment.

The social dimension is about the social costs and effects of environmental governance, while the social support for and the effectiveness of particular governance measures is tightly connected with the motivations and preferences of different actors, an aspect that is captured by the psychological dimension (see more on this in Chapter 9).

Last but not least, the technological dimension of environmental governance includes the use of different technologies and their feasibility, including renewable energies such as tidal energy or the potential use of so-called 'geo-engineering techniques'.

As argued earlier in the book, one key element we believe to be crucial for strengthening the enforceability and stringency of environmental governance are environmental rights (see Chapter 2). However, environmental rights come in many ways, shapes and forms. Normatively speaking one first of all needs to differentiate between individual environmental rights and collective environmental rights, as well as between rights whose bearers are humans only, humans and other animals, or no humans but the environment as such. Depending on which normative framework one chooses one can end up with very different environmental rights, not only in terms of their direct content, but also their scope and demandingness. Generally speaking – with regard to the content of environmental rights – large differences exist, since some environmental rights express general claims to a vaguely defined valuable good, such as rights to a safe environment. Other environmental rights express direct entitlement rights, such as rights to clean and sufficient water, or rights to life-sustaining ecosystem services. However, it is also possible to frame environmental rights as rights of the environment, or of animals or ecosystems; this way of framing environmental rights intends to establish strong non-human rights claims in order to curb humans' negative influence on the planet and its non-human inhabitants. In many other cases environmental rights are intended to express the idea that a healthy and safe environment is a necessary condition for the prolonged fulfilment of most other rights.[4] Therefore, environmental rights are sometimes seen as meta-rights, or the legal expression of meta-capabilities (that is, the things we need to be able to do in order to be able to be capable of anything – if we are to work, for instance, we need to be able to breathe) (for a detailed argumentation on this, see Chapter 2). Furthermore, one of course needs to distinguish between philosophical theories and accounts of environmental rights and politically and legally existing environmental rights. The distinction between the moral dimension of rights as different from political and legal rights is important, since the practice of environmental rights and laws can obviously deviate quite significantly from the initial normative underpinnings and intentions. While legal and political interpretations of constitutional environmental rights naturally vary, the existence of such rights provides a huge normative resource for progressive sustainable governance. At the same time, the legal acceptance of environmental rights can always only be part of a more complex solution, since rights – in order to be effective – need enforceability, accountability and responsibility to go along with them. Our discussion throughout the remainder of this chapter will highlight the importance of rights-based environmental governance across a range of issues.

Global and international environmental governance touches upon all of the issues discussed earlier in this book, including risks, rights, economics and the relationship between affluent and poor countries. We will discuss these issues throughout the following four sections, using three particularly informative examples in order to explain the issues at hand: the case of the Guangdong fisheries (case 1); the Sardar Sarovar (Narvada dams) in India (case 2), and the failure of the Yasuni–ITT Initiative (case 3). Cases 1 and 2 illustrate a huge range of governance issues related to: lack of coordination, context-blind coordination of Agenda 1, misplaced expertise, conflicting interests between nutrition and sustainable politics, lack of solidarity within the current generation, and the need for collective environmental rights. Case 3 relates in particular to developing countries, and analyses the case from diverse angles, thus aiming to shed light on normative dilemmas. All these cases illustrate the complexity of the normative, social, political and economic demands shaping environmental governance and allow us to flesh out the normative potential of using a rights-based approach to sustainable governance.

3 Governance towards intergenerational justice

In this section of the chapter we will focus on the difficulty of representing future generations in democratic and international decision-making practices, especially with regard to possibly fulfilling the wide-ranging demands of intergenerational justice. In so doing we shed light on both the utter dependence of future generations on the decisions and policies of current people, as well as the worrying lack of long-termism in current democratic institutions (see more on this in Chapter 6).

3.1 Representation of future generations

Initially we need to decide how to define 'future generations'. We shall argue that there is a need to extend the scope beyond national societies, and also beyond the human species, i.e. to an anthropocentric view that also includes nature not just as an object to serve human interests. Further, we shall argue that our current ethical commitments are internally connected with our obligations towards future generations (Alvarez and Thorseth 2015). The question whether and how to represent future generations is complex, as it raises questions such as whether we can harm people we do not yet know, and who have not yet been born. We shall leave aside the non-identity question discussed extensively by Parfit (1986). Rather, we shall argue that currently living people have commitments towards future generations for reciprocity reasons. Reciprocity can be considered a possible moral motivation to conserve natural resources for the sake of future generations. There are reasons for paying forward the benefits we enjoyed from past residents of our common planet earth. One reason is akin to John Rawls's idea of just savings for the stability of the basic structure of the society of future generations (see Rawls 1971, section 44; see Meyer 2008). The amount of savings should be sufficient for future generations to continue with a society stable enough for members to meet their own needs, to fulfil their obligations to one another and to contribute to their just savings for their future generations (Alvarez and Thorseth 2015). This is also based on the most prevailing definition of 'sustainable development':

> Sustainable development is development that meets the needs of the present without compromising the ability of future generations to meet their own needs.
> *(World Commission on Environment and Development 1987*
> *aka Brundtland Commission 1987)*

Governance towards intergenerational justice thus presupposes intragenerational justice as well, or so we shall argue. Briefly, this is because we do face conflicts having to do with the fact that we may have to choose between, on the one hand, protecting the environment in order to meet intergenerational challenges, and on the other, avoiding the exacerbation of inequalities among those presently living (see Chapter 8 on developing countries).

3.2 Sufficientarianism, frugality and the rebound effect

Sufficientarianism is a theory of distributive justice. Rather than being concerned with inequalities as such or with making the situation of the least well off as good as possible, sufficientarian justice aims at making sure that each of us has enough. The problem is, however, that we need to make sure that limited resources are compatible with a certain standard of living for all. Thus, frugality among the rich should in principle contribute to the right direction, i.e. towards inter- and intra-generational justice. In order to govern towards inter- and intragenerational justice there is one particular obstacle that has to be overcome, though. This is the rebound effect. Briefly speaking, the rebound effect may be described as an unin-tended effect of frugal behaviour in the rich world. The reason is that frugal behaviour causes new consumption by others (Alcott 2008: 7). As an example, technological improvement results in improved fuel efficiency, which in turn leads to more consumption of fuel, as it becomes cheaper.

Frugality through for instance purchase of emission certificates is often con-sidered a transfer in the name of equity (Alcott 2008: 15). The problem is that such affluence-lowering measures address only the rich. In order to make frugality contribute to a sufficiency level for all, i.e. to a more equal distribution of available resources, there has to be a possibility of transfer in purchasing power. It does not help much if frugality among the affluent is not transferred to purchasing power for the poor. Briefly, the problem remains as long as the poor have no power to change their consumption. Without a transfer in purchasing power to either pre-sent or future poorer people, frugality among the rich will have no sustainable impact, with respect neither to intragenerational equity, nor to intergenerational justice (Alcott 2008: 15). In order to illustrate this point Alcott mentions that without an explicit transfer, the beneficiary of the income effect could be an affluent neighbour who heats his swimming pool more often. We are sympathetic to this approach to the rebound dilemma as it gives a fruitful starting point for criticism of a prevailing regime within sustainability discourses.

In this paragraph we aimed at showing that in order to govern towards intra- and intergenerational justice we need to enable a transfer of purchasing power in order to accommodate equality more equal distribution of available resources. Frugality among the current living will only serve the purpose of sufficiency while at the same time avoiding the rebound effect. Only then will frugality among the rich serve the poor. More importantly, though, is to extend environmental rights to include non-human nature, which should not be treated as commodities, but instead as commons. In view of this it is probably misleading to discuss sufficiency in terms of a transfer in purchasing power in the first place.

While Alcott's main point is that personal shifts to frugality guarantee neither present nor intergenerational equality, we would like to focus on the idea that environmental rights need to be extended to non-human nature as well. Then it becomes obvious that even if it were possible to implement a transfer of purchasing power, this would still be inadequate with regard to environmental rights that include non-human nature. Such rights cannot be treated as purchasable commodities. Rather, there is a need for another kind of transfer, namely of the sustainability vocabulary with respect to environmental rights.

4 Uncertainties and risk concerns in future-oriented governance

While law- and policymaking is, at some level, always future-oriented, some people hold that environmental policies should be particularly 'future-proof'. In this section, we will briefly discuss what this might actually mean and how the taking of certain risks might be deemed acceptable. In the context of global environmental change, the scale and nature of the relevant risks, the different layers of uncertainty besetting the issue of large-scale and long-term environmental governance, the temporal scope of the problems (and their possible solutions), and the evident time lag between decision-making and the materialisation of future positive and negative consequences make decision-making particularly difficult. The temporal problem of climate policy is thus a dual one. On the one hand, it takes relatively long for emissions to negatively affect the climate. Yet policies also come with a distinct time lag problem of their own, since the presumed benefits of many policy decisions will only materialise in the not-to-near future. Moreover, many of these benefits are actually the avoidance of major risks/harms, and thus might not even be particularly tangible. Many policymakers seem to face (or at least think they face) a dilemma between choosing policy A and saying to their voters 'You should thank me because I just made sure you will have access to affordable energy, great shopping malls and high speed internet in a year' and choosing policy B and saying 'You should thank me because if I had acted differently your children would be much more likely to be killed in a flood'. While this contrast is obviously too crude to be particularly helpful in thinking about the issue, it is important to keep these concerns in mind for the discussion in this section and the next (section 5).

Further major issues for policymakers with regard to governing climate change are related to issues mentioned earlier in this book: people's poor understanding of the relevant differences between predictions, models, scenarios and probabilistic forecasts (see Chapter 4); people's difficulty to understand and normatively assess the nature of the kinds of risks connected to climate change; the scope and nature of the various kinds of uncertainties involved. However, the risks associated with global climate change are so large and serious that it is crucial that we carefully distinguish between predictions, scenarios and probabilistic forecasts and that we establish reliable mechanisms for governing issues, technologies and processes and the corresponding risks (see Chapter 3).

Probably the most often used and most successful attempt at establishing a reliable risk governance protocol is the precautionary principle, which has become a cornerstone of international environmental governance. However, the effectiveness of the principle is contested, especially since at the national level precaution is interpreted in various ways with different degrees of stringency (Feintuck 2005). Moreover, in the context of anthropogenic climate change, policymakers face real difficulties in assessing and regulating future risks. This is particularly true for risks that are the outcomes of cumulative processes, since it is often difficult to establish clear chains of causality – which leads to a denial of responsibility – and to give accurate prognoses of exact effects. One of the key benefits of using a precautionary approach to environmental governance is that it establishes a justificatory logic which forces policies to make the case for their being future-proof. However, at the same time precautionary governance can only be effective and helpful if it goes hand in hand with the establishment of clear risk thresholds, since taking a zero-risk approach to technological and political change is simply unfeasible. That is to say, successful precautionary governance requires a sound normative and practical understanding of different forms of risk and their acceptability.

In order to establish acceptability thresholds for risk-taking scenarios, a rights-based framework proves invaluable. Defining key basic rights, including environmental rights, allows us to carve out the difference between morally permissible and impermissible risk-taking. However, we want to emphasise that the determination of acceptability thresholds should be based on a multidimensional metric, not a monodimensional one. That is to say, instead of calculating risks simply as 'negative utility of P times probability of P' we should be sensitive to the different values that can be affected by particular instances of risk-taking, such as well-being, fairness and equality, all three of which can be understood either intragenerationally or inter-generationally. Moreover, one's framework should be sensitive to different kinds of risks, since irreversible systemic risks should probably be treated differently from recoverable isolated risks, even though the latter might involve huge negative utility.

Risk governance, irrespective of the level at which it operates, needs to be context sensitive, though. That is to say, when dealing with complex environmental problems it seems naive to assume that we could settle for one-size-fits-all approaches. Policies that might work in one case may not work in a seemingly similar case because of a range of external factors (see section 5). Moreover, we live in a multirisk world (Wiener 2002), so in most cases risk governance is not about the complete avoidance of certain risks, but about a careful balancing and controlling of a myriad of potential risks.[5] Here we simply aimed to show that the determination of acceptability thresholds for particular risks and risk governance in general often have to be settled on a context-sensitive basis.

5 Obstacles to sustainable governance

There are many obstacles to achieving sustainable governance. Additional to the generic part of this chapter we want to highlight the need for context sensitivity and real-life implementation by looking into concrete cases of governance challenges. Within this section and the next, though, we want to leave the more principled and abstract discussions of the previous sections behind and focus on two real-world cases, in order to illustrate the nature and extent of the problems sustainable governance faces. In this section we first describe cases 1 and 2, followed by an analysis in terms of institutional and motivational obstacles. Case 3 is further developed in the following section. In focusing on these cases, we want to draw out the different kinds of obstacles that stand in the way of more sustainable governance. The most serious obstacles are institutional, motivational or both. Let us first present the cases, and thereafter proceed to identifying the character or nature of the obstacles.

Case 1 Guangdong fisheries in southern China

This case (Ferraro and Brans 2012) concerns the rapid economic growth followed by strong exploitation of fishery resources in the Guangdong province in southern China, relating to both the fish stock and marine environmental deterioration. One obvious tension here is rather general as it points to the conflict between environmental protection and economic development. The case in view demonstrates how this conflict pans out at a local level, due to a range of institutional obstacles. One remarkable conflict is about diverging objectives both at an inter- and intraorganisational level. Briefly, the conflict occurs between the national State Oceanic Administration (SOA) and the Fisheries Management Bureau (FMB), i.e. the national and the subnational levels. Whereas the former acts as 'the ruler of the sea', the latter acts as 'the servant of the fishers' (Ferraro and Brans 2012: 41). The conflict is thus about protection on the one hand and increasing economic growth on the other. According to Agenda 21 and other international regulations there are some international conventions to be implemented at the local level in different countries. However, when such objectives are implemented at the local level, responsibility is often delegated to the subordinate level, which in the *Guangdong* case is the provincial level regulated by the FMB. Several obstacles are present: (i) the policy implementation is captured by informal patron–client-type relationships (local governmental level); (ii) management responsibility is transferred to the FMB, which owns a huge fishing company; and (iii) the FMB is responsible for its own budget.

This case demonstrates how fiscal decentralisation leads to bureaucratic fragmentation and vertical specialisation: those who are responsible for environmental protection have no direct say in the implementation of the protection policies, which are governed by those who also have ownership interests in the fisheries production. In the *Guangdong* case there is even a further complication having to do with a certain division at the central level, so that fisheries management and environmental protection remain separate competencies. Now, this case most likely demonstrates more than an average amount of institutional obstacles. Additionally, as pointed out above, the authors found the 'ruler' and the 'ruled' to coexist in the same agency, that is, the Federal Management Bureau being responsible for policy implementation and also being the owner of an important fishing company.

The *Guangdong* case serves as an illustration of institutional obstacles to sustainability, mainly concerning the lack of adequate coordination of action. This flaw could be described in different ways. It is partly a demonstration of the problem of the public to the extent that the coordination of action at the local level is corrupted, partly due to lack of well-informed actors and institutions. There clearly also is an institutional obstacle having to do with the strong belief in one technological model applied indiscriminately, including to contexts where it does not work – that is, acting according to general international rules and regulations according to Agenda 21.

Furthermore, the empowerment of people through participation seems to have little to do with concern for the environment, and a whole lot with the safeguarding of nutrition and income. In this particular case there are several reasons why environmental responsibility is evaporating. Some have to do with patron–client relationships at the local level, which prevent natural resources and environments to be governed along democratic lines.

The main point of the authors describing the *Guangdong* case was to show how Agenda 21 and other international regulations often work poorly at the level of policy implementation. Besides, the objective here is not only to illustrate how overlap of authorities and double accountability may complicate the political process. Obviously, there is a need for looking in a different direction, since the coordination of formal agencies regulating sustainability policies does not work, at least not in developing and non-democratic countries.

Some of the problems in the *Guangdong fisheries* case have to do with the absence of alternative sources of nutrition and livelihood. In this particular case one may ask whether responsible fishery is an achievable objective at all. We believe it requires no further argument that the international organisations' capacity for solving the problem institutionally is doomed to fail as long as actions at the global, national and local levels are poorly coordinated. In the *Guangdong* case there are certain values in conflict that obviously prevent efficient coordination of action, as we have seen. The most obvious conflicting values have been observed as the double role of owner and controller co-residing in the same body.

Case 2 The Narmada dams (Sardar Sarovar) in India

This is a project aiming to provide irrigation water to drought-prone areas of Gujarat (India), as well as electricity to all three states sharing the project. Sardar Sarovar is a developmental project resulting in the displacement of many rural people and in environmental degradation, while urban dwellers profited through an increase in their already high standard of living (Cullet 1995: 33).

Thus, there are different groups with claims to the same resources. Intragenerational solidarity becomes an issue when e.g. economic development entails the improvement of someone's environment or quality of life balanced by the loss of other resources and by deprivation for other people (Cullet 1995). What happened in this case is that the project fed new water-intensive industries near the main urban centres without delivering water to its final destination – after having displaced an estimated 100,000 people who had to be relocated on new land, which is not freely available in India. Many rural people were displaced, causing significant environmental degradation, while at the same time urban dwellers already enjoying a comparatively high standard of living benefited. According to Cullet, Sardar Sarovar stands out clearly as a failure to make all people, or at least the least well off, benefit from a development project partly aimed at improving environmental conditions on a regional scale.

In addition to compromising solidarity *within* the same generation, the Sardar Sarovar project also illustrates how sustainable development still may entail environmental deterioration that is not captured by the prevailing concept of sustainable development. This is a reason why we need to address environmental rights as a kind of collective right, across and between generations. In the particular case of the Sardar Sarovar project, an intragenerational injustice is committed towards one among several groups with claims to the same resources. The case in view demonstrates how economic development may entail an improvement in the environment for certain people balanced by loss of other resources for other people, e.g. the displacement of rural people and environmental degradation benefiting urban dwellers. This case also illustrates the kind of injustice discussed in Rawls, notably the difference principle – a principle according to which the only differences allowed are those that do not disadvantage those less privileged (Rawls 1971). Against this background we may now understand environmental rights as collective rights aiming at improving the situation of the less advantaged. How could we make sense of such a concept of environmental rights?

5.1 Institutional obstacles

Lack of coordination (case 1)

Several problems of insufficient or inadequate coordination of action have been discussed in connection with the *Guangdong fisheries* case. One main issue relates to problems of delegating governance to sublevels without safeguarding communication between the global, national and local levels of governance. This problem has been identified as a challenge to the implementation of Agenda 21 locally, where the aim is to enhance sustainability, to empower people through participation, and to create ownership of the local project. These goals sound good as long as they are considered without reference to concrete contexts. However, as shown by the implementation in the *Guangdong* case, local conditions are not always consistent with these aims. This is proved by the lack of enhanced sustainability. Overfishing and environmental pollution were not reduced despite the implementation of Agenda 21. This case of overfishing and pollution also partly illustrates what has been discussed in terms of the 'tragedy of the commons', i.e. the problem of each individual trying to gain own profit while at the same time causing damage to the commons.[6]

Context-blind implementation of Agenda 21 (case 1)

Local Agenda 21 is an example of a transnational policy aimed at sustainable development in a broad sense. The protection of fragile environments and the strengthening of the role of local authorities are among the objectives. In the *Guangdong* case there are several reasons why these universal intentions do not translate to the local context. A major problem seems to consist in indiscriminate and context-blind implementation of a project that is not adjusted to the local conditions of governance (see Chapter 7 on developing countries). In the particular case of the Guangdong fisheries, responsibility is delegated to the subordinate level, which in this case is the provincial level regulated by the FMB. As such, it meets several obstacles: the policy implementation is (i) captured by informal patron–client-type relationships (at the local governmental level); (ii) management responsibility is transferred to the FMB, which owns a huge fishing company; and (iii) the FMB is responsible for its own budget.

Misplaced expertise (case 1)

Additional to the problem of context-blind implementation of Agenda 21, there is also a problem in the *Guangdong* case of misplaced expertise. One aspect of fiscal decentralisation is vertical specialisation, which in this case means that the fishery management and environmental protection belong to separate organising units. This is a separation within the Ministry of Agriculture, which governs two main branches divided between fisheries and marine protection. As a consequence, those two competencies are kept separate. In order to obtain the goals of less environmental deterioration and less exploitation of fishery resources, it is necessary that the competencies, or expertise, resides within the same organisational branch. Instead, in a situation such as in Guangdong, those who are responsible for environmental protection have no say in the implementation of the protection policies.

Conflict nutrition vs. sustainable politics (case 1)

Some of the problems of the *Guangdong fisheries* case have to do with the absence of alternative sources of nutrition and livelihood. Thus, there is an initial incompatibility between the aims of environmental protection and those of economic growth, a problem often referred to as the 'entrapment problem'. This problem is typical of many underdeveloped countries (see Chapter 7 on developing countries). The conflict is amplified because the Federal Management Bureau is responsible for policy implementation while also being the owner of an important fishing company.

Lack of solidarity within same generation (case 2)

A different aspect of institutional obstacles concerns lack of solidarity across current generations. In the *Saradar Sarovar* case we witnessed a situation of solidarity within the same generation being compromised, that is, among different people having claims to the same resources. Although the project benefits some of those concerned, others – primarily poor and rural people – are disempowered. In this case both disempowered people and nature fall victim to deterioration. In a similar way, a lack of solidarity with future generations may cause damage to future people, as well as to the non-human environments, due to pollution and the overuse of natural resources by the current generation.

Need for collective environmental rights (cases 1 and 2)

The idea of environmental rights draws upon human rights in one important respect: broadly similarly to the way in which we allocate certain universal rights to humans, we are urged to think about the environment. The rationale for doing so is that the environment affects both human and non-human nature, and because emissions and the utilisation of natural resources affect people and environments far beyond the contexts in which the actions are carried out. Unlike individual human rights, environmental rights should be conceived as collective and solidarity rights (see also Chapter 2). On this account, the rights would be given to communities of peoples rather than to individuals. This perspective appears to be the most suitable one, as 'environment' does not seem comparable to individual human rights, one main reason being that it is hard to tell who should be held accountable and responsible for environmental damages. Talking of protection of the environment in terms of collective rights also turns the corresponding responsibilities into a collective concern. Further, such a perspective also requires that the rights encompass non-human nature, even if it is otherwise anthropocentric.

5.2 Motivational obstacles

Time preferences (case 1)

Short-termism in attitudes and policies has frequently been referred to as an obstacle to sustainable development for further discussion of motivational obstacles (see Chapter 9). Partly this has to do with shifting political regimes of different shapes, within democratic as well as non-democratic contexts. Several solutions have been suggested, among them transnational governance as an alternative to national and local forms of governance. Some of the arguments emphasise the need for considering non-human nature and the environment as commons rather than commodities. As such, nature and the environment are unlike many other tradable goods and services. In the cases discussed above we have witnessed vulnerabilities due to short-termism. In the *Guangdong* case the concern for meeting the needs for nutrition of the currently living overrides the need to protect the environments in the interest of other currently living and future generations. The *Sardar Sarovar* case, although in a different manner, also runs victim to short-termism, since neither the needs of all concerned people in the area nor those of future generations are accommodated, as the project leads to environmental deterioration.

6 Developed and developing countries

Apart from the many obstacles to sustainable governance discussed above, there is another issue that further complicates the government of climate change, sustainability and intergenerational justice, namely, the unequal politics between more developed and less developed states (see Chapter 7 on developing countries). After setting out some of the general problems surrounding the currently often glossed-over differences between developed and less developed states, we will again use a real-world case: the government of Ecuador's Yasuni ITT Fund Initiative. This case nicely illustrates the pitfalls and complexities underlying the common suggestion of differentiated responsibilities of more and less developed states.

It is highly important to consider the differences between individual developed countries (DCs) and less developed countries (LDCs), since subscribing to universal moral principles and a human rights-based approach should not be mistaken for proposing abstract context-blind governance principles. As was pointed out in Chapter 7, many countries face difficult choices when it comes to where to invest and which of their obligations to fulfil, since economic development, environmental protection and addressing domestic poverty and intergenerational inequity will not always go hand in hand. In fact, in some cases they might be diametrically opposed. At the same time, one should be cautious not to let the perceived conflict between development and environmental protection, or between intra- and intergenerational justice, hegemonise the thinking and discourse around global environmental governance. There are many different ways in which countries can develop economically, though many of these paths will require certain forms of international collaboration.

However, in a world marred by unequal trade relations, exploitative foreign investment practices and a deeply unequal international political system, international collaboration is a thorny issue. While international collaboration and support appear to be a crucial element for successfully dealing with an issue as complex as global environmental change, we need to flesh out firmly what the slogan of common but differentiated responsibilities actually entails for potential duties of DCs to support environmentally sustainable development in LDCs without reproducing neocolonial power structures and dependencies. Current practices such as land grabbing, natural resource exploitation by foreign countries, or the disposal of toxic electronic waste in LDCs, obviously run counter to the ideal of fruitful collaboration.

The idea of common but differentiated responsibilities can be cashed out along different normative fault lines, depending on what is taken to be the origin of the differentiated responsibilities. Some see the origin of the differentiated responsibilities in countries' historical behaviour and the benefits they might have accrued; others connect the responsibilities countries have to wealth and the ability to pay. Either way, it is widely assumed that one of the major dividing lines is the separation of highly developed countries from less developed ones. However, whether this distinction is the correct one remains controversial. Moreover, even if we were to agree on the origin of the differentiated responsibilities it is not at all clear how the differences in responsibility should be translated into action, since DCs are reluctant to see themselves as the ones who have to take the first step, and vice versa.

Case 3 The Yasuni ITTI

Take the question of global carbon sink conservation as a practical example: global carbon sink conservation raises a host of normative issues, since it is debatable, for instance, who should pay the costs of carbon sink conservation, who has the duty to protect which sinks (especially since not all sinks are terrestrial) and how far the duty to conserve one's carbon sinks extends (e.g. is it morally impermissible to cut down a small part of one's forests if that creates major benefits for the local population?). These normative questions are not of a mere theoretical nature. When Ecuador discovered major oil reserves under the area of its Yasuni National Park, the government founded the Yasuni Ishpingo–Tambococha–Tiputini Initiative (Yasuni ITTI), which asked foreign governments, NGOs and individual stakeholders to pay into a fund for the conservation of the Yasuni National Park. If by 2023 the fund would have generated donations of around US$3.6 billion, Ecuador would leave the oil reserves in the ground; if not, Ecuador would go ahead and extract the oil. The rationale behind the Yasuni ITTI was clear. Ecuador would preserve parts of its crucial global carbon sinks (and of the park's amazing biodiversity), but the costs of doing so (both direct and indirect) would have to be borne by foreign governments and other parties. In August 2013, the Yasuni ITTI was declared unsuccessful, due to insufficient contributions to the UN-administered fund.

The Yasuni ITTI was politically controversial, since some took it to be a case of ecological hostage taking: instead of finding a multilateral solution to the environmental challenges we face, Ecuador threatened to destroy part of its public good-providing carbon sinks in case the international community was not willing to pay. This seems problematic, since many would hold that Ecuador has a duty of justice to conserve its tropical forests, as part of global and intergenerational climate justice and as part of doing their share in governing the global commons. At the same time, many people hold that the developed states of the global North have a duty to bear (most of) the costs of fulfilling these duties of justice, since the only reason that Ecuador is in the difficult position to either protect its forests or exploit the oil, is anthropogenic climate change, which was largely caused by emissions from the global North. What is absent from this framing of the issue, though, is the question of the environmental and other rights violated.

Analysis of the Yasuni ITTI

Assessing whether setting up the Yasuni ITTI was legitimate and who is to blame for its failure, which means that large parts of the national park will be destroyed and climate-damaging oil is going to be extracted, very much depends on how one conceptualises the very problem at hand. If one sees the *Yasuni* case as part of the global governance of the commons it seems fair to conclude that by even considering drilling for oil Ecuador's government failed to do its share in preserving the global commons. If one focuses on the idea that the national park with its massive rain forest is a crucial part of the global carbon cycle, it seems clear that Ecuador should have a duty to preserve its precious rain forests.

However, one could choose a different angle and see the rain forest in the national park as just one natural resource among many under national control. On this reading, it goes without saying that Ecuador – like any other country in the world – has the right to sovereign control over its natural wealth and resources, meaning that it is up to the people of Ecuador to decide what to do with its forests and oil reserves. In other words, Ecuador as a self-determining state has the right to control its resources and to do as it sees fit, which includes the right to extract the oil and to use the proceeds to advance economic development.

However, there is another rights angle that allows us to advance important normative claims regarding the Yasuni National Park and its oil reserves: on the one hand, there are the rights of the citizens of Ecuador, who have a right to be protected by their state against major risks and harms (whether that is future climate risks or the current risk of economic deprivation); on the other hand, there are the rights of the indigenous population within the Yasuni National Park, a group of Ecuador's population that lacks equal political rights. These indigenous people would lose their natural habitat if oil drillings went ahead, without ever being consulted on what should be done with the national park.

Moreover, one can approach the Yasuni ITTI from a global justice perspective, focusing on the fact that Ecuador did very little to cause global climate change, that the most powerful states in the world do little to help countries like Ecuador to develop economically, and that interfering with Ecuador's right to self-determination in the name of global climate governance seems paternalistic and hypocritical, considering how little DCs do to reduce their own emission footprints.

No matter which of these readings and claims one finds the most plausible, it seems that all of the voiced concerns and claims are relevant in this context. This goes to show that governing natural resources often cuts across a whole range of levels, from the local level (e.g. the indigenous people living in the Yasuni park), to the regional level (e.g. locals directly affected by use changes), to the national level (e.g. the people of Ecuador and the country's government), to the international level (e.g. other governments), to the global level (e.g. the users of the global commons). This of course raises the question at which level decisions should be made, whose claims should be heard and how legitimacy can be bestowed on such decisions if it is clear that not all relevantly affected parties can have an equal say in such matters. Furthermore, one can wonder whether in such cases democratic procedures help or hinder to achieve the goal of just and sustainable environmental governance.

Having considered the three case studies above and drawing on our analysis from sections 1–6, the next section will bring the key findings of the other chapters of the book into our governance context, looking for common concerns where we can profit from further developing our interdisciplinary discussion of ethics of a green future.

7 Governance in view of remaining chapters of the book

The previous chapters of this book shed light on challenges, hopes and visions for human rights to a sustainable future for humankind and the environment. In dealing with rights (Chapter 2) it is claimed that protection of environmental goods is basic to human rights. Such rights need to be governed. One of the basic challenges is how to oblige current living people to take upon duties towards future people who are not yet brought into existence. As an example, there are no people in the future to reciprocate current people's actions directed at advantaging future generations. Perhaps some sort of indirect reciprocity would make sense. One concrete suggestion is to establish a system where future people could be represented politically, an arrangement that is further discussed in a separate chapter on political representation (Chapter 6). One basic question that is raised is whether there is a need for environmental rights as such, partly analogous to human rights. One obvious constraint for being a rights holder is to be capable of taking upon responsibilities and corresponding duties. In this respect, it is clear that environmental rights cannot be compared to individual human rights. This is also a reason why caring for the environment for all – current and future generations – need to be understood in terms of a different kind of rights for all. Governance of rights privileging current and future generations on a global scale needs to undertake a careful examination of the particular contextual conditions. This is what this book aims for, in considering e.g. legal, economic, motivational and risk aspects in their various contexts.

One reason why general models, or a one-size-fits-all mentality works poorly when discussing rights to a sustainable future has to do with risks (Chapter 3). Not only are environmental risks hard to predict in environmental contexts, particularly due to uncertainty. This is mainly due to the fact that the kind of risks in view are exempted from the possibility of calculating probabilities. Thus, we have to act upon the precautionary principle without being able to know exactly what kind of precautions need to be taken. Besides, one complicating matter is to what extent people may have rights against risking, as some risks are necessary in order to appreciate a right to a meaningful life. Additionally, there is also the case that people experience risks differently. The contextual stakes are obviously high. At a governance level a rights-based approach may give a rough guidance with respect to risks, but this has to be context sensitive.

The lack of knowledge about the future is highlighted in the chapter on scenarios (Chapter 4). Any discussion of what might happen in the future has to be based upon uncertainties, as also discussed in the chapter on risks. In the scenario chapter, it is argued that scenarios must be based on narratives and informed qualitative and fact-based reasoning, warning that policies on environmental rights must not be based on unchangeable and decontextualised 'iron laws'.

The right to life for future generations raises a question whether it would be possible to safeguard future generations through legal arrangements. A move in such a rights-based direction has been done in the past, in the United Nations Conference held in Stockholm 1972, but has not been developed further since then, e.g. in Rio 1992 (Chapter 5). The way to safeguard future generation was discussed in terms of environmental rights, as distinct from human rights. As is pointed out in this chapter there has ever since 1972 been a question of more soft law, focusing on moral and political rather than legal rights. Still, there is an environmental linkage in the legal debate between human rights and future generations. Since it is difficult to allocate rights be it to the environments as such, or to future generations, there has instead taken place a greening of existing human rights. A legal approach has to be based in protection of identifiable lives, not life as such. Thus, the current juridical framework puts limits to how far it is possible to go in the direction of rights to the environments or to future people we do not yet know who they are. The most promising attempt to accommodate future generations' rights to life after the Stockholm 1972 has been the 1998 Aarhus Convention on Access to Information, Public Participation in Decision-making and Access to Justice in Environmental Matters, through the *actio popularis* claim, which includes future people in terms of 'members of the public'. As argued in this chapter, without *actio popularis* in relation to the environmental damage it is hard to make claims on behalf of those who will suffer in the future. One strategy suggested in this chapter is to broaden the concept of 'victim' and to give room for group-based rights. Another possible route which was mentioned earlier in this chapter would be to establish an international court for the environment, which would need to go hand in hand with a strengthening and extension of existing environmental rights frameworks, along the lines discussed in Chapter 2.

The possibility of safeguarding future people has been extensively discussed in terms of political representation of future generations (Chapter 6). The idea to include future generations through representatives has been set to work in some democratic contexts, notably within governmental bodies. This far such arrangements, e.g. through an Ombudsman, has not succeeded in coming up with a model to be embraced by a majority of democratic states. One reason may be because the focus this far has been on political institutions. As suggested in Chapter 6, one should rather look to NGOs, firms and educational institutions in order to engage the public more directly. Apart from that, one idea suggested here is to have separate institutions for environmental protection, which could then be a tool to represent future generations. Again, like in most of the chapters of this book, we face the problem of assigning particular rights to non-identifiable future people.

Economics is still another frame for discussing accommodation of future generations. The most prevailing problem from an economics aspect is probably the overuse of common property such that there is not enough left for future people (Chapter 8). Along with the overuse of common property resources there is also the underproduction of collective common goods, as well as negative externalities. Anthropogenic climate change causes negative externalities, and in this chapter, it is argued that we cannot escape them. Rather, it is a question of how much environmental pollution should be justified? If this argument is sound, the question still remains to what extent negative externalities in terms of an optimal amount of environmental pollution is possible to apply to future generations, not least given the uncertainties and risks discussed in Chapter 3.

The quest for more contextualised or tailor-made arrangements for accommodating future generations becomes particularly urgent when discussing developing countries (Chapter 7). One approach is to focus on economic and ecological depths, and the question of uncompensated disadvantages for people in developing countries. One alerting problem is how countries that are not able to accommodate the current generation should make sacrifices for safeguarding future generations. The resource curse is a particular case in view, i.e. countries who are rich in natural resources still remain in poverty due to e.g. bad governance, dictatorship, economic usurpation and others, the main problem often being that political institutions fail to act impartially in the public interest. The problem of entrapment appears to be a general problem across the diversity of developing countries, one example being that investment for future generations seems undoable as long as the current living are starving. In this chapter, it is argued that there should be less duty for developing countries to spend resources to protect future generations, as compared to developed countries. The 'polluter pay principle', or 'beneficiary pays principle' is advanced as an argument in favour of justifying less duties for developing countries. The main appeal being made is to the following general, although contextual circumstances of developing countries: economic vulnerability, institutional weakness and entrapment. It is further claimed that the problem ought to be viewed as global rather than national, i.e. we should look for cooperative solutions to the problems. Besides, it is necessary to look for tailor-made solutions, as developing countries are diverse with respect to what cases the problems in each particular context.

The need to look carefully into particular contexts is also emphasised in the chapter om motivation (Chapter 9). The motivational problem connected with ethics of a green future is identified as a gap between norms and conformity, i.e. the problem to act upon what we believe. Four particular obstacles are identified in this chapter: time preference, non-reciprocity and uncertainty, of which the latter two are also discussed in the chapters on rights, risk and political representation. Additionally, there is also the threat of maintenance of habitualised lifestyles. These are held to be motivational obstacles to safeguarding a sustainability for future generations. One main problem discussed in this chapter is the problem of abstract risks where, in dealing with statistical rather than identified victims (see Chapter 5 on legal implementation). Given these problems of motivation, rather than acting on direct motivations we should instead focus on indirect motivations (love, pity, care, solidarity), then appealing to the heart, captured in the concept of 'chain of love'. Self-binding is further discussed as a strategy to handle the motivational problem, internally or through institutions. In doing so, we need to confront the abstract models for such arrangements with real-life problems, a task recommended for ethics as a philosophical discipline.

8 Concluding remarks

At the beginning of this chapter we said that we would highlight possible roads to sustainable politics and governance. As our discussion above showed it is indeed necessary to think of different roads rather than a single road in order to address the problems and challenges that lie before us. The demands of intergenerational justice and environmental sustainability cut across a host of different dimensions and levels, making it necessary to devise context-sensitive policies. However, in so doing, we think that three crucial aspects should be kept in mind. First, any lifestyle and production changes in the most developed countries ultimately only contribute to a solution if rebound effects are minimised. Similarly, second, a possible move to sufficiency and/or frugality has to go hand in hand with a shift in resources and power to those currently disadvantaged. Consequently, third, following Caney (2012), environmental policymaking needs to avoid the pitfalls of atomism and isolationism, that is, climate policy must be contextualised within the wider context of existing inequalities in economic and political power, vulnerability and coping capacity. In other words, environmental governance needs to be problem-solving and context-sensitive, and it needs to address wider inequalities.

Governance in view of the other chapters of this book points to a need for careful consideration of the particular context for governance of *rights* to a green future. In discussing rights there is a quest for adequate human rights, and a corresponding need to find ways of regulating such rights. A rights-based approach to *risk* problems give us a rough guidance, but then we need to be sensitive to the context in implementing this at a governance-level. Further in creating *scenarios,* politics should not be based on decontextualised hard laws, and when looking for good ways of governing *legal* arrangements we should leave room for group-based rights and a broadened concept of 'victim'. When setting out to find out how to *represent future generations* politically it is suggested that we look for suitable NGOs, firms and educational institutions rather than embedding the representation in general political institutions. *Economics* questions of negative externalities also need to pay attention to particular contexts in order to decide how much environmental pollution should be justified. The discussion of duties of *developing countries* to accommodate future generations asks for tailor-made governance arrangements. Lastly, when it comes to governance aspects of the motivation problem we need to confront our abstract models with real-life problems, asking what is needed in the particular context in question. This is a challenge for ethics, which we have tried to accommodate in cooperation with the other fields of inquiry presented in this book.

In the beginning of this chapter, we raised the question of whether effective global environmental governance requires the establishment of a global environmental agency or an international court for the environment in terms of a global enforcing mechanism. However, central decision-making and enforceability are only two of a range of important aspects which might contribute toward a better environmental governance system. Therefore, coming to the end of this chapter, while we still believe that there is a need to look at least in part for global solutions, we want to highlight what we emphasised throughout this chapter, namely, that we should build our solutions around contextualised models of governance mechanisms. This points to a need for better fit methodologies for governance implementation, while not losing sight of a global perspective as such. After all, intergenerational justice, rights to a green future and environmental rights cannot be obtained at local or national levels in isolation. Still, the governing mechanisms have to work at all levels in each particular context. The requested context sensitivity seems to be missing in the governance arrangements we have witnessed thus far.

In light of the issues discussed in this book in general and this chapter in particular, academics should aim to provide policymakers and activists with at least a rough road map of how to conceptualise people's rights to a green future, how to regulate intergenerational risks and how to implement pathways to sustainable governance. This is precisely the aim of the research agenda in the next chapter; it sets out where further research is needed, which issues must be given priority and how we might address the practical questions surrounding people's rights to a green future.

Notes

1 Agenda 21 is a non-binding, voluntarily implemented action plan of the United Nations with regard to sustainable development. It is a product of the 1992 Earth Summit (UN Conference on Environment and Development). Agenda 21 is an action agenda for the UN, other multilateral organisations, and individual governments around the world that can be executed at local, national and global levels. It has been affirmed and modified at subsequent UN conferences.
2 Some people of course claim that a lack of democratic control might be a good thing, since environmental policy (and possibly other policies, too) should not depend on public support and applause form the constituency, especially in cases in which present well-being's losses are necessary for the securing of future well-being opportunities.
3 For a detailed discussion of this case, see Weber (2015).
4 An example of the former kind of rights of the non-human environment is Bolivia's Law of the Rights of Mother Earth, while an example of the latter kind of environmental human right can be found in the South African constitution, ch. two s. 24, which affirms every citizen's right to a non-harmful environment.
5 This of course also means that people are vulnerable to risk in more than one way, making it thus policymakers' task to socially distribute risks in light of existing inequalities in risk vulnerability.
6 See Hardin (1968) and Ostrom (1990/2015).

Bibliography

Alcott, Blake. 2008. 'The sufficiency strategy: would rich-world frugality lower environmental impact?'. *Ecological Economics* 64(4): 770–786.
Alvarez, Allen Andrew and May Thorseth. Forthcoming. 'Intergenerational justice and obligations towards future generations: towards environmental rights in land use policy'. Forthcoming in an anthology at the University of Toronto Press from the RCN funded project FORFOOD: *Frogs, Fuel, Finance or Food*.
Birnbacher, Dieter. 2015. 'Some moral pragmatics of climate change'. In D. Birnbacher and M. Thorseth (eds), *The Politics of Sustainability: Philosophical Perspectives*. Abingdon: Routledge, 153–173.

Boyle, Alan. 2007. 'Human rights or environmental rights-a reassessment'. *Fordham Environmental Law Review* 18: 471–511.

Caney, Simon. 2012. 'Just emissions'. *Philosophy & Public Affairs* 40: 255–300.

Cullet, Philippe. 1995. 'Definition of an environmental right in a human rights context'. *Netherlands Quarterly of Human Rights* 13: 25–40.

Feintuck, Mike. 2005. 'Precautionary maybe, but what's the principle? The precautionary principle, the regulation of risk, and the public domain'. *Journal of Law & Society* 32(3): 371–398.

Ferraro, Gianluca and Marleen Brans. 2000. 'Trade-offs between environmental protection and economic development in China's fisheries policy: a political analysis in the adoption and implementation of the Fisheries Law'. *Natural Resources Forum* 36: 38–49.

Gosseries, Axel. 2009. 'Three models of intergenerational reciprocity'. In A. Gosseries and L. H. Meyer (eds), *Intergenerational Justice*. Oxford: Oxford University Press, 119–146.

Gray, Kurt, Adrian F. Ward and Michael I. Norton. 2014. 'Paying it forward: generalized reciprocity and the limits of generosity'. *Journal of Experimental Psychology: General* 143(1): 247–254.

Hardin, Garrett. 1968. 'The tragedy of the commons'. *Science* 162(3859): 1243–1248. Available at: doi:10.1126/science.162.3859.1243

Howarth, Richard B. 1992. 'Intergenerational justice and the chain of obligation'. *Environmental Values* 1(2): 133–140.

Meyer, Lukas. 2008. 'Intergenerational justice'. Available at: http://plato.stanford.edu/entries/justice-intergenerational (last accessed 9 April 2018)

Mitchell, Ronald. 2003. 'International environmental agreements: a survey of their features, formation, and effects'. *Annual Review of Environment and Resources* 28: 429–461.

Mitchell, Ronald. 2012. 'Technology is not enough: climate change, population, affluence, and consumption'. *Journal of Environment & Development* 21(1): 24–27. doi:10.1177/1070496511435670

Ostrom, Elinor. 2015 [1990]. *Governing the Commons: The Evolution of Institutions for Collective Action*. Cambridge: Cambridge University Press.

Parfit, Derek. 1986. *Reasons and Persons*. Oxford: Oxford University Press.

Rawls, John. 1971. *A Theory of Justice*. Cambridge, MA: Belknap Press of Harvard University Press.

Rawls, John. 1985. 'Justice as fairness: political not metaphysical'. *Philosophy & Public Affairs*: 223–251.

Stephens, Tim. 2009. *International Courts and Environmental Protection*. Cambridge: Cambridge University Press.

Weber, Rolf. 2015. 'Border tax adjustment – legal perspective'. *Climatic Change*. doi:10.1007/s10584–10015–1414–1412

Wiener, Jonathan. 2002. 'Precaution in a multirisk world'. In Dennis Paustenbach (ed.), *Human and Ecological Risk Assessment: Theory and Practice*. London: Wiley, 1509–1531.

Woods, Kerri. 2015. 'Climate justice, motivation and harm'. In D. Birnbacher and M. Thorseth (eds), *The Politics of Sustainability: Philosophical Perspectives*. Abingdon: Routledge, 92–109.

11

ETHICS OF A GREEN FUTURE

A research agenda

Marcus Düwell and Karsten Klint Jensen

Introduction

The aim of this book has been to investigate, quite comprehensively and in an interdisciplinary setting, our long-term responsibilities from a rights-based perspective. One can see three recurring topics.

First, long-term responsibility implies that we have to face a fundamental uncertainty: we simply don't know the future and thinking about our responsibilities should start with this insight (particularly Chapters 3 and 4). However, we *can* know specific biological and ecological constraints within which the future may develop, and we *are* aware of the biological and anthropological conditions of human life and the needs that have to be fulfilled to enable human beings to lead a human life. All relevant ethical considerations have to take those constraints into account. But we cannot know what consequences climate change in detail will have, nor can we know how social life and political institutions will develop. We have to develop views and models regarding the future that take these uncertainties into account and we have to wonder what kind of normative commitments we may have in light of this unknown future.

Second, long-term responsibilities have a clear collective dimension, ultimately a global dimension. This implies that thinking about long-term responsibilities has to involve rethinking the structures of political decision-making and other governance structures (Chapter 10); it also involves thinking about the psychology of human beings living in those institutions and who ultimately are the driving forces of decision-making (Chapter 9). The necessary coordination in meeting our long-term responsibilities concerning the climate will only be possible as an integrated part of these structures. This means that we have to investigate the connections between the international political and legal institutions and the way the economy works (Chapters 7 and 8) in order to understand how these structures are related to motives human beings may have concerning long-term responsibilities.

This implies, *third*, that the details of these responsibilities are dependent on further questions regarding citizenship, inclusion, democratic participation and global human rights (Chapters 2, 5 and 6). This book has worked from a rights-based perspective which emphasises that political institutions have to be built on respect for the rights of individuals, on the rule of law and legitimate democratic procedures – the starting points on which the international normative order is built (at least in theory). But in light of the discussions in this book it seems clear that such a rights-based ethics will have to be developed much further if it is to be capable of providing convincing normative answers to the current ecological challenges.

It is clear that this book has opened a lot of issues that lead to further questions. It will be the task of this concluding chapter to outline some further lines of discussion and academic research on the bases of those considerations. The chapter will: discuss foundations of a future-oriented rights-based approach (section 1); sketch some questions regarding the political dimension of the topic (section 2); discuss the ethical significance of risk and uncertainty (section 3); outline how those questions are related to issues of more general cultural and philosophical significance (section 4); and conclude with some methodological issues regarding the appropriate form of an ethical debate (section 5).

1 An ethics of rights?

The current book has taken a rights-based ethics as a normative starting point for its investigation. This starting point has various advantages: it is firmly embedded in the current national legal systems and in international law; it is furthermore an approach which is compatible with many theories of justice in so far as they assume that in a just society equal rights should be respected. The idea that human beings have equal rights is also deeply embedded in political theory of the last centuries, not only in Western countries, but also in the movements of protest and emancipation in non-Western countries. The critique of racist and colonialist traditions is based on the idea that all human beings deserve equal respect. It seems therefore natural to ask what kind of duties with regard to the future would follow from such an ethics. To think about duties to future generations in terms of 'rights', however, makes it necessary to rethink dominant interpretations of the traditional notion of a 'right'. This deserves further consideration and research; we shall mention some issues here.

First, it would have to make sense in the first place to have duties towards people that do not yet exist and whose identity we do not know. This appears to imply a certain impersonal or generic understanding of a right. But if we assume that the entire human rights regime is based on the idea that the dignity of all human beings, regardless of their identity, requires our respect and should be promoted, it seems clear that this would hold also for future people. In that case, the mere anticipation of their existence would create duties for us. Those duties would be concerned with the life opportunities and interests of future people. They are part of the idea of 'sustainable development', as understood in the Brundtland definition: a development that respects the needs of future people.

A *second* revision is concerned with the ideas that there are only a few negative rights with 'absolute' authority, such as rights that protect human beings against torture, genocide, arbitrary violation of privacy, enslavement, deprivation etc. A duty to respect the dignity of future humans appears to involve a broader scope of rights, which the current generation actually can infringe. This, however, is not a strange revision. The entire contemporary human rights-regime and national constitutions are implicitly built on this assumption. But a broader scope of rights only appears plausible if those rights are not all on the same level of importance. Hence, it must be possible to prioritise rights and assign them different weight. However, this also opens up space for trade-offs which rights are supposed to protect against. So there is a challenge for the revised notion of rights to find a non-arbitrary ways to restrict possible trade-offs.

Third, another revision has to do with the normally shared assumption that rights have to be seen as individual rights only. However, there are some important issues about the possibility of 'collective rights'. Consider, for instance, goods that are important for ethnic identities, and situations where we have to ask whether rights to those goods can legitimately restrict the exercise of individual liberties in order to protect ethnic or other collective entities to maintain their traditional way of life. We will not go into the details of those debates because they are not the topic of this volume. But (as discussed in Chapter 2) there are some collective goods necessarily implied by the idea of individual rights. If a human being has the right to exercise his basic liberties and not be vulnerable to arbitrary interventions of others, there might be a right which protects the ecological circumstances that are required for being able to exercise these basic liberties. It seems that the entire idea of a sustainable development implies that we have certain rights to ecological conditions that are important for the life of human beings and that, correlatively, other agents have duties to refrain from damaging those conditions. This cannot mean that human beings are condemned to do nothing at all – because most of our activities will be accompanied by negative effects on the environment – but it would certainly be a reason for restricting those activities that have particularly high costs for the important aspects of the environment.

It must be further discussed what these considerations will imply for our understanding of political institutions, but we should emphasise that this overview of issues is only a sketch. However, we strongly believe that it is important for the human rights discourse to take the entire idea of rights of future people seriously. If the human rights regime and rights-based legal system is not able to provide orientation with regard to the ecological challenges, this implies that they are not really able to function as an orientation for the challenges of the future – they are normative models of the past. So far, we have no reason to assume that this is the case. It is, however, clear from the outset that it would require some methodological revisions of the current philosophical notions of human rights, namely the strict opposition between a practical approach to human rights on the one hand and a more natural rights-based approach on the other hand (see Chapter 2). The way we propose to understand rights here is not restricted to existent human rights practices, but it is an attempt to reconstruct presuppositions that are incorporated in the human rights idea, and to elaborate the implications of those presuppositions. This does not mean that human rights have to be understood as a kind of earthly representation of an eternal natural law–idea. Likewise, it does not presuppose any form of moral realism. Instead, we propose to critically reflect on the presupposition behind the practice of ascribing rights to human beings and try to understand how this practice should be developed in a world that is characterised by challenges other than those that were dominant when the current legal practices were formulated.

2 Our understanding of politics and political institutions

If we understand the duties towards future people in terms of rights, the implications for those duties within the political order will have to be investigated. It should not just be an arbitrary decision of the current generation to protect the interests of future people or to decide not to do so – it should be an essential element of the normative self-understanding of political institutions. This would appear to imply that the protection of the basic life conditions of future people should be integrated in the hardware of political institutions; it should be part of the institutional setting itself. When political institutions develop mechanisms to ensure the rights of minorities and vulnerable groups, and ensure that political majorities cannot infringe upon those rights, they would also have to ensure that the life conditions of future people are protected.

One possibility is to develop a concept of citizenship that includes future generations. By doing so, future people can be granted a normative status within the political system, and this status would have to be respected by the current generation. Current citizens would be entitled to take decisions about matters that are important for them in so far as those decisions do not seriously harm the life conditions of future people. All decisions that would have a significant impact on future people would need justification. It is hard to see how we do not already implicitly assume that future people have such standing. Furthermore, this is supported by the simple insight that there are no strict borderlines between generations: generations are overlapping and continuously developing. A position that regards citizenship limited to the present living generation could not ignore the dynamics and fluent character of political responsibility. To regard it as an arbitrary decision of current people whether to care about future people is not really consistent in the first place. We hope that there will be more discussion in political philosophy on this subject.

If this possibility makes sense, it raises the further question of how future people and their basic interests can have a safe place in the political system (see Chapter 6). If we have rights-based duties to respect the interests of future people, it is important to ensure that those interests are protected on a structural basis, independent of changing political majorities. The existing proposals about this topic are so far in a rather embryonic stage. We think that there are important reasons for a more intense discussion concerning how a representation of future generations could and should look like.

However, this raises a challenge for democratic institutions. It will likely lead to the political process becoming more dependent on technocrats and their assessments, and will it make it more difficult for policymakers and for citizens to have influence on those technocratic processes. Also, it will mean that political decisions will have to deal with a lot of questions concerning probabilities, risks and uncertainties. Citizens would need a lot of 'empowerment' by intermediary institutions, education, new forms of participation to be able to intervene in this process. The danger is of course that the current erosion of political institutions would only be intensified by an amplification of technocratic processes.

Many topics currently politically discussed have significant impact on the future, ranging from the introduction of new technologies, energy use, housing, food habits and travelling to procreation. To treat all such topics as requiring that political decisions on them would not have severely harmful consequences for future people may not leave much room for political decision-making in the first place. It requires continuous assessment of the long-term effects of decisions, an assessment of the uncertainties and risks accompanied by those decisions, etc. A morally acceptable form of politics requires not only that citizens can trust the experts that provide them with the relevant information about fact and forecast. It also requires a sophisticated form of interpretation of the significance of risks and uncertainties for the life conditions and interests of citizens, and a framework that allows us to understand the impact of such (partly speculative and uncertain) information on our normative commitments. We will come back to this in the next section. Moreover, the entire tendency for a morally globalised and international form of politics and the tendency to form political institutions on higher levels (e.g. Europe, the UN) is not only driven by the interests of economic actors but is to some extent also necessary from the perspective of sustainable governance. This also has the danger that it may enforce a more technocratic form of politics with higher distance from citizens.

From a normative perspective this is quite an ambivalent picture. On the one hand one could say that it is the price of technological progress. If we choose to make our life easier, richer or more exciting with specific technologies (and there are normative reasons to do so), we need a higher level of control and a more technocratic system to deal with the consequences of those technologies (and there are also normative reasons for that). On the other hand, as citizens significantly forfeit influence on political decisions and it becomes increasingly more difficult to decide important political matters by ourselves, this is, from a normative point of view, problematic. The gap between those matters that are discussed in the political sphere and the matters that would have to be disputed if one were to regulate matters of long-term responsibilities is growing. We already see a growing number of citizens not taking part in any form of political decision-making, particularly in elections. But if citizens are not participating in political debates in the first place, it is unlikely that they will be committed to the predicament of future people. Nudging people to act sustainably without deliberation is perhaps effective and to some extent morally required. But nudging cannot compensate this lack of political commitment. From the perspective of democracy, it is normatively dubious to have a central dimension of political decision-making that develops to a great extend outside the awareness of a great part of citizenry.

All these observations are far from original or new – governance scholars have observed them for a long time. But the normative significance is not sufficiently acknowledged in ethical debates. If a life in accordance with the normative requirements of respect for the interests of future generations is only possible with a high level of technocratic governance that would exclude significant parts of the citizenry from the political process we would have a serious moral problem. It should be a central aspect of the normative debates in political philosophy.

Respect for the basic rights of people requires likewise that we ensure that future people are able to live an autonomous life and that current people are able to decide themselves about basic aspects of their life. Hence, there is a duty to implement democratic institutions worldwide for future generations to inherit.

3 Prediction, risk and uncertainty

It has been emphasised in this book at various places that an ethics of long-term responsibilities is confronted by fundamental risks and uncertainties. While it is uncontested that climate change is in the first instance the result of human activity, there is a significant level of uncertainty about the ecological consequences of climate change. We can make some models and work with different scenarios, but we can only predict to a degree what the consequences of climate development in different parts of the world will look like. This uncertainty of the level of biology and ecology will have further consequences concerning uncertainty from social and political perspectives. Depending on climate development, certain regions of the world will be very inhospitable; perhaps it will be impossible to live there. Parts of the Middle East will perhaps be too hot to live in, some African regions – which at the same time are expected to have a high level of population growth - may become very dry, Northern Europe may warm up or – depending on e.g. the behaviour of the Gulf Stream – cool down. Those possible developments will have all kinds of consequences for the possibilities of human beings to live in those regions, it will affect their behaviour, migration, economic activities and techno-logical patterns. Depending on the development of the climate in Europe e.g. people will have very different needs concerning housing, food production and cultural habits, and different technological paths will be needed to fulfil those needs. Each approach to an ethics of long-term responsibilities will have to deal with such unpredictability and uncertainties on different levels. We mention here four relevant implications.

First, as Chapter 4 outlined, it is fundamental to ask what methods we use to predict the future. Chapter 4 makes a case for models that try to be as inclusive and self-reflexive as possible. We have to be aware that all models depend on specific conceptual presuppositions which determine the kind of information we are to take into account. The current trend of selecting models on the basis of whether they are amenable to computer simulation counteracts such a self-reflexive trend. The complexity of ecological systems makes it, however, necessary to work with methodologies with awareness of their conceptual presuppositions, being able to understand how those presuppositions are filtering information and excluding other information and that are permanently able to rethink those exclusion mechanisms. The choice of mechanisms for prediction are also relevant in an ethical perspective since those models determine to which extent we are able to integrate a normative perspective in the first place.

Second, this uncertainty of the future also requires some new ways of thinking about the future. We need to some extent overcome traditional ways of predictions that are primarily extrapolations of current trends into the future. If we expect that in the future some characteristics of our ecological circumstances will change, this will have unexpected impacts on certain regions of the world and on the life people were used to. It requires creativity and imagination to figure out what kind of future will be possible and what life might look like. That does not mean that human beings have just to adapt to all kinds of ecological changes; if we imagine the future, this can also be a strong reason for restraints when it comes to significant ecological changes. But it is necessary to use the creative potential that human beings are capable of to develop views on the future to understand the complexities of ecological and social interrelationships. Normative assessments of our actions should be based not just on facts in idealised models but on concrete anticipations of possible future developments that try to understand the complex interrelationship of possible future developments. And we should use our creativity to figure out what different models of a social, economic and political life might look like.

Third, to deal with those uncertainties requires also political institutions that are capable of such learning processes. It would be necessary to have institutions that are capable of dealing with uncertainties and to work under the awareness that we are not capable of fully understanding the ecological and social complexities of climate change. The challenge is here that those political institutions would have to realise various expectations at the same time. They should be able to anticipate long-term consequences, they must be capable of learning processes, they must work on an international or even global level to have sufficient influence and at the same time it must be possible to democratically control them. At the moment, it is hard to see how current political institutions can be transformed in a way that they are capable of fulfilling all of these expectations.

Fourth, uncertainties and risks were also discussed in Chapter 3 (rights and risks) and Chapter 8 (economy). It is clear that an ethics of a green future would have to have a stance with regard to risk and uncertainties. This is at the moment the case to a very limited degree. A particular problem is in this context that a lot of moral philosophers would assume that a rights-based approach would be incapable right from the beginning to deal with those questions. According to various philosophers, a rights-based approach would have to be blind to the consequences of actions and would protect individual liberties, irrespective of the (short or long-term) consequences. Against those prejudices this volume has proposed revisions which also indicate how a rights-based ethics could deal with questions of risks and uncertainties. It should be clear right now that this discussion is of utmost importance for the prospects of an ethics of a green future. If a rights-approach is not capable of dealing with risks, this implies that the current normative frameworks that national constitutions and international law presuppose are fundamentally unfit to deal with climate change. The challenge is to reformulate those frameworks in a way that they are able to incorporate a dimension of risk and uncertainty.

4 Implications for our moral and practical self-understanding in general

We have already seen that broadening the scope of ethical debates to the future is not only a challenge for technology and the organisation of governmental processes, it also affects the understanding of basic concepts like human rights, citizenship and political institutions. It would be a wrong picture if we would think about questions of intergenerational justice in the way that we know criteria to measure whether a distribution of goods, opportunities and chances are fair and now we only have to apply these criteria on future people as well. Such an idea of fair distribution would presuppose an Archimedean position from which we would be able to oversee the entire history and assess how criteria for fair distribution could work. But we are not in this position atop of history, we are subjects within a historical process. We have to consider how to relate to a future that is unknown and one for which we do not have the knowledge for such a fair distribution. It is fundamental to reconsider our moral outlook on the world, political institutions and central aspects of modern life in a way that ensure that options to shape the future in a humane way will remain open.

This openness for the future will, however, not be independent of any kind of world views. Human beings have always developed views about the future, they have imagined apocalyptic scenarios, peaceful pictures of salvation and eternal peace or have interpreted the cosmos in terms of recurring historical cycles. These views are not only a relic of pre-modern times; in modernity people have also interpreted the world in terms of a teleological view on historical progress, have dreamed of a dialectics in the development of history, have thought in terms of the 'fall of the occident', have thought in terms of historical necessity, in terms of progress or decline. Human beings have developed a grand picture of historical processes and those pictures have influenced their interpretation of the world and their actions. It is inevitable that human beings develop views about history, to have patterns of interpretation that allow them to make sense of their actions.

Those interpretations necessarily go beyond that which human beings can know. We cannot know the future but nevertheless we have to relate to this broader horizon under which we act, even if we would be completely agnostic with regard to the future. Even such agnosticism would already be a very specific attitude towards the future and concerning this attitude like all other possible attitude we would have to show that it is an appropriate one. If due to current ecological challenges we extend our moral considerations to the future, we have to take all those broader questions into considerations. Specific views on history will influence the way we think about responsibility for the future. If we knew that the apocalypse was imminent, we would have no reason to worry about the long-term effects of our actions. And those interpretations are deeply embedded in broader cultural outlooks of the world, a cyclic interpretation of history will differ from a teleological view.

Emphasising the relevance of those bigger interpretations of history is not pleading for cultural relativism. We can – on the contrary – ask whether we have moral reasons for embracing or rejecting specific views on history. If we have good moral reasons to respect future people and to ensure safe life conditions for them, this could also mean that we have reasons to reject specific forms of historical determinism and develop instead an attitude of hope with regard to the future. If the future is open and unknown to us, it is morally important to take a critical look at world views that pretend to have comprehensive knowledge about the future. But if it is correct that moral duties regarding the future are interrelated to the way we think about the future, then it is difficult to avoid taking about those bigger philosophical questions about the place of human beings in the world and in history. A tendency in modern political philosophy to claim that moral and political convictions should be neutral with regard to comprehensive views on the world, should be at least again a topic of discussion. Perhaps the pretention of neutrality is difficult to defend, and it should be the task of debates of the ethics of long-responsibilities to discover new ways of discussing those broader comprehensive views. This is not to say that we should go back to the 1960s and discuss ethical questions in terms of historical materialism or in terms of sin and forgiveness. But it is necessary to be aware that those broader philosophical perspectives cannot be avoided in ethical debates. And it is necessary for find forms to discuss those matters in a constructive and productive way.

5 What might an appropriate 'ethics of the future' look like?

This final chapter, like the entire book, attempts to outline what an appropriate attitude towards an 'ethics of the future' might be. Of course, the different authors of the book are themselves responsible for the approach they have chosen – and it is perhaps not necessary to stress that different authors are committed to different approaches and theoretical background convictions. But what we can see in the different discussion are steps in the direction of a philosophical attempt to take the complexity of the topic serious. We have to deal with the empirical complexities of the topic, we have to understand the political, economic and juridical contexts in which we are shaping the future and we have to take human psychological limitations into account. An appropriate ethical discussion of the topic will not be possible if we attempt to bypass real-world complexities. And this empirical aspect of ethics is not primarily concerned with the question of how people – empirically speaking think about long-term responsibilities. Rather, the task is to aim for a comprehensive understanding of all those empirical aspects that determine the current situation in which we ask ourselves what kind of long-term responsibilities we may have.

But at the same time it is our task as philosophers to support an appropriate understanding of the normative concepts we are dealing with, the possibilities of dealing with the uncertainty of the future and the normative commitments human beings may have. And it is impossible to do justice to the problem without discussing quite fundamental questions of our understanding of politics, history and the place of human beings in the world. At the end of the day, asking ethical questions is part of the more fundamental attempts of human beings to understand what it means to be a human being. To be confronted with the question of our responsibilities with regard to the future forces us to go further with regard to the question and it is perhaps important to understand the significance of the challenge; otherwise it will be difficult to find appropriate responses to it and to find appropriate responses is perhaps one of the biggest challenges humanity is confronted with at the moment – and probably also for decades to come.

INDEX

POLITICAL BODIES, AGREEMENTS AND LEGAL DOCUMENTS

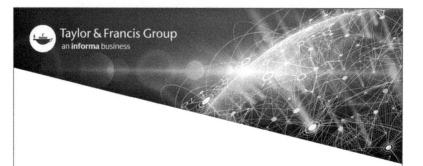

For Product Safety Concerns and Information please contact our EU
representative GPSR@taylorandfrancis.com
Taylor & Francis Verlag GmbH, Kaufingerstraße 24, 80331 München, Germany

www.ingramcontent.com/pod-product-compliance
Ingram Content Group UK Ltd.
Pitfield, Milton Keynes, MK11 3LW, UK
UKHW021031180425
457613UK00021B/1124